BRIDGE BUILDERS
African Experiences with Information and Communication Technology

Office of International Affairs
National Research Council

NATIONAL ACADEMY PRESS
Washington, D.C. 1996

NATIONAL ACADEMY PRESS • 2101 Constitution Avenue, N.W. • Washington, DC 20418

NOTICE: The project that is the subject of this report was approved by the Governing Board of the National Research Council, whose members are drawn from the councils of the National Academy of Sciences, the National Academy of Engineering, and the Institute of Medicine for their special competence and with regard for appropriate balance.

This report has been reviewed by a group other than the authors according to procedures approved by a Report Review Committee consisting of members of the National Academy of Sciences, the National Academy of Engineering, and the Institute of Medicine.

This report has been prepared by the editorial subcommittee of the Advisory Panel on Planning for Scientific and Technological Information (STI) Systems in Sub-Saharan Africa. Support for the project and for this report was provided by the Carnegie Corporation of New York.

A limited number of copies of this report are available from:

Office of International Affairs
National Research Council
2101 Constitution Avenue, N.W.
Washington, D.C. 20418

Additional copies are available for sale from:

National Academy Press
2101 Constitution Avenue. N.W.
Box 285
Washington, D.C. 20418
Tel: 1-800-624-6242 or (202)334-3313
(in the Washington Metropolitan Area).

Library of Congress Catalog Card Number 96-68711

International Standard Book Number 0-309-05483-4

PANEL ON PLANNING FOR SCIENTIFIC
AND TECHNOLOGICAL INFORMATION (STI) SYSTEMS
IN SUB-SAHARAN AFRICA

Co-chairs

DR. JOHN BLACK, Chief Librarian (retired), University of Guelph, Guelph, Ontario, Canada

JANE BORTNICK GRIFFITH, Chief, Science Policy Research Division, Congressional Research Service, Library of Congress, Washington, D.C.

Members

DR. GBADE A. ALABI, Department of Library, Archival, and Information Studies, Faculty of Education, University of Ibadan, Ibadan, Nigeria

STEVE CISLER, Senior Scientist, Apple Computer, Inc., Cupertino, California

DR. NANCY HAFKIN, Head, Pan African Development Information Systems (PADIS), United Nations/Economic Commission for Africa, Addis Ababa, Ethiopia

DR. HEATHER HUDSON, Director, Telecommunications Program, University of San Francisco, McLaren College of Business, San Francisco, California

DR. BERNARD LOWN (IOM), Lown Cardiovascular Center, Brookline, Massachusetts

THEOPHILUS E. MLAKI, Director of Information and Documentation, Tanzania Commission for Science and Technology, Dar es Salaam, Tanzania

DR. ALEX TINDIMUBONA, African Science and Technology Exchange, Kampala, Uganda

Staff

WENDY D. WHITE, Senior Progam Officer, Office of International Affairs

PAMELA GAMBLE, Assistant, Office of International Affairs

iii

The National Academy of Sciences is a private, nonprofit, self-perpetuating society of distinguished scholars engaged in scientific and engineering research, dedicated to the furtherance of science and technology and to their use for the general welfare. Upon the authority of the charter granted to it by the Congress in 1863, the Academy has a mandate that requires it to advise the federal government on scientific and technical matters. Dr. Bruce M. Alberts is president of the National Academy of Sciences.

The National Academy of Engineering was established in 1964, under the charter of the National Academy of Sciences, as a parallel organization of outstanding engineers. It is autonomous in its administration and in the selection of its members, sharing with the National Academy of Sciences the responsibility for advising the federal government. The National Academy of Engineering also sponsors engineering programs aimed at meeting national needs, encourages education and research, and recognizes the superior achievements of engineers. Dr. Harold Liebowitz is president of the National Academy of Engineering.

The Institute of Medicine was established in 1970 by the National Academy of Sciences to secure the services of eminent members of appropriate professions in the examination of policy matters pertaining to the health of the public. The Institute acts under the responsibility given to the National Academy of Sciences by its congressional charter to be an adviser to the federal government and, upon its own initiative, to identify issues of medical care, research, and education. Dr. Kenneth I. Shine is president of the Institute of Medicine.

The National Research Council was organized by the National Academy of Sciences in 1916 to associate the broad community of science and technology with the Academy's purposes of furthering knowledge and advising the federal government. Functioning in accordance with general policies determined by the Academy, the Council has become the principal operating agency of both the National Academy of Sciences and the National Academy of Engineering in providing services to the government, the public, and the scientific and engineering communities. The Council is administered jointly by both Academies and the Institute of Medicine. Dr. Bruce M. Alberts and Dr. Harold Liebowitz are chairman and vice chairman, respectively, of the National Research Council.

The Office of International Affairs (OIA) is concerned with the development of international and national policies to promote effective application of science and technology to economic and social problems facing both industrialized and developing countries. OIA participates in international cooperative activities, engages in joint studies and projects with counterpart organizations, manages scientific exchange programs, and represents the Academy complex at many national and international meetings directed toward facilitating international cooperation in science and engineering. Dr. F. Sherwood Rowland, Dr. Harold Forsen, and Dr. David Rall are the foreign secretaries of the National Academy of Sciences, the National Academy of Engineering, and the Institute of Medicine, respectively.

Preface

Bridge-Builders: African Experiences with Information and Communication Technology brings good news from that continent. This volume tells sixteen remarkable stories—first-person accounts of how information and communication technologies (ICT) have been successfully introduced into institutions for the benefit of scientists and engineers in sub-Saharan Africa. The projects described by the authors are case studies that focus on the lessons learned in designing and implementing projects dealing with scientific and technological information (STI) and that examine the impacts these projects have had. For the most part, these are not big projects in terms of funding. They do, however, demonstrate just how much can be accomplished through leadership, dedication, and determination. The authors are very honest in discussing the problems they faced and the lessons they learned.

By providing this systematic examination of the lessons learned by these project managers, the National Research Council's Advisory Panel on Planning for STI Systems in Sub-Saharan Africa hopes to encourage the donor community and many others in the STI community to engage in strategic planning for STI and to strengthen the design and management of scientific and technical systems. The Advisory Panel expects this volume to contribute to the development of national STI projects that are based on a firm and educated comprehension of what is already in place and to catalyze necessary linkages between STI institutions and actors so that national STI networks can be developed to support African scientists and engineers. The stories told by these authors should also encourage managers of other fledgling STI initiatives whose objectives are similar or complementary.

This volume has been a long time in the making. Since 1989, the Advisory Panel has observed the STI scene in Africa with growing interest. Through a number of workshops and seminars in Africa and through the travel of staff and panel members, we have had the opportunity to observe, first-hand, the growing impact of STI in Africa. We have also been privileged to meet the authors from the volume and many others who are struggling to bring ICT to their institutions and countries.

The authors included in this volume are not the only successful ICT project managers in Africa and the panel regrets that it had neither the time nor the resources to bring more success stories to light. We hope that the NRC can salute additional projects in future volumes of case studies. In the meantime, we trust that those bridge builders whose work is not described in this volume will be encouraged to share their activities with us and with others in their countries who can benefit from their experiences.

This volume would not have been possible without the tireless efforts of the authors themselves. They patiently wrote, rewrote, answered questions, and brought their contributions to the standards demanded of them. The editorial review committee, which I also chaired and which was composed of panel members Nancy Hafkin, Theo Mlaki, G.B. Alabi, and Alex Tindimubona, gave much of their time to read drafts of the studies and make queries of the authors. Their knowledge of the field and their expertise on the situation in Africa have been invaluable.

As chair of the Advisory Panel, I wish to acknowledge the Carnegie Corporation of New York, whose generous support of this project made this volume possible. Realizing that information and communication technologies could only be tools of empowerment for those who had access to them, Carnegie helped to "jumpstart" the information revolution in Africa by supporting many of the projects described in *Bridge Builders*. By supporting small pilot and demonstration projects, Carnegie has helped innovative project managers overcome the social, technical, political, and economic barriers to introducing new ideas and technologies.

I also wish to acknowledge the leadership role of the Office of International Affairs (OIA) of the National Research Council. Since 1989, they have been helping donors, policy-makers, and project managers realize the benefits and problems associated with the introduction of information and communication technologies. Through this and proceeding projects, they have encouraged the Advisory Panel and others to study many aspects of STI activities and to concentrate on the role information and communication services can play in decreasing scientific isolation and in improving the effectiveness of scientific research.

Most of all the OIA, through this Advisory Panel, and Carnegie have proven that small projects can have a big impact. Projects that encourage the process of learning, familiarize users with computers and other information technologies, and demonstrate the use of these technologies in an everyday setting often have a greater impact than large projects that tax scarce resources.

Finally, on behalf of the Advisory Panel, I want to give particular thanks to several OIA staff members. First, our appreciation goes to Pamela Gamble, who made sure everyone arrived at the writing workshops when they were supposed to be there and who handled all other logistical concerns with grace, good humor, and her usual efficiency. We also want to thank Wendy White, the NRC program officer who assisted the Advisory Panel throughout its activities. Her knowledge of the African STI environment and the people involved, combined with her sensitivity to the African context, has been invaluable to the work of the panel and, in particular, to the completion of this volume. Her willingness to share her expertise and to provide moral support to all involved goes far beyond the line of duty.

Together, the Advisory Panel members, the case study authors, and the OIA staff have a broad understanding of STI, an appreciation for the unique opportunities and challenges in Africa, a thorough knowledge of ongoing STI activities, and a demonstrated commitment to create an enabling environment within which African STI networks can flourish. Their wisdom, vision, and dedication are reflected in this report.

John B. Black, *Chairman*
Advisory Panel

Contents

ix

Introduction

BACKGROUND

Since 1989, with support from the Carnegie Corporation of New York, the National Research Council (NRC) through its Office of International Affairs (OIA) has reviewed and identified ways to strengthen the state of planning, design, and management of scientific and technical information (STI) services in selected African countries. The program has studied many aspects of STI activities, including database access and management, library development, scientific publishing and communication, and the role information technologies play in supporting these. The OIA program has concentrated on the role information and communication services play in decreasing scientific isolation and in improving the effectiveness of scientific research.

In 1989, an OIA-sponsored meeting in Nairobi identified the information and communication technologies that held the most potential for the African scientific and research community.[1] Looking at information and communication both as inputs to and results of the scientific process, the workshop participants identified CD-ROM, desktop publishing, and electronic networking as key information technologies for African scientists. In addition, they identified the collection, management and dissemination of local information resources as an area of both great need and potential in Africa.

Since that workshop, OIA's Advisory Panel on Planning for STI Systems in sub-Saharan Africa has provided advice to the managers of the diverse STI projects that the Corporation and others are supporting in Africa. The panel found that some of these projects are models for the further development of STI services in their communities and that the project managers are in a unique position to contribute to their own country's national STI planning efforts.

They could play this important role, however, only if they first analyzed their own projects and looked closely at the experience and knowledge they had gained. The panel recommended to Carnegie that it draw on its knowledge of STI projects in Africa to produce a volume of case studies that would:

- focus on the lessons learned in designing and implementing STI projects;
- examine the impacts these projects have had;
- identify gaps in our information base;
- share innovative and cost-effective ways to market new products and services and ways to measure the impact of these on the users; and
- share information on proposal formulation, evaluation methods, and information marketing.

THE EDITORIAL AND SELECTION PROCESSES

To collect the case studies, the Advisory Panel appointed an editorial subcommittee to design and manage the process in an efficient manner and to formally select the authors to be invited. This subcommittee met in Addis Ababa, Ethiopia in April 1995. The subcommittee decided that the projects selected for inclusion in the case study volume should demonstrate the use of the key information technologies and services that had been identified as most critical in the 1989 Nairobi Conference.

The subcommittee then debated the criteria to be used in the final selection of case study authors. They decided that each project selected for inclusion in the case study volume must:

- Be catalytic—it should promote STI beyond the original parameters of the project and have an effect beyond what might have been expected;
- Demonstrate the use of local resources and not be totally dependent on external funding;
- Be relatively small in terms of the amount of external funding available to it;
- Have demonstrable results; that is, the project must be beyond the planning stages and be offering services to users; and
- Highlight the personal commitment and leadership of an STI pioneer.

After identifying many projects that fit these criteria, the subcommittee looked for gender and geographical balance and selected projects to represent as many countries in sub-Saharan Africa as possible. Following much debate, the subcommittee reached a consensus and nominated 18 projects to be included in the case study volume. (One nomination was later withdrawn after the subcommittee determined that it did not meet the criteria; and one nominee did not accept the invitation.)

The panel chairman wrote to the nominees and invited them to draft personal and informal accounts of their specific projects. The authors received an outline that detailed the common elements that they were to include in their accounts. Those authors who committed to writing a case study then participated in one of three writing workshops that took place in July and August 1995 in Harare, Nairobi, and Accra. Authors came to these workshops with all the background materials they needed to write their chapters. In a collegial atmosphere, far from the pressures of their offices, they worked hard to produce first drafts of their studies. These drafts were reviewed by the subcommittee and the authors have had the opportunity to submit revised versions of their case studies.

The title of this volume, *Bridge Builders: African Experiences with Information and Communication Technology*, is meant to describe the active role these authors have played in introducing new information technologies into their institutions. Their personal accounts will illustrate the steps they are taking to bridge the gap between the "information haves" and the "information have-nots" and to build bridges between their countries and the worldwide movements related to the global information infrastructure (GII). Step-by-step they are contributing in a major way to the development of Africa's information culture.

THE INFORMATION AND COMMUNICATION
TECHNOLOGY (ICT) SCENE IN AFRICA

The pace and complexity of modern research have greatly increased the information and communication needs of researchers, scientists, engineers, and their institutions. Research and development relies heavily on the ability to gather reliable data; have access to widely dispersed data and information; collaborate on projects; hold discussions and conferences; and disseminate the results. Information and communication technologies can help the scientist at each step of his or her research endeavor.

Taken together, this collection of case studies reflects a changing ICT scene in Africa. In 1989, the Nairobi workshop participants were concerned about *which* information technologies would be most suited to their situations. By 1995, project managers had proven just how successful the introduction of ICT could be in order to support science and research.

The problems are a long way from being solved. In some areas, the paucity of software written in local languages hinders adoption of information technologies. In other areas, basic information-processing tools are still in short supply. Computer equipment is expensive and hard to maintain. Consumables, such as paper, ink, toner, and other necessities of the computer age, almost always have to be imported and are thus terribly expensive. Regular contact among colleagues or experts in the field is still difficult. Many times, it is just as difficult to communicate with scientists within a country as it is to communicate with scientists abroad. African scientists and engineers still face isolation because of poor or expensive communication channels and because of a chronic shortage of funds, particularly hard currency, for purchasing books, periodicals, and subscriptions to international sources of information.

In 1989, the Advisory Panel sensed that policy-makers and donors were not well focused on these problems. Now, six years later, project managers, government ministers, donors, and scientists seem more prepared to recognize that developments in the fields of information and communications services and technologies offer vast opportunities to make real progress. The pace at which the price of communications and information systems has fallen has undermined the previously rigid link between a nation's wealth and its information richness. Through the efforts of individuals such as the ones featured in this volume, more and more people recognize that informatics (the merger of communication and information technologies) plays a fundamental role in the development of a science culture and the building of a scientific infrastructure in developing countries.

There have been several highly-visible initiatives since the 1989 meeting in Nairobi. In March 1994, Vice President Gore of the United States advanced the concept of a Global Information Infrastructure (GII) in a speech to the International Telecommunications Union's World Telecommunication Development Conference in Buenos Aires, Argentina. He proposed that the GII be composed of local, national, and regional networks. As a "network of networks," the GII should facilitate the global sharing of information, interconnection and communication—creating a global information marketplace.

The prominent support of the GII, or the information superhighway, has served to focus unprecedented attention (and much hype) on the importance of information and communication technologies. In the last few years, Africa has taken several important steps to be a part of the GII.

First, in April 1995, the Economic Commission of Africa (ECA) hosted the African Regional Symposium on Telematics for Development. Shortly after that, the Conference of African Ministers responsible for Economic and Social Development and Planning passed a resolution entitled *Building Africa's Information Highway*, which called for the establishment of a high-level working group on information technologies and communications in Africa made up of African technical experts.

Under the leadership of the Pan African Development Information System (PADIS), this group has met twice. It is studying the economic and social and the scientific and technological implications of the information highway for Africa. It will advise the Executive Secretary of the ECA and African governments on policies and strategies that will assist in confronting and taking full advantage of this global phenomenon. In May 1996, there will be meeting of the ECA Conference of Ministers in Addis Ababa at which the high-level working group will issue a paper called "An African Information and Communication Initiative to Accelerate Socio-Economic Development."

In addition, the South African government is organizing a Ministerial Conference on the Information Society and Developing Countries, also in May 1996. This meeting, which is inspired by the 1995 G-7 meeting on the same topic, might further advance the international consensus on the fundamental principles underlying the development of the Global Information Infrastructure.

Finally, of special interest to Africa, is the authorization of the Leland Initiative, or the Africa Global Information Infrastructure Gateway Project. This is a $15 million cross-cutting project managed by the U.S. Agency for International Development (USAID). Its primary purpose is to disseminate the benefits of the Internet and other GII technologies to people in 20 countries in sub-Saharan Africa in which USAID works. Those countries closest to attaining connectivity will receive benefits from the initial phases of the project.

So, while the promises of the information age may be something less than the media attention would have us believe, there is no question that people are paying increased attention to the potential of information and communication technologies in support of science and development.

LESSONS LEARNED IN THE CASE STUDIES

The sixteen case study authors whose stories appear in this volume represent important stepping stones in the development of Africa's information highway. In many ways, they are pioneers—introducing new technologies before they have achieved widespread acceptance. They have paved the way for others because they have proven that, with enough perseverance and personal energy, the technologies can work and can improve information services to the scientific community. Nothing is more basic to scientific institutions than the tools needed to conduct research, engage in discussions with other scientists, and publish the results of research in a form accessible to all. The case studies include descriptions of how ICT can help support and build capacity for all of these functions.

CD-ROM

The first three studies, written by John Newa, Regina Shakakata, and Helga Patrikios, describe the introduction of CD-ROM into university libraries. At the 1989 Nairobi conference, the participants expressed great excitement over the potential of this technology. Since then, CD-ROM has achieved widespread recognition as a highly cost-effective and locally viable medium for accessing international databases. It also has potential for delivering full text documents to areas where the source documents are hard to obtain. Its qualities of speed, power, and, above all, user-friendliness in information retrieval, and its value as a training medium for online searching are detailed in these three studies.

Here are some of the lessons learned by these case study authors:

- High-level support of the projects has been critical to their success. Such support often allows for the provision of local funding and helps to publicize the service.
- The selection of the right vendors, not only for the equipment but for the databases, is extremely important. The products vary in content, user friendliness, and search capability and some are more suited to the equipment found in Africa than others.
- Planners must face and meet the costs associated with maintaining the equipment and subscribing to the databases. The one-time provision of set-up costs is not sufficient.
- CD-ROM projects can have side benefits. Two of the case studies discuss the authors' roles in supplying records for the African Index Medicus Project (described on pages 45–46).
- Document delivery is still a problem. Many CD-ROM databases help researchers identify articles that they cannot obtain locally. Detailed abstracts are very helpful, as are full text CD-ROMs containing, perhaps, documents in the public domain.

Desktop Publishing

The next four studies are written by Xavier Carelse, Albina Kasango, Agnes Katama, and Alex Tindimubona. Desktop publishing (or DTP) is the product of technological advances in personal computing, print graphics, and computer-generated typography. DTP can be used to design and produce anything that can be printed: newspapers, books, posters, catalogs, journals, articles, or annual reports.

Each of these case studies emphasizes a slightly different aspect of publishing. Xavier Carelse discusses the equipment needed and lays out a logical progression for upgrades; Albina Kasango talks about training and personal commitment; Agnes Katama discusses the steps taken to create a sustainable DTP unit and gives some creative examples of internship, or attachment, programs; and Alex Tindimubona discusses peer review systems and other aspects of a high-quality, scientific press.

Some of the lessons learned by the desktop publishing authors include:

- Training of the DTP operator took unexpected time and resources.
- It is important to select equipment that is compatible with what the institution is using. Buying the most popular or the easiest-to-use equipment is not always the best course.
- DTP takes more than the basic computer: peripherals such as scanners, printers, and photocopiers are also essential.

- DTP should not be confused with simple typesetting or design on a computer. A DTP operation should be organized as much like a professional press as possible. Project managers need to pay attention to deadlines, peer review, organization, and cost recovery.

Electronic Networking

The GII—and its system of interconnected networks—has dramatic implications for broadening the knowledge base in most scientific fields. It is becoming more important than ever for African scientists to be *electronically* connected to colleagues, information, and literature in order to keep up with advances in their field, exchange ideas and information, and communicate the results of their research. Easier communication and more readily available channels for information exchange create new opportunities for international cooperation. Scientists can: collaborate more easily; develop problem-solving models; tap the information resources of other scientists and institutions; and discuss important issues without the need for expensive or time-consuming travel. Systems operators and scientists can also benefit from remote systems in order to share software and gain access to computing resources. Indeed, access to networks and digital libraries may well be as important to economic and social well-being in the Information Age as access to trade routes and natural resources was in the Agricultural and Industrial Ages. [2]

Building and sustaining electronic networks in Africa has been challenging but, as the next five case study authors prove, it is possible. Lishan Adam, Moussa Fall, Charles Musisi, Paulos Nyirenda, and Neil Robinson describe their efforts to bring electronic networks and, eventually, the Internet to their institutions or countries.

The lessons they have learned include:

- Training is the main aspect of infrastructure development and should not be under-played.
- Building local networks first helps develop a user base that will be willing to sustain international connections and more sophisticated applications.
- Good network management, which includes marketing, accounting, and statistical analysis, is important, no matter how small the network.
- Network start-up takes considerable time and energy. Often users are unsure of the technology and require extra support in order to get started.
- Certain hardware is more suitable to poor telecommunication lines and harsh environmental conditions than others. It pays to study what has worked well for others.
- Software written in local languages helps users adapt faster to computer-based communications.

- The transition from subsidized to fee-based email services can be difficult and controversial; while subsidies might be critical in introducing networking technologies, they can contribute to a climate in which users demand free information services.

Collection, Management, and Dissemination of Local Information Resources

The final four case study authors focus less on a specific technology and more on developing local information resources and services for a specific group of people. Ermias Dagne describes how a group of scientists interested in natural products research has formed its own network in order to convene professional meetings, sponsor special training opportunities, and publish journals and conference proceedings. Stella Monageng discusses her activities in creating and managing a specialized database for Botswana's socioeconomic development information. James Muttunga writes about his efforts to introduce computer technology and information management systems at the Kenyan Medical Research Institute. John Villars describes a national information network that his institution has developed for Ghana.

The lessons learned by these four authors are broad-ranging but include:

- Too little attention is paid to collecting locally-produced information. What is available is often not distributed to those who could use it most.
- Funding for these types of projects is extremely difficult to come by and virtually impossible if support for the project does not come from the highest levels of the institution.
- Equipment purchase, maintenance, and repair can be difficult. It is hard to get reliable and unbiased information about technology resources.
- Training must be an essential component of the project.
- If the project is to be implemented in phases, then it is best to install equipment first in those units that have an existing and specific need for automation; otherwise, the equipment may go unused and this will cause frustration all around.
- Network programs thrive on a give-and-take basis. All members must be willing to shoulder some of the burden.

CONCLUSION

Information and communication technologies over the past few years have changed the way in which we work and communicate with each other and these case studies demonstrate in a very personal way just how much has changed in the way science is learned, communicated, and disseminated. These changes are so vast that the authors demonstrate that they, and the scientists and researchers they serve, need to learn an entirely new set of skills related to the current ways of conducting, writing about, and disseminating scientific research to policy makers and the public.

These case study authors have made very specific and measurable contributions to their institutions. They have also made contributions that are less obvious. They are, for example, contributing to *information literacy,* or the ability to access, evaluate, and use information from a variety of sources. They are teaching the scientists and researchers they serve to use computers and other information technologies competently, to work with others productively, and to access and use information resources. The authors also address how important it is for them to promote policy changes within their institutions and countries that favor the gathering and sharing of information.

These case studies provide valuable insights into project management and design. While they might describe very specific situations, the experience of these authors should prove helpful to anyone implementing projects in these areas:

- national STI network building;
- electronic network development;
- library collection or services development;
- document delivery schemes;
- cooperative database development;
- standardization efforts;
- marketing of information services;
- implementing cost-recovery schemes;
- operating STI projects on a sustainable basis;
- training programs for information technologies and services;
- introduction or application of information technologies;
- collection and description of locally-produced information; or
- scientific communication or publishing.

By examining the lessons learned by these authors and the impacts their projects have had, policy makers will see how important it is to become engaged in the effort to give equitable information access to all Africans. In addition, governments, foundations, development assistance agencies, and other members of the donor community can look at these lessons to develop a new generation of projects that are based on a firm and educated comprehension of what is already in place. Finally, project managers in Africa can use these case studies to learn how to implement necessary linkages among their institutions so that national STI networks can be developed. Many others who have been reluctant to begin projects in this field should be inspired to follow these leaders and to design activities that will help multiply the positive impact of information and communication technologies for everyone.

NOTES

1. National Research Council, Board on Science and Technology for International Development (1989) *Science and Technology Information Systems and Services in Africa: Report of a Workshop Held in Nairobi, April 19-22, 1989.* National Academy Press, Washington, D.C.

2. Peters, Paul Evan (1995) Networked intellectual property: brain-ache of the decade. *Educom Review* 30 (3).

CASE STUDIES ON THE INTRODUCTION OF CD-ROM TO UNIVERSITY LIBRARIES

CD-ROM (*Compact Disc, Read-Only Memory*) is a high density storage medium on which electronic data are etched by laser onto a compact disc master. A single CD-ROM can hold still images, motion video, audio, and digital data. With its vast storage capacity (a single CD-ROM can store as much data as 1,500 floppy disks or 200,000 printed pages of text), ease of mailing, and tolerance of harsh environmental conditions, CD-ROM offers a practical solution to the information isolation experienced by researchers, information professionals, and scientists in many developing countries.

These case study authors live in areas where high costs and technical difficulties deter online access and searching. They demonstrate that CD-ROM can bring the following gains:

- user-friendly, interactive online searching of databases by library staff and end-users;
- current citations, with abstracts that often provide sufficient information to negate the need for source documents;
- selected citations and abstracts that can be used for national digests of relevant material;
- an enhanced image of library staff due to their dramatically improved ability to deliver current information and to demonstrate computer skills; and
- demystification of microcomputer technology for staff and end-users.

CD-ROM has proven appropriate to these authors because it reduces the need for online links and it operates under difficult conditions, such as heat, humidity, dust, and unstable power supply. The authors did find, however, that while there is a relatively low capital cost for the equipment, the cost of sustaining the subscriptions to the databases is still a problem.

These case study authors demonstrate how they have used CD-ROM as a powerful tool to develop local computer literacy by providing the opportunity for hands-on use of a sophisticated system. They also describe how CD-ROM has been used to develop both local and pan-African databases and digests of relevant information.

The CD-ROM Service
for the University of Dar es Salaam
by John M. Newa

Dr. John Newa is Director of Library Services at the University of Dar es Salaam. He has worked on the promotion and development of information centers in Tanzania. Since 1990, he has been concerned with the introduction and application of information technologies in libraries.

BACKGROUND AND CONTEXT OF THE PROJECT

The University of Dar es Salaam was the first university for Tanzania. The United Republic of Tanzania was the outcome of the political union in 1964 between the former British Protectorates of Tanganyika (independent in 1961) and Zanzibar (independent in 1964 following a bloody revolt against the Arab Sultan). It is located on the Indian Ocean between Kenya and Uganda in the north, Burundi, Rwanda and Zaire in the west, Zambia and Mozambique in the south. The country has a population of about 27 million and is growing at the rate of 3.1 percent (1991).[1] People use Kiswahili as the national language. English is a second language and the language used in institutions of higher learning.

Tanzania is ranked second from the bottom worldwide in terms of its gross domestic product and its economy is mainly agricultural-based. It was reportedly growing at the rate of 3.6 percent in 1992. The industrial sector is increasing and accounts for 40 percent of the national economy. Through the International Monetary Fund's policies of structural adjustment, the economy is said to be improving, although the man on the street says life is getting more difficult.

The country recorded a literacy rate of over 80 percent in the late 1980s. The policy of Universal Primary Education—introduced in the early 1970s and calling for all girls and boys to have a basic seven years of primary education—is in place.

Yet the total number of children enrolled in secondary schools is less than 10 percent of primary school graduates, and the number of those who struggle and make it to the universities hardly reaches 0.05 percent. In recent years deliberate efforts have been made to increase the amount of science and technology in the curriculum at all levels of education.

Scientific and technological training is given more emphasis in the Teachers and Technical Colleges, as well as in the several vocational institutes spread all over the country. The government, through the Ministry of Science, Technology and Higher Education, is making deliberate efforts to prepare the country for the 21st century when scientific and technological information developments will be critical for national socioeconomic development.

At the national level, the Commission for Science and Technology (COSTECH) is responsible for the adoption, development, and dissemination of scientific and technological information. The target of the Ministry of Science, Technology and Higher Education is to raise the national expenditure on research and development (R&D) from the present 0.2 percent to 1 percent by the year 2000. Besides creating the scientific and technological infrastructure in R&D institutions, COSTECH is in the process of creating three databases: a directory of scientists and technologists; a directory of scientific and technological institutions; and an inventory of scientific and technological equipment.

The need for adequate scientific and technological information (STI) is felt in the research institutes of all sectors, including agriculture, forestry, health, industry, wildlife, and fisheries. However, I feel that the greatest need for the provision of STI is in the institutions of higher learning, especially the universities that are expected to support teaching, research, and consultancy activities.

When the CD-ROM project was first being prepared in 1991, the STI infrastructure at the University of Dar es Salaam (UDSM) and throughout the country was still underdeveloped. There were only a few international vendor agencies for STI hardware and software in the country: among them, IBM, International Computers Limited (ICL) and Wang. There were two electronic mail nodes: one at the Medical Library in connection with the HealthNet Project and another at COSTECH. At the UDSM, besides the University Computer Centre, there were personal computers in only some departments. The library had two computers. There was also a ground station for communication using a low-earth orbiting (LEO) satellite connection between the Department of Electrical Engineering and Essex University, in England. As far as CD-ROM services are concerned there was one CD-ROM workstation each at the United States Information Center Library (for the Books in Print database), at the British Council Library (for the British Books in Print database), at the Demographic Unit of the University of Dar es Salaam (for the POPLINE database), and in the Department of Crop Science at the Sokoine University of Agriculture (for a few databases from the Commonwealth Agricultural Bureaux).

As the CD-ROM Service project was getting under way in 1993, an electronic mail node was installed at the University Computer Centre, with connections to various departments of the University. For a variety of reasons, including the lack of email technicians and the need for a secure location to place the equipment, the library did not get its email connection until May 1995. Until then the University Library used the Medical Library and Computer Centre email nodes for sending and receiving messages. The University Computer Centre expected to install an Internet connection via leased line to South Africa in November 1995; however that proved too expensive and the Computer Centre is currently waiting for the arrival a satellite dish that they will use to connect to the Internet.

At this point the University of Dar es Salaam is in the process of adopting a technology information policy that will encompass the various university operations, including administration, student administration, finance, and the automation of the library.

PROJECT DESCRIPTION

The University of Dar es Salaam academic community was facing the problem of availability of and access to current information for its teaching, learning, and research activities. Our scholars and researchers were isolated from their colleagues in the region and overseas. Limited resources made it difficult to acquire and provide current information resources, including the maintenance of adequate periodical subscriptions. The lack of information technology resources and the poor telecommunication infrastructure ruled out online connections with information databases in the region and abroad.

For all of these reasons, we decided to introduce CD-ROM service to the University. We had heard about the successful introduction of CD-ROM at the medical library in Zimbabwe and wanted to provide our own library users with the same benefits: especially convenient and relatively inexpensive access to current scientific, technological, and socioeconomic information.

The financial support provided by the Carnegie Corporation of New York allowed for the purchase of two CD-ROM workstations, their accessories, a laser printer, and initial subscriptions to two CD-ROM databases. The Institute of Scientific Information's (ISI) *Science Citation Index* and the *Social Science Citation Index* were selected for their breadth in providing for the teaching, learning, and research needs of a large section of the university academic community. We hoped that this broad appeal would give the new service good publicity.

The CD-ROM service started operation with two donated engineering databases provided by American Association for the Advancement of Science (AAAS)—Engineering Index Page One and Compendex Plus—and the Distance Education Database from the International Centre for Distance Learning (ICDL), donated by the Commonwealth Association for Distance Education. The Library also decided to acquire two additional databases, ERIC and TROPAG, which we believed to be of more general interest to the larger section of the academic and research community at the university and in other R&D institutions in the country.

Within its interlibrary loan program, the library had provision for document delivery through coupons purchased from the British Library Lending Division in Boston Spa. This provision enabled the Library to provide a modest document delivery service emanating from the CD-ROM database searches. In order to cope with the increasing demand from the CD-ROM service, the document delivery financial allocation had to be more than doubled.

The library was also maintaining a total of about 800 current journal subscriptions, 40 percent of which came through the assistance of the Swedish Agency for Research and Economic Cooperation (SAREC), 20 percent through AAAS's support within the sub-Saharan Africa program, and 40 percent from the library's own resources. The photocopying service of the library was also improved by the purchase of additional heavy-duty machines. The photocopying machines had been purchased with funds from SAREC within its Library Support to Tanzania Libraries Programme.

As originally intended, the CD-ROM service has provided the academic and research community at the university, in particular, and in Tanzania, in general, access to current information and has relieved the isolation of scholars and scientists in the region and abroad. In brief, the service provides scholars and researchers with the capacity of 15 different and updated CD-ROM databases in their subjects of interest and provides document delivery to most items requested. The databases include subjects in Science and Applied Technology, Social Science and the Humanities, and Law. Document requests from database searches were met by services from the British Lending Library and recently from the Massachusetts Institute of Technology through the AAAS. Our assessment is that the document delivery service, in terms of documents requested and time it takes to get the documents, has not been found satisfactory by our CD-ROM service users.

When we acquired the CD-ROM service, the only other operational service I knew about was at the Medical Library, which was part of the HealthNet project. My visit to the Department of Crop Science at the Sokoine University of Agriculture in the company of a team of experts from BOSTID indicated that the facility was not being used. I am also informed that about 1993 a CD-ROM facility was introduced at the Uyole Ministry of Agriculture, Research and Training Institute. It is not known which databases were donated to the Institute but I guess these might be products of the Commonwealth Agricultural Bureaux. Again the state of its functionality and extent of use is not known.

COSTECH acquired one CD-ROM workstation about 1993, which became operational in the same year, using patent databases from the U.S. Patent and Trademark Office and the European Patent Application Bibliography. When I visited the facility recently, the CD-ROM drive was out of order. The Ministry of Trade and Industry Registry Office is also reported to have one CD-ROM workstation.

BOX 1 The Art of Proposal Writing

The personal contacts who gave us information on the technology—and where and how to get it—made a large difference in the quality of our proposal. The library had earlier contacted Dr. Patricia Rosenfield at the Carnegie Corporation of New York. She suggested that we meet with Wendy White of the U.S. National Research Council, who was scheduled to visit Tanzania in 1991 as a guest of COSTECH. The project proposal for the CD-ROM service was revised with her help and expertise before we submitted it to Carnegie. When you are new to proposal writing like we were, it is very helpful to have someone come along and help you compose answers to the reviewers' criticisms! For example, we thought that we had to address the reviewers' comments by changing our proposal to agree with them. We didn't know that we could *challenge* the reviewer by giving our justification for why we proposed to do things in a certain way or to use a certain product vendor.

The Office has also received a wide range of patent CD-ROM databases. However the facility is not yet operational awaiting the training of staff. So as far as the general academic and research community is concerned, the CD-ROM at the University Library was the first facility with a reasonable degree of usage.

Since our CD-ROM facility has been operational, there has been keen interest to spread the technology to other institutions in the country. As seen above the CD-ROM service has since been introduced in other information institutions in the country. The UDSM Library service has built upon the library's and the university's interest to acquire more personal computers. Since then the Library has acquired six computers, which are used in a variety of operations, including the creation of three local databases, in education, environment, and biodiversity. Under the UDSM Library's coordinating role for the SAREC Library Support Programme to Tanzania, we have also acquired four personal computers for other universities and research institutes. As will be seen below, the tempo generated is now helping us make a credible case for the library's partial or complete automation.

PROJECT EXPERIENCE AND IMPLEMENTATION

Correct decisions concerning how to go about writing an acceptable and externally-funded project proposal, the handling of the grant, and the acquisition of hardware, software, and databases have been critical to the effective and efficient operation of the CD-ROM service. The story of how we learned about the technology, what it could do for us, and how and from whom to acquire it has been given above and in Box 1. Because we had little expertise and experience at the UDSM Library on appropriate equipment and databases, contacts with other African librarians in the region and individuals abroad at meetings organized by the AAAS and the U.S. National Research Council were very helpful. Still, our lack of experience resulted in heavy reliance on vendor recommendations for hardware and software and little control over the versions and price paid.

We decided to use the ICL local agent as a vendor for the hardware and software, so as to ensure the availability of spare parts, service, and consumables. Lengthy and cumbersome customs procedures were avoided by asking the Carnegie Corporation to make direct purchases from the vendor's parent company in London. A two-year service contract with the local vendor at the time of purchase solved the problem of installation and maintenance. The local back-up service has proved to be critical to the smooth operation of the service. Yet I have heard criticism from the Director, AAAS Library Program for sub-Saharan Africa, that the price paid for the UDSM's CD-ROM hardware was the highest in Africa. I swear that it was not caused by the Library Director's demand for kick-backs! It could be a factor of international and local vendors' price mark-ups, or a result of the country's customs duty structure for computer products imported into the country. The first two CD-ROM workstations were actually bought directly by the donor from ICL London and sent to the UDSM Library.

We faced a number of problems before the service got under way. First, the cost of the entire package from the local vendor was comparatively high. Then, the installation of the facility took longer than our donor could understand. We had peculiar local problems of security and high humidity. It took about six months for the Estates Department of the University to fix security grills and provide air conditioning for the CD-ROM facility. That was to ensure that the equipment was safe from possible theft and could not be damaged by the high Dar es Salaam humidity. So, although it took us longer than expected to become operational, we have had no serious problems in the safety and operation of the facility.

The purchase of CD-ROM database subscriptions has also been problematic from the outset. First of all, the CD-ROM databases selected were very expensive by our standards. In addition, financial transactions with database dealers overseas were long and difficult to execute, partly because of financial regulations at home and partly because of some irksome conditions set by the vendors. For example, the vendors required that we sign lease agreements before purchase and delivery. The database vendors contacted would not accept UNESCO coupons. Because of that initial experience, we have in subsequent years paid our database subscriptions through a London-based book agent who accepts payment in UNESCO coupons. We also learned that, in some cases, the CD-ROM databases actually belong to the publisher and were only being *leased* to us: we would have to return one disc before an update would be issued or if we had to cancel the subscription at a future date.[2]

From the beginning we realized that it was our responsibility to have a few database subscriptions that were rather popular, rather than rely completely on the grant. We chose a department with high visibility—Reference—to house the CD-ROM service. This department was fortunately headed by a very able, effective, and efficient

---

BOX 2   The Benefits of CD-ROM

"Now that we have an efficient CD-ROM Service in the Library, there is no valid excuse for one not to register for a Ph.D. locally nor to produce scholarly publications, or go overseas for literature review."

Chairperson, Appointments Committee for Academic Staff at the UDSM, June 1993.

---

scholar and professional who had great personal drive. This has proved to be an asset to the service.

Effective March 1994, we formed a CD-ROM Service committee whose membership includes two end-users (people of senior academic ranks in the faculties of Engineering and Science) and four library professionals (the Director, and the Heads of the Reference, Periodicals, and Readers Services departments).

In a concrete way, the university teaching and research community have reacted very positively to the project. (See Box 2.) Since the CD-ROM service became operational more and more users have turned up. The CD-ROM service is now the most important part of the library for teaching staff and postgraduate students and researchers. The library's 1994/95 Annual Report indicates that there has been an average of 53 searches per month and a total of 1,540 since the service started in October 1993.

The image of the library staff has also been significantly boosted among university professors, students, and committees. The CD-ROM service has frequently been cited by the Higher Degrees Committee as reason for academic staff and postgraduate students to enroll in the university. Since the CD-ROM service became operational, the Appointments Committee for Academic Staff no longer accepts complaints about lack of access to scholarly publications. Everyone on campus is expected to use the new service to improve their own scholarship.

Promotion and Publicity for the CD-ROM Services

We widely publicized the CD-ROM service within the university community and outside. We initially announced the service in various university committees, including faculty boards and the Senate. We sent circular letters to all heads of departments within the university and to all academic staff members, and we posted notices on all bulletin boards. We sent similar letters announcing and explaining the service to other universities and research institutes. We prepared special publicity leaflets and spread them all over the campus and outside. The 1993/94 Library Guide and University Prospectus and subsequent annual editions have included a sizable section on the CD-ROM service.

Word of mouth still plays a very important part in African communication channels. Since the 1993/94 academic year the service has featured prominently in all freshman and postgraduate orientation programs. I have spoken about the service in various forums, including the Senate, the Committee of Deans, Faculty Boards, and other academic gatherings to both announce and explain the service and its benefit for teaching, learning, and research.

The Library CD-ROM Committee took part in a number of departmental seminars as well as in postgraduate research seminar programs. So far the library has organized two Exposition Days for the CD-ROM service that were very well attended by both the university and external community. We organized the first Exposition Day when the service was just getting under way. We held the second Exposition Day during the university's Silver Jubilee week in July 1995; it was officiated by the former President and Chancellor of the University, Mwalimu J.K. Nyerere. The mass media, including newspapers and television, widely covered the event. Recently we decided to place one of the three CD-ROM workstations in the public area near the public catalog. The visibility of the facility may attract more users. We trust that these marketing and promotional efforts will improve and increase the use of the CD-ROM service.

Outreach Activities

In fact we are already providing outreach service to users in sister universities and research institutes. We have given access to a number of external users. In connection with other Library Current Awareness Services, we provide searches for users from outside the University. We have desktop publishing equipment on order that will allow us to produce and disseminate an information bulletin to users in the university and outside. The major limitation that we are facing now is poor and slow communication with institutions that do not have email or other telecommunication facilities. Thus in addition to providing traditional library products and services, such as bibliographies and newsletters, we plan to use the CD-ROM service as a launching pad for direct and aggressive services, directed at answering specific needs of S&T practitioners and researchers. This will include SDI (selective dissemination of information), retrospective searches, assistance in question formulation, bibliographies on demand, question and answer services, referral, photocopying, and citation tracing. These are in addition to the document delivery service.

RESULTS, IMPACT, AND BENEFITS OF THE PROJECT

We put a monitoring system in place when the service was launched. We keep records for users and their particulars, as well as records of searches. We are in the process of installing a system that can do that automatically. Currently all is done on daily record sheets which are cumulated weekly, monthly and yearly. Table 1 shows usage according to the broad categories of staff, postgraduate and undergraduate students, and others. Table 2 shows the number of searches requested according to the database.

TABLE 1   Usage Statistics, 1993–1995

	Staff	Postgraduate	Undergraduate	Others	Total
1993	18	42	2	5	67
1994	195	404	126	27	752
1995	104	338	251	28	721

Since May 1995, the library has embarked on a project to evaluate the CD-ROM service, particularly the various CD-ROM databases held by the library. We identified senior academics and postgraduate students who had used the service and asked them to evaluate the databases in their various aspects, including the amount of information and its usefulness, relevance, currency, and coverage of the Africa region. From this evaluation and others to be conducted in the future, we will determine whether or not the CD-ROM service is having the desired effect. Unfortunately because of a change of the Librarian in charge of the CD-ROM service in the Library, this important report is not yet out.

We are bearing in mind Erick Baard's injunction that: "A correct assessment of an information technology innovation should include an examination of its requirements as regards physical and social infrastructure, its possible effects on new environments, and finally the nature of the limitations to information utilization which it is designed to alleviate."[3]

TABLE 2   Searches by Database

Database	1993	1994	1995
Compendex Plus	32	154	199
Social Science Citation Index	9	154	199
Science Citation Index	8	65	51
Tropag and Rural Economy	8	41	21
Educational Resources Information Center	4	93	51
Agecond	6	46	16
Arts and Humanities	-	11	-
International Centre for Distance Learning	-	6	-
Public Affairs Information services	-	33	12
Life Sciences	-	47	56
Social Science Index	-	20	-
POPLINE	-	10	35
Applied Sciences	-	22	12
Current Citation	-	-	4
Current Contents	-	-	4
Biotechnology	-	-	5
TOTAL	67	702	721

Training

We have also taken serious steps to take care of the training aspect for both library staff and users. We expect staff to have basic computer skills and some ability in trouble-shooting, in case of minor operating problems. In order to undertake database searches effectively, CD-ROM operators need knowledge and experience in information retrieval techniques. So far all this has been only partially accomplished because, although professional staff had some exposure in their professional training, the rest of it, especially for the support staff, has been done on the job. Many academic staff members have had some database searching experience during their studies overseas. The bigger problem is with those who trained locally. The training of this group, together with that of students, is done by the library staff during their early database search sessions. The library has persuaded some teaching staff to have demonstrations in their classes or during seminars. The problem has always been whether to take the equipment to the class or to bring the group to the library CD-ROM facility. We have also used the Exposition Days as an opportunity to train both teaching and research staff and students in conducting database searches. We are still struggling to get training in trouble-shooting for our staff, but opportunities in the region and abroad have not presented themselves.

ANALYSIS OF LESSONS LEARNED

In hindsight we can say what went right:

- It was critical to have a good and acceptable CD-ROM project proposal and we were lucky that somebody happened to be there at the right time.
- We consulted and got the support of the university authorities before we sent out our project proposal. That support has been very critical in a number of ways, including provision of adequate local funding, and in publicizing the service.
- The decision to choose that particular vendor for the purchase of the equipment was also right. Back-up service has been very critical and the local ICL agent has generally not let us down.

There is no doubt that the CD-ROM service technology has done a wonderful job in alleviating our problems of availability of and access to current information. It is definitely a technology that we can afford. In implementing the technological innovation at the Dar es Salaam University, we did our level best to make the right decisions, and some of the problems are beyond our control.

So far our user statistics are still low. We should have made the CD-ROM service accessible to undergraduate students. That should have boosted our user statistics to an optimal level. We are discussing that issue in the CD-ROM Service

Committee and the idea is likely to be accepted and adopted. We are also experimenting with various ways of making the document delivery service easier and cheaper for users.

There is little that we can do about the high cost of hardware and the ISI database products. We wished we had started with cheaper products. We could also have shortened the period of waiting for the purchase and the delivery of the equipment. That might have required us to use the services of another local agent, other than the ICL agent. But then that might have meant compromising on the back-up service. Unfortunately practically all hardware and software has to be ordered from overseas, and not locally or in the region. We had to resort to using personal contacts in the region and abroad from the beginning to the implementation stage of the project in order to obtain all the equipment and programs we needed.

At this point we have managed to convince our major CD-ROM database dealers, ISI and Silver Platter, to accept payment in UNESCO coupons. By this method, we have managed to bypass the cumbersome bank transfer procedures.

The application of information and communication technology (ICT), however, raises some old problems: if not used properly, ICT could perpetuate the dependency syndrome of the poorer African countries on the western countries. Of course this is a controversial issue like "appropriate technology" or "aid" in both the North and the South. As other case studies have shown, however, the technology can also be used to Africa's advantage. For instance, cataloging and capturing locally-produced material for distribution on CD-ROM will be of great benefit to Africa. Dissemination of local information databases to the North can provide a give and take situation between the South and the North.

The sustainability issue is very critical. The donor agency and the university have raised it on numerous occasions. The library and the university must have the necessary resources to carry on the project, when the donor's project period comes to an end. Here the need to make provision for local resources is critical. The local contribution is actually important throughout the functional operation of the project.

We have made significant efforts to cultivate individuals, departments, and research institutes inside and outside the university to contribute to the sustainability of the CD-ROM service. We have indicated that all users of the service must contribute to the cost of the service in one way or another. During the initial and launching period everything has been provided free-of-charge; however, as the service becomes critical to users, the users will be requested to pay at least a nominal cost for printing. We also ask users to pay for photocopies of documents delivered. We charge outside users a small user fee.

Teaching departments of the university are requested to consider subscribing to CD-ROM databases in their respective subjects within their link agreements with overseas universities or include the databases within their documentation components when presenting proposals to donor agencies. The faculties of Education and Engineering, for example, will take up subscriptions to ERIC and Engineering

Index, respectively, should the Library fail to pay for those subscriptions. The Faculty of Science will take up databases in the sciences. Recently the Faculty of Law consulted the Library on the acquisition of hardware and software, including databases in law. Some departments also have arrangements to pay for the cost of document delivery for their staff and postgraduate students.

It is also important to think about twinning arrangements with other projects going on in the Library. This ensures the successful implementation and mutual support of the projects. For the University of Dar es Salaam Library this has included project support from SAREC, the AAAS Journal Donation Program, and the UNO/RAF/006/GEF Biodiversity Project. One project seems to have a multiplier effect on others. It is after you have one project running smoothly that you attract other, related information technology projects. Since we started the CD-ROM service project in 1993, we have had two other local database creation projects.

CONCLUSIONS AND RECOMMENDATIONS

The introduction of the CD-ROM service technology has solved a critical information problem for the UDSM and Tanzania. But there are several challenges, beyond the issue of sustainability. Recognizing that the UDSM Library cannot afford to ignore the CD-ROM technology—for fear of being left further behind—we have some concerns about whether the CD-ROM technology can be technically maintained. Do we have enough local expertise to repair and replace the technology, for example? So far we have depended on back-up service from the vendor. So the problem of maintenance is not difficult in the country, but it could be cheaper and faster if we had the qualified personnel at the University or in the Library.

The CD-ROM databases we have from overseas cannot meet all of our STI needs. For development purposes, Tanzania's scientists need to have access to local and regional information resources, as well. There is considerable information in the form of grey literature—unpublished or unindexed reports, studies, and surveys by government and R&D institutions. A start has been made by the UDSM Library to create databases of local literature on environment, education, and biodiversity. The next important step is to create regional and continent-wide databases. This effort should be coupled with a campaign to convince scholars, scientists and practitioners to publish locally. Although the UDSM Library is one of the African University Libraries participating in the evaluation of international databases, the outcome of that evaluation is not yet complete at our University, and results from other African universities are not yet out.

As stated above, CD-ROM database information providers and vendors set conditions that are difficult to meet in developing countries. Should we, for example, cancel subscriptions to print indexes and rely on their compact disc equivalents? If we do, what will happen if we cancel the CD-ROM subscription and we are asked to return the discs?

This technological innovation also gives STI workers in the Third World an opportunity to think seriously about the development of appropriate STI technologies in the South and the adaptation of STI technologies from the North. It is our hope that our friends in the North will support this noble endeavor.

It is important to operate a project in accordance with the agreement and expectations of the donor agency. We tried as much as possible to keep to these conditions. We are convinced that because of this, besides the growing user demand for the service, the Carnegie Corporation accepted our application for the extension of the project by supplying an additional CD-ROM workstation and two CD-ROM database subscriptions, a desk-top publishing facility, and support to outreach activities.

NOTES

1. Statistical data in this report is taken from Jamhuri ya Muungano wa Tanzania. Hotuba ya Waziri wa Nchi katika Ofisi ya Rais na Makamu Mwenyekiti wa Tume ya Mipango, Mh. S. A.Kibona (Mbunge) wakati akiwakilisha Bungeni Taarifa ya Uchumi wa Taifa ya Mwaka 1992 na Mapendekezo ya Mpango wa Bajeti (Rolling Plan and Forward Budget) kwa kipindi cha 1993/94 - 1995/96, tarehe 17 Julai, 1993. Dar es Salaam: Government Printer, 1993.

2. We have since learned that this is a problem faced around the world—in both developed and developing countries.

3. Baard, Erick (1982) Appropriate Information Technology: A Cross-Cultural Perspective, UJISLAA, 4(4):263-268.

CD-ROM for Health Information in Zimbabwe

by Helga Patrikios

Helga Patrikios went to school in New York and Belfast, and to university at Trinity College Dublin, where she read French and Italian language and literature. She worked as a TV documentaries researcher, teacher and editor until her marriage to a Rhodesian brought her to Harare (then Salisbury) in 1972. She took a Higher Diploma in Library Science by correspondence with the University of South Africa in 1978, and has worked ever since at the Library of the University of Zimbabwe. She has been Medical Librarian since 1985, and has published and presented many papers on her work there. She was appointed Deputy University Librarian in 1994.

BACKGROUND AND CONTEXT OF THE PROJECT

In recent decades, throughout sub-Saharan Africa, academics, scientists and researchers have seen the decline of once flourishing institutes and universities as economic conditions worsened, and inflation and devaluation of local currencies exacerbated the chronic shortage of hard currencies. The deficiencies in traditional information sources, arising from economic, geographical and cultural factors, have worsened perceptibly in the past two decades. And while the information explosion in the North is fuelled by dramatic developments in information technologies, the South must watch the gap between its own information sources and those available in the industrialized countries grow ever wider. Can that gap be narrowed or even bridged, or will the poorer countries be further marginalized in terms of technology and information access?

Fortunately, in many African countries, the advent of the personal computer has enabled libraries to leapfrog two decades of development in information technology, and move straight into effective and appropriate solutions to some of the problems of information storage and retrieval. Institutions and private companies which had never seen a mainframe or minicomputer began in the mid-1980s to acquire microcomputers—often initially only for word processing, but increasingly for compiling databases and other specific applications.

In Zimbabwe, at the Medical Library of the University of Zimbabwe (UZML), the process began with CD-ROM. This case study will describe how and why that process was set in motion, and its immediate and longer-term effects on the services of the library and on its staff and users.

Zimbabwe has a population of 11 million people, 70 percent of whom are based in the rural areas. Independence from the illegal white minority rule of Ian Smith's Rhodesia was achieved in 1980; by 1990 Zimbabwe's development programs were well advanced, particularly in the fields of education and the health services.

The colonial legacy included a centralized health service, with a concentration of sophisticated curative services for a minority in the urban centers. (See Box 1.) The goal of the new Ministry of Health was to create an extensive network of primary health care outlets in the rural areas, reallocating existing resources to establish new clinics and upgrade general and district hospitals. The success of their policies was seen in a steady improvement in health status indicators during the middle and late 1980s, including maternal and child morbidity and mortality; nutritional status; and expanded immunization programs.

Harare, the capital, is the home of the University of Zimbabwe, established in 1958, which includes the country's only Medical School—added in 1963. As well as the 500 medical students, the Faculty has departments of Nursing Science, Pharmacy and Rehabilitation, and the School is a regional center for postgraduate programs in the medical specialties. The present total of students approaches 1,000, and student intakes continue to grow.

The Medical Library was well planned from the outset, with a good collection of journals and textbooks, and a current awareness service for academics. As the country's only medical library it was in principle accessible to members of the health professions outside the University; but since it was situated in the main University Library on the campus in an outlying suburb, it was little used other than by staff and students of the Faculty. In 1978 the library moved to the spacious premises of the new medical school and teaching hospital close to the city center, where more non-university health workers began to make use of it.

BOX 1   Pre-Independence Health Services

Pre-Independence health services had neglected information support; medical and nursing education were historically centralized, and the only other sources of information and educational material lay in the small collections at the nursing schools. The library at the Ministry was a dusty storeroom piled high with government reports. The achievement of Independence made rapid growth and change possible not only for the health services but for health information too.

In 1983, following recommendations from a World Health Organization-sponsored workshop in Tanzania, the UZML, as the only major medical library in Zimbabwe, was designated National Focal Point for Health Sciences Information Services, by both the Ministry and the University. An outreach librarian was appointed to deliver services to health workers in provincial and rural hospitals and health centers. In 1984, we carried out a survey of their information needs and priorities.[1]

Anecdotal evidence from rural health professionals of a dire lack of access to information—an absence of current textbooks and journals, or indeed any considerable hospital library—had prompted the survey, which had a 74 percent response rate; this evidence was emphatically confirmed by the 63 doctors and 10 senior nurses who responded. Their expressed priorities were to have core collections of books and journals at their workplaces, and 90 percent considered the lack of current medical information to be a serious difficulty or disadvantage.

Some of these needs were addressed by a Joint Health Information Committee, which we established with the Ministry of Health for this purpose—core collections of 40 textbooks and 13 manuals were provided by a Scandinavian donor for all hospitals and clinics. Adequate journal collections could not be provided to all hospitals, so we compiled instead a digest of MEDLINE abstracts on Zimbabwe's health issues, *Current Health Information Zimbabwe (CHIZ)*, a free update for all Zimbabwe's health professionals. The abstracts were provided for us by the World Health Organization (WHO) in Geneva, who sent us the monthly MEDLINE printouts produced by the Swiss host Datastar. Datastar ran searches using a profile of Zimbabwe's major health problems, compiled with advice from former district medical officers.

We tried, in the mid-1980s, to gain access to the online databases of the U.S. National Library of Medicine and to MEDLINE in particular—the index, with abstracts, to over 3,700 of the world's major biomedical journals, with over 8 million records. The obstacles—high and unpredictable costs in scarce foreign currency (for passwords, telecommunications, connect time and printouts)—were too great. A further disincentive were the complex command syntaxes of the databases, and the need for considerable familiarity with the medical terminology.

A less demanding more user-friendly medium was needed to access MEDLINE. In 1988, while visiting a London medical school library, we saw it—in the shape of CD-ROM, in full-color action—a technology based on laser discs that was just then beginning to penetrate European markets. The advantages of CD-ROM were immediately obvious: the powerful laser discs, used in conjunction with an ultra-friendly search engine, mounted in the homely personal computer, bringing international bibliographic databases into the most remote centers—and at a predictable cost. Unlimited online searching and training time, unlimited information retrieval, unlimited access to the almost mythical databases of the world's most advanced scientific institutions—these were suddenly within our reach.

PROJECT DESCRIPTION

In mid-1988, a project proposal went off to the Carnegie Corporation of New York—for the acquisition of CD-ROM equipment with a subscription to the MEDLINE database. The general objective of the project was to improve the health information service at the UZML, with the specific objective of providing users in the Medical School and throughout Zimbabwe with MEDLINE literature searches.

The Medical Library had three professional (graduate) staff, three diplomates, and adequate secretarial and other support staff. The reference librarian had nursing training behind her, as well as her library qualifications. Most of her working hours hitherto were spent scanning the latest journal issues for individuals requiring current awareness updates—a Selective Dissemination of Information (SDI) service. We did not yet know that this task could be reduced to some minutes a month. All of us were excited by the prospect of introducing a computerized service into the Library at last.

Neither I nor any of my colleagues had ever laid hands on a computer. No one in the University Library had computer skills. Many of us were conscious of being left behind while libraries in the North were forging ahead with newer and better computer applications for information storage and retrieval, and library housekeeping systems. Among the major benefits of the project would be the familiarization of library staff with microcomputer technology.

We also counted on providing our own MEDLINE searches for *CHIZ*, and relieving WHO's Library in Geneva of that expensive burden. We could also revise our search strategy at will without incurring further expense or trouble for WHO.

The response from Carnegie was rapid and positive—we received a discretionary grant for a feasibility study of a MEDLINE on CD-ROM search service. The grant also enabled us to buy a personal computer, the two drives needed to search the current five-year MEDLINE file, and a two-year subscription to the MEDLINE database.

PROJECT EXPERIENCE AND IMPLEMENTATION

What were our problems, errors, and successes in implementing the three phases of our project?

Hardware

Our initial choice of hardware was poor. Since we did not even know which questions to ask, we were guided by earlier advice from another donor's program officer, which stressed the importance of securing reliable local (IBM) maintenance. We ordered the smallest cheapest IBM: a PS2 Model 30. We were guided by excessive thrift, rather than by criteria of power and speed, of which we then knew nothing except what we learned from the conflicting advice given by local computer experts. They in turn knew nothing of the rapidly growing exigencies of CD-ROM—an unknown technology in Zimbabwe in 1988.

In reality the Harare private sector offered more than enough microcomputer support to go round; furthermore, a snippet of local lore that we absorbed has proved to be well founded: in Harare's temperate and relatively dust-free climatic conditions microcomputers, even the cheaper IBM clones, generally give little trouble. We rightly did not budget or contract for an expensive maintenance agreement with the local IBM agents—a hefty 10 percent of the equipment's cost per year, the local standard charge. (The high cost of equipment in Africa shocks buyers in the North—the addition of transport and duties almost double prices of any imported goods.)

Instead we allowed in our budget for (lower) maintenance costs and have always spent less than was budgeted on hardware and software problems. A piece of late news: recent extensive building operations next to our library have created a reddish-grey dust—clay and cement—which now thickly coats the edges and insides of our drives. They are giving occasional trouble now.

The pioneer personal computer, within three years of purchase, was unable to process the burgeoning MEDLINE database. We ran out of space on the 20 megabyte hard disk before the end of the first phase of the project—there was barely room for MEDLINE software (13 megabyte) and word processing software, and ultimately everything but MEDLINE had to be deleted. When MEDLINE needed 28 megabytes of disk space and at least one megabyte of RAM, and we found the machine's hard disk and RAM could not be upgraded, it was relegated to word processing use.

Clearly, as novices, we should have sought and found more expert advice outside Zimbabwe before deciding what to buy. (See Box 2.) It was a colleague in New York who discovered that the drives we had ordered were incompatible with the personal computer—just in time to prevent their shipment; it took several months to rectify that error; and when the equipment was all finally assembled, we found that the driver extension software was superseded, so that more weeks passed while we awaited the current version.

BOX 2   Relative Speed of Equipment

When, before ordering, I contacted the MEDLINE vendors in New York to ask whether our choice of equipment was appropriate for their database software, they said it would be fine, but warned that its performance would be a bit sluggish. I responded, quite seriously, that was just fine, since we too were sluggish . . . . It turned out that we could go off and brew tea during some of the lengthier search processes, and still find the search in progress on our return.

Professional advice provided by Carnegie, and first-hand experience, helped us in making better decisions on equipment in later phases of the project. Four years later, for instance, we were encouraged by a local supplier—and were very tempted—to network existing and new personal computers so that all workstations in the library could access all CD-ROMs. We learned, though, that not only would the proprietary networking costs of our database vendors have been beyond our long-term means, but also the absence of expertise in the library system needed to maintain the network would have left me with that responsibility. We knew that neither I nor my colleagues could muster the time or skills needed.

As time passed our local suppliers learned much more about CD-ROM; we too learned, as personal computers became cheaper, faster and more powerful in terms of clock speed, disk and memory size, that we needed to allow for rapid growth in the number and size of databases, for much more RAM, for Windows software for the databases which would, before long, be available only in Windows; for anti-virus packages to check the diskettes on which our users increasingly needed to download their search results.

Our initial choice of a vendor for the MEDLINE database (from a product range of eight competing companies) was based on advice from a large medical library in Milwaukee, which had closely examined all the options, and on journal articles which rigorously evaluated the search features of the different versions. Our chosen vendor, Ovid Technologies (formerly CD Plus), has prospered, multiplied and improved its products, and supported us with discounts. CD Plus responded, though not always promptly, to the software difficulties that arose from time to time as new features were developed. We learned to correct some of them by the simple expedient of reinstalling the software. Other software failures needed input from our suppliers. The only personal computer in which we failed to install the recent much larger DOS version of Ovid's MEDLINE is an IBM PS2 Model 70; it accepts only the Windows version of MEDLINE.

Delays

Our greatest frustrations came from the delays that held up the first phase by one year. There were delays in obtaining the correct drives and software; it took more time to cajole duty free certificates and import permits from the State's then ponderous bureaucratic machinery. The wasted year, 1988-1989, nonetheless saw a degree of progress in STI at UZML. We learned word processing on the personal computer, which was delivered within only a few months. Once the library had at least one functioning workstation (and by the second phase of support we had three) and could keep our search service going, we could tolerate subsequent delays. The cliff-hanging saga of the supplier who held us up in the third phase of the project by converting funds for equipment to his own use must be documented elsewhere; he delivered our goods in the end, but a year later than planned.

RESULTS, IMPACTS, AND BENEFITS OF THE PROJECT

What have CD-ROM technology and the microcomputer—the availability of in-house biomedical and health databases—brought to the library, to the Medical School, its staff and students, and to the country's health workers? Who uses MEDLINE most? Why do they want MEDLINE searches? The data gathered from our search request forms give some answers.

Numbers of MEDLINE Searches Made

The average number of searches rose from 80 searches per month (1989-1990) to 450 per month in 1995 (November). (See Figure 1.) In March 1995 a record 700 individual searches and monthly updates (SDIs) were recorded.

Categories of Search Requesters

Undergraduate and postgraduate students represented 36 percent and 15 percent, respectively, of all searchers in a 6-month sample of 1,660 search request forms in 1994. (The 58 monthly SDIs that are automatically generated as updates for individuals were not categorized.) Other searchers were academic staff, non-academic staff, or government workers, or from NGOs, parastatals, or the private sector. (See Figure 2.)

Purpose of Searches

In the same six-month period, research and assignments (in which there may be overlap) accounted for 41 percent and 13 percent, respectively; teaching 4 percent; updates and SDIs 20 percent; patient care 8 percent; publications 2 percent; in 12 percent no purpose was given. (n = 2008 searches including SDIs.)

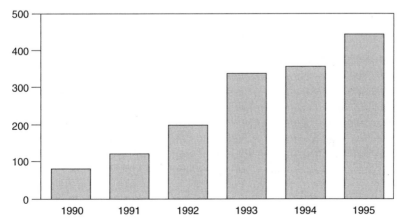

FIGURE 1   Monthly average of CD-ROM searches conducted, January 1990 to November 1995.

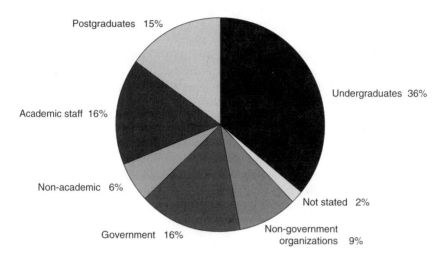

FIGURE 2   MEDLINE searches by user categories.

Survey on the Use of MEDLINE and Its Abstracts

In March 1995 we carried out a survey on the use of MEDLINE by staff and students of the Medical Faculty.[2] A questionnaire sent to 252 staff and under-graduates sought to gain information on:

•   numbers of MEDLINE users and non-users;
•   frequency of use;
•   the value of searches and of abstracts;
•   the number of end users and the need for training in end user searching; and
•   reasons for non-use of MEDLINE.

We had a response rate of 50 percent (n = 252). Of 122 academic staff to whom we sent questionnaires, 49 responded. Of the 130 final-year students to whom we sent questionnaires, 67 responded. Of the total 126 respondents, 119 used MEDLINE and only seven had never used MEDLINE. (See Table 1.)

We can surmise that those who have used MEDLINE are much more likely to respond to a questionnaire on its use than those who have not used it; thus a much greater proportion of the 50 percent who did not respond may have been non-users. The reasons given by respondents who had never used the service were lack of knowledge about it and lack of time to use it. Additional survey results are given in Tables 2–5.

TABLE 1   MEDLINE Users/Non-users

	Academics		Final-year Students	
MEDLINE Users	(n = 54)	92%	(n = 65)	97%
MEDLINE Non-users	(n = 5)	8%	(n = 2)	3%

TABLE 2   Frequency of Use of MEDLINE

Use of MEDLINE per month	(n = 114)	%
Use it often (5 times or more)	12	11
Use it regularly (2-3 times)	24	21
Use it occasionally (once)	41	36
Use it rarely (less than once)	37	32

TABLE 3   Value of Search Results

Search results satisfactory	(n = 117)	%
Usually	78	67
Sometimes	32	27
Rarely	7	6
Never	0	0

TABLE 4   Usefulness of Abstracts

Abstracts as a source of information	(n = 116)	%
Very useful	74	64
Moderately useful	41	35
Not useful	1	1

TABLE 5   Completeness of Information in Abstracts

Abstracts provide information complete in itself:	(n = 117)	%
Usually	23	20
Sometimes	62	53
Rarely	23	20
Never	9	7

Training in MEDLINE Searching

The library has periodically offered training in MEDLINE searching to users: 49 percent of respondents had received some training. Most of these were students: only 17 (31 percent) academic staff had received training.

The survey showed that most staff and students did searches assisted by a librarian; only 25 percent of respondents (n = 29) were able or willing to do their own searches, although half had received some training. Training was thus deficient in some way for half the participants. Ninety percent (n = 87) were interested in receiving training from library staff and/or the MEDLINE tutorial program.

It is important that we enable more end users to make searches independently of library staff. Because few of our staff have a strong grasp of medical terminology we are concerned that the quality of more complex searches may be uneven. The more end users with search skills, the higher the potential relevance of search results, and the more staff time saved.

Availability of Full-text Articles

MEDLINE citations carry a note if the journal cited is held by our library, and most users reported making some effort, sometimes, to locate such journal articles. But less than half of our users attempt to obtain articles through the Library's Inter-Library Loans (ILL) service. There had been a boom in ILL requests, almost matching the growth in the numbers of searches, from 1990 to mid-1994. The service then declined sharply when ILL funds ran out.

Users have little confidence in the library's runs of journals, which are broken by frequent temporary or permanent stoppages of subscriptions; they are unwilling, too, to depend on the unreliable and very slow ILL service. When its funds run out we are dependent on the goodwill of two or three South African libraries, which cannot, of course, meet all our needs. In response to the library's attempts to improve ILL services, the University has recently approved, in principle, the introduction of realistic (almost full cost-recovery) charges, as opposed to highly subsidized minimal charges for ILL documents. While students will continue to be subsidized to some extent, researchers (academic staff) will be expected to pay for ILL services.

Immediate and Long-term Outcomes of the Service: Products and Spinoffs

Searches

MEDLINE now produces over 380 individual searches each month, as well as 58 monthly updates for individual researchers and clinicians; it also produces the monthly printouts of abstracts for our national digest *Current Health Information Zimbabwe (CHIZ)*.

Journal selection

CD-ROM (used with the bibliographic database management program Papyrus) enables us to use MEDLINE in bibliometric studies to identify those journals which most frequently publish articles of relevance to Zimbabwe's health problems—the citations selected for *CHIZ* and those selected for printing out by our users. The most frequently cited titles are included in a revised core collection of most-needed journal titles.

The Bradford's Law of Scatter (illustrated in many studies including one at the National Library of Medicine, where it was found that only 300 titles of its 22,000 periodicals satisfied 70 percent of all requests[3]) reinforces the benefits of accessing journals through a document delivery service, rather than "owning" expensive subscriptions to little-used journals. The "ownership versus access" algorithm we have developed[4] can be brought to bear on the selection process now that lists of most frequently cited titles can be built on objective criteria rather than relying solely on manual analyses of inter-library loans, or on the possibly idiosyncratic or unrepresentative demands of often transient specialists and other academics.

Abstracts

The survey demonstrates the dissatisfaction of users with our journal collection and inter-library loans service, and a considerable—and certainly lamentable—dependence on abstracts rather than on full-text articles, with 73 percent "usually" or "sometimes" making do with abstracts alone. How valuable can abstracts be, how complete the information they contain? No clinician, researcher, or librarian would advocate total dependence on abstracts. Many of them do not accurately reflect the main findings or conclusions of their full papers, and rarely (except in terms of the unassailable reputation of the source publication) enable a critical evaluation of a paper's real worth in terms of methodology and other criteria. A recent study on the reliability of reviews of abstracts for scientific meetings found that reviewers disagreed substantially when evaluating the same abstracts and that structured review criteria were needed.[5] The proportion of structured abstracts in the medical literature is increasing, however, and enhances the value and useful-

---

BOX 3   The Importance of Abstracts

We have learned anecdotally too that our users find that abstracts can and do provide critical information in a crisis—our Drug and Toxicology Information Service, for example, inevitably has to rely on abstracts in emergencies. Abstracts inform policy and assist planning. They have had to satisfy our users for information on management of diseases and poisoning cases for decisions on drug prescribing and dosages, for literature reviews, for preparing lectures, for updating practical knowledge and skills—because the back-up of full texts is not available quickly enough. It may be deplorable but it is also true that in many contexts, including our own, the back-up texts will never be available, or will arrive too late. It must be recognized that in the poorer countries of the world an abstract is likely to be all the reader will ever see of journal articles.

---

ness of bibliographic databases. (See Box 3.)

Outcomes for health professionals, patients?

While published data demonstrate the impact of MEDLINE on patient outcomes in the USA[6,7,8] we are not able in Zimbabwe to quantify what the direct and indirect benefits of CD-ROM databases and their abstracts are, in terms of improved efficacy of health professionals, or improved health status indicators, for instance. There were considerable gains in the health status indicators of Zimbabwe's people after the country won its Independence in 1980, but these are now being rapidly eroded by the combined effects of the AIDS pandemic, and of the economic structural adjustment programs being implemented in recent years in many African countries.

In a 1993 snap survey of opinions of senior academic staff on MEDLINE's effects the following were among their comments: "its comprehensiveness and currency [make it] revolutionary"; "it makes life so easy . . . very helpful for research and teaching"; "it plays a very important role in teaching Med students enabling them to keep up with the latest information . . . is invaluable for their clinical presentations"; "it helps me keep up with appropriate management of clinical problems"; "it is indispensable for research protocols and write ups of research projects"; "in the recent meningitis epidemic it provided essential epidemiological and serotyping data for appropriate measures for prevention, control and management"; "it plays a major role for me as a consultant teaching juniors."

Some examples (from the 1995 survey) of respondents' reactions to a question on the effects on their work of NOT having access to MEDLINE: "dramatic—my research and teaching capability would collapse without it"; one urologist declared he "would scream"; others spoke of "catastrophic", "devastating" and "drastic" effects, and "the end of the road."

Promotion of the CD-ROM Literature Search Service

We promoted the service initially only to Medical School staff and not to students, anticipating an unmanageable demand on our single workstation. Only two members of staff (out of over 100 in 21 departments to whose chairmen we sent promotional circulars) appeared at our MEDLINE open day. We assume that initially news of MEDLINE and POPLINE spread largely by word of mouth, since there was a steady increase in use after the first few weeks.

After a formal presentation of the first workstation, involving the United States Information Service (USIS), the small paragraph on the event which appeared in the daily paper showed a total lack of understanding of the technology on the part of the reporter. Our handout about CD-ROM was beyond his comprehension — we realized how important it is to recognize the impenetrability of new technologies to those who have no experience of them, and to learn how to communicate their capabilities in the simplest possible way.

We reinforced our initial low-key circulars and notices only when we had acquired two more workstations in the second phase of the project, by promotional demonstrations of MEDLINE (using a Datashow projector we acquired in the second phase of the project) at professional meetings of interest groups (such as pharmacists, physiotherapists, primary care physicians). To provide these demonstrations our reference librarian, with help sometimes from me or another colleague, had to load her car with a personal computer, four drives and a printer, drive to the meeting venue and reassemble the workstation there—a considerable undertaking. From follow-up visits and search requests from those sectors we knew the demonstrations made an impact—seeing is believing. (Recently staff in our Main Library took CD-ROM to individual faculties, and they too found that an immediate increase in use of the databases resulted.)

Demonstrations of CD-ROM searches get the most attention in our library orientation sessions for students; post-graduate students are given a longer introduction than undergraduates, and are strongly encouraged to read database tutorials and take the training which is always available from our staff. However, offers to academic staff and students of training for individuals or small groups have had little response thus far. The lack of interest in our offers of training is not surprising—very few students and staff have had the opportunity to acquire computer skills, and most still have no access to any computer other than ours. They will have to start by learning basic computer skills, and only then attempt to use the (relatively user-friendly) interface software.

Training is more likely to be accepted if it is informally given, by way of explanations to a search requestor as he helps a librarian make his search. Our understanding of the problem of low uptake of training is that, unless users practice and enlarge on newly acquired search skills on a regular basis, they forget them between visits and have to start again. Many of our users have very little spare time for acquiring new skills outside their daily work schedule.

BOX 4   The African Index Medicus Project

Our database, *Utano* (the Shona word for Health), provides records for us to contribute to WHO's recent database initiative, the African Index Medicus (AIM). The innovative AIM project assembles (at WHO headquarters in Brazzaville) abstracts of mainly unpublished "grey" literature collected from a growing number of African countries. WHO produces and circulates regular printed updates to libraries in Africa, and to subscribers in African institutes throughout the United States and Europe.

The Medical School is constructing a new Health Sciences building and plans to incorporate considerable computer-aided learning facilities in the building. Easy access to computers will then no longer be limited to the library's CD-ROM facilities.

Other Uses of Microcomputers in the Medical Library

A database of local health literature

This project to create and compile a database of local unpublished health literature was funded by IDRC and implemented in 1991-1992, concurrently with our expanding CD-ROM service. (See Box 4.) The contract staff, the training in database use (UNESCO's Micro CDS/ISIS) and the hardware brought to the library by the project reinforced our understanding and appreciation of the potential and value of computerization, and has since offered continuing opportunities to all our professional staff to widen their computer skills. The database, after the expiry of the contracts of project staff, has continued its slow but steady growth, as two of our staff members gradually master the complexities of the ISIS software.

Email: local and international access to information

Email now enables health workers outside the capital to get access to MEDLINE searches and other material from the Harare library and beyond. In our third year of reliable email access, we now operate through Zimbabwe's upgraded telephone system, through SatelLife's local HealthNet node in Harare, which links us with other major international email networks as well as with the HealthNet users in provincial medical directorates and many of the district offices. The number of MEDLINE search requests emailed to our outreach librarian from the provinces doubled last year. We download and return search results to users by email, and can at last scan and email photocopies of articles in the library instead of mailing photocopies (which may take a week to deliver). The main limiting factor in the use of email is the still small number of health professionals with easy access to and familiarity with personal computers; but the time taken to scan and run an Optical Character Recognition program against the copy is also something of a deterrent.

Moves to bring us online into the Internet may bear fruit in the next year or two. Meanwhile email and the Grateful Med search interface give us easy and low-cost access to the MEDLARS databases of the National Library of Medicine, through the BITNIS program,[9] which enables a turn-around time of 24-48 hours. The costs of our email services are modest: each of our two stations costs about $7.00 per month, less than the cost of one five-page fax.

The impact of microcomputer technologies on library staff

Many libraries in Africa, including our own, have become shelters for dwindling and aging printed resources. The effects on library staff of acquiring computer skills and delivering computerized and very current information are all the more positive in this context. The image of traditionally low-status professionals has been subtly but unquestionably enhanced by their new capabilities—doctors and nurses now request appointments for searches with library staff . . . who have something valuable to offer at last. This empowerment of librarians increases their morale at a time when economic forces have a contrary effect on the work force; computers make the job more fun for the majority of staff who enthusiastically embrace the new technologies.

The growing use of personal computers in our library imposes on us the need to re-examine our management structure; lines of authority have to be redefined. There is need for greater flexibility in job descriptions and responsibilities, need for recognition and monitoring by senior management of any radical increases or reductions in workloads brought about by automation, need for rewarding exceptional skills and providing opportunities for the development of those skills to those who show aptitude. If sustained progress in use of the new technologies is to be made, the old rigid and hierarchical structures of libraries must bend and expand to allow for new patterns and areas of growth. The application of performance indicators to services and processes is one obvious method of planning and managing the changes which automation inevitably brings in its wake.

ANALYSIS OF LESSONS LEARNED

Unquestionably CD-ROM databases, MEDLINE in particular, have brought about a radical change in the information seeking behavior of our users: unprecedented rapid and easy access to current and archival journal literature; and an increased awareness and documented increased use of the journal literature.[10] We believe, however, that the most significant and valuable outcome of this service has been the growing awareness in its users of a range, literally a world of otherwise unknown information sources. It has been by far the greatest force for progress in information access that our users have experienced.

However, while the advent of CD-ROM has been a dramatic success in our library, and while email is the cheapest known method, *pro rata*, for the speedy transmission of data, there are funding and technical issues that cannot be ignored. We have learned—painlessly so far, thanks to the generosity and flexibility of our donors—that one-time set-up costs are not a reality.

Planners must face and meet the costs of maintaining and updating expensive hardware to keep pace with changes in database sizes and interfaces; they must have access to expert and unbiased information on the new technologies to avoid costly mistakes in purchasing inappropriate equipment. They must allow for the relentless growth of RAM requirements; the need for multiple workstations when multiple users want access to databases; the need for the more expensive laser printers when printing out images from full-text CD-ROMs or other electronic sources such as World Wide Web. The Internet has come to neighboring countries and is likely to reach us too before very long, with further implications for hardware, training and other costs. Growth and development in the technologies are inevitable and expensive. Institutional support and involvement become increasingly vital if the technologies are to survive and prosper in the long term in Africa.

The lack of concern of institutional planners for information supply may be attributable to negative experiences and low expectations in the libraries they have known, as much as to the failure of educational systems to include information retrieval skills in their curricula. We expect MEDLINE to break that cycle in Zimbabwe, by sensitizing students—the planners of the future—to the existence of vast and formerly unknown resources. The cost of introducing and maintaining a MEDLINE search service, represented as a proportion of the budget of a Medical School or a Health Ministry, would be insignificant. That cost calculated as a percentage of the salary of each health professional in government service would be negligible; its cost effectiveness in terms of the development of human resources and services would be obvious.

Our survey, made after five years of use of MEDLINE, shows that this database has become essential to the work of many of our academic staff: eighty per cent of respondents stated that they would elect that the library cancel ten journal subscriptions rather than the MEDLINE subscription. We are likely to have to make just such a substitute in the near future. As a first step it is essential to expose present and future generations of planners, teachers and practitioners to these databases. The fact that the library has been able to offer four or five workstations providing MEDLINE and other databases to all comers has meant quick, easy, and free access to vast quantities of medical literature, which would otherwise be inaccessible.

CONCLUSIONS AND RECOMMENDATIONS

We have realized to a considerable extent the potential of CD-ROM technology at the UZML. The primary effects of the medium have been a vastly increased access to and use of current health information sources, whether in the form of abstracts or full-text journal articles or segments from constantly updated textbooks; and along with this increase there have been very significant changes in the information seeking behavior of large proportions of academic staff and students in the Medical Faculty and of health professionals in government service and the private sector. There is evidence elsewhere, and we must to a great extent assume, that the increased use of the literature and the resulting increased knowledge base of health professionals must produce the secondary and most important benefits of improved health services in general and better patient care in particular.

Our experiences in providing CD-ROM literature search services suggest that increased and more effective use would be made of the databases, and of other computer technologies such as email and eventually the Internet, if more of our present and potential users had been previously exposed to computers, or had some computer training. Economic circumstances in Zimbabwe have hitherto prevented all but the most privileged sections of our present and potential user community from owning or having easy access to computers. However, the rate of growth in the computer industry, and growing awareness among members of the health care community of the immeasurable benefits of personal computers—to which our project has made a major contribution—suggest that a critical mass of computer users will have been reached in the longer term.

Once this critical mass has been achieved, the question of sustainability will cease to be such a worrisome issue. Institutions, health services, and individuals will have their own strong motivation to supply the material and human resources necessary to exploit and develop the new technologies.

NOTES

1. Patrikios, H.M. (1985) Socio-economic changes in developing countries: the concern of the medical librarian? In: *Medical Libraries, One World: Resources, Cooperation, Services. Proceedings of the Fifth International Congress on Medical Librarianship.* Tokyo: Keio University Medical Library.

2. Patrikios, M.M. (1995) Effects of MEDLINE abstracts on information use in an African medical Library. Paper presented at 7th International Congress on Medical Librarianship: Health Information for the Global Village, Washington, D.C.

3. Warren, K. (1987) The evolution of selective biomedical libraries and their use in the developing world. *Journal of the American Medical Association* 257(19):2628-9.

4. Patrikios, H.M. (1994, 1996) A minimal acquisitions policy for journals at the University of Zimbabwe Medical Library. In: *Survival strategies in African university libraries.* American Association for the Advancement of Science.

5. Rubin, H.R. et al. (1993) How reliable is peer review of scientific abstracts? Looking back at the 1991 Annual Meeting of the Society of General Internal Medicine. *Journal of General Internal Medicine* 8(5)255-8.

6. Lindberg, D.A., et al (1993) Use of MEDLINE by physicians for clinical problem solving. *Journal of the American Medical Association* 269(24):3129.

7. Wilson, S.R., et al. (1989) *Use of the Critical Incident Technique to evaluate the impact of MEDLINE: Final report.* Palo Alto, CA: American Institutes for Research.

8. Klein, M.S. et al. (1994) Effect of on-line literature searching on length of stay and patient care costs. *Academic Medicine* 69(6)489-95.

9. Search costs are currently being funded by SatelLife, Cambridge, Massachusetts.

10. Patrikios, H.M. (1993) A minimal acquisitions policy for journals at the University of Zimbabwe Medical Library. In: *Survival Strategies in African University Libraries: New Technologies in the Service of Information.* American Association for the Advancement of Science, Washington, D.C., p. 96.

The African Index Medicus (AIM) Project

The need for improved access to bibliographic and other information related to health issues of African countries has long been felt by researchers, development agents, health administrators, and planners both inside and outside the continent. Very few African health and biomedical information sources are included in the world's leading bibliographic databases. Thus, access to information on health and medical research in the region is inadequate and, unless researchers publish in non-African journals, their work may be overlooked or duplicated. Further, there is a wealth of untapped information in books, reports and studies from international development agencies, nongovernmental organizations and local institutions.

The *African Index Medicus (AIM)* was initiated by the Association for Health Information and Libraries in Africa (AHILA) to provide improved access to health information published in or related to Africa. At its consultative meeting in January 1993, in Accra, Ghana, AHILA members made decisions regarding contents, standard data-input format, methods of exchange of database records, and training needs. Participants at this meeting included AHILA committee members, potential pilot-site librarians from Ghana, Kenya, Nigeria, Zambia, and Zimbabwe, and technical support staff from the World Health Organization. With sponsorship from the Health Foundation (New York), WHO has recently completed training of librarians in Cameroon, Ethiopia, Ghana, Kenya, Nigeria, Tanzania, and Uganda.

With technical assistance from the World Health Organization (WHO) and support in the form of training and equipment from the Health Foundation and other agencies, the project is steadily growing with the motivation and hard work

continued

of the African health librarians. Indeed, Regina Shakakata, one of the contributors to *AIM,* calls the project "the pride of Africa because it developed with the efforts of AHILA members." Ms. Shakakata says that, in Zambia, the *AIM* project means that the local literature created by health professionals is indexed and disseminated widely using the printed media intra-nationally and the Internet gophers internationally. As a spin-off service, her Medical Library collects the full text articles of the indexed items and integrates them into the University of Zambia Medical Library collection.

The project is a decentralized one that gives participating institutions greater bibliographic control of their national health information materials. Databases of bibliographic records of local health materials are created at the national level, using CDS-ISIS software. They are then merged with records relating to health in Africa emanating from other international databases, such as WHO's WHOLIS, POPLINE, and others. The bibliographic database is only one of the components of the project. AIM also intends to create files on health-related research, health information experts, and health information resources and services. Seven issues of *AIM* have appeared. Input centers are in anglophone and lusophone countries and francophone countries have been encouraged to join in the project.

A sample file from the database is available on the Internet from the WHO gopher (gopher.who.ch) in order to give visibility to the project in developed countries. Through increased visibility, WHO and the AIM participants hope to garner support for AHILA's efforts by encouraging people and institutions to become affiliated members in order to receive the latest print version of AIM. AHILA's existence depends on its membership. Many of the AIM participants have pointed out the difficulty of getting such a project off the ground with little or no funding. They encourage other African countries to join the AIM project and welcome partnerships with bilateral agencies and others interested in this unique grassroots, south-south project.

The success of the *African Index Medicus Project* is due, in large part, to the efforts of Dr. Deborah Avriel, who joined WHO in 1984 and was Chief Librarian from 1987 until her death in June 1995. Dr. Avriel's global vision consistently emphasized the importance of library and information services for health professionals in the developing world. Her enthusiasm and commitment to the cause of health information in the poorer countries motivated and encouraged her colleagues even at a distance. As a vocal supporter and untiring friend of Africa, she gave vigorous backing to the launching of the *AIM* Project.

Communications for Better Health Project in Zambia
by Regina Shakakata

Regina Shakakata is Medical Librarian at the University of Zambia Medical Library. She is Coordinator for the Communications for Better Health project and the National Coordinator for Healthnet. She has managed the Medical Library since 1986.

BACKGROUND AND CONTEXT OF THE PROJECT

About Zambia

Zambia has an area of 752,600 square kilometers and a population of 8.09 million people (1990 census). It has a national average density of 10.8 per square kilometer. Children under 15 years and women of child bearing age (15-49) constitute almost 75 percent of the population in any given year.

The country has a fairly good health service infrastructure and a reasonable cadre of health professionals, at least by standards of the developing world. The health system is heavily biased in favor of curative services rather than in preventive medicine and, even then, it favors urban population over rural populations.

Health resources and status are influenced by the economic development of the country. The consequences of the economic crisis in Zambia include among others the following:

*   Erosion of the health infrastructure;
*   A decline in the quantity and quality of access to health services;
*   An increase in the cases of malnutrition;
*   An inadequate supply of drugs;

- An unsatisfactory rate of infant mortality;
- Poor staff morale due to unfavorable working conditions; and
- The neglect of health information provision in national programs.

The University of Zambia (UNZA)

The link between the University of Zambia and the Ministry of Health (MOH) is the School of Medicine. When the School of Medicine was established in 1970, it had a book collection which was housed at the then Oppenheimer College of Social Services. The years that followed the establishment of the Medical Library saw a steady growth of health information at the library, with a book stock of 25,000 volumes of books and 781 periodical titles on the current subscriptions list in 1985 (Stock-taking report, 1985). Although the proportion of the books and periodicals budget which was given to the Medical Library was not rationally divided, the Medical Library was able to purchase all the recommended books and to pay for the periodicals on the current subscriptions list in any given year. (See Box 1.)

The Medical Library collection was supplemented by generous donations from friends of the University of Zambia, mainly from abroad and through gifts and exchange programs within and outside Africa. The only technology that was available at the Medical library was an audio/visual collection, which was composed of slides, microfiche, microfilm, filmstrips, reel-to-reel tapes, and texts. This collection was not easily accessible because the library did not have, and still does not have, the hardware with which to view the collection. The collection was and is still only usable with the help of the equipment from the UNZA Medical Illustrations Unit of the School of Medicine.

The Medical library struggled to survive through all the economic turmoil that Zambia faced from 1985 to 1990. Health information provision at the Medical Library suffered much since 1985. The last regular subscriptions to periodicals was in 1984. The book budgets were last fulfilled at about the same time. There

---

BOX 1   The UNZA Medical Library

The economic conditions that prevailed in the country due to extensive mining activities at the time of the inception of the Medical Library made it possible for the UNZA to be very well supported financially. The UNZA in turn gave 5 percent of its budget to the UNZA Library. As the local book industry was not developed and is still not developed, all required medical books and periodicals were obtained from either the United Kingdom or the United States, with less than 5 percent coming from Africa and other parts of the world (annual reports, 1970-1985).

was near total dependency on donor support to acquire current health literature. The World Health Organization (WHO) played a major role to sustain subscriptions to critical journal titles in the Medical Library. Initially, the total number of periodicals subscribed to by WHO was 50, which was reduced to 15 in 1987 and which has remained at that level to date. The book collections were slowly becoming redundant as new acquisitions diminished in number year after year. The academic and research programs were dependent upon the ingenuity of the medical librarians and the goodwill of their partners outside the country. The host institution did not have the funding required to support the library services.

In this situation of real information poverty, genuine financial support was sought to try and alleviate or reduce the lack of information to less destructive levels. It was not possible to seek assistance in-country because the entire nation existed in an information poverty trap. Neighboring states were in no better situation either, except in the case of the University of Zimbabwe Medical Library, which survived the scourge of the rash economies of developing countries due to late independence.

The Carnegie Corporation of New York, the International Development Research Centre of Canada (IDRC), the Commonwealth of Learning, WHO, the Ford Foundation, and others have, at one time or another, sponsored meetings that brought together African medical librarians and persons working in the area of science and technology information systems and communication technologies to discuss access to information and other professional developments. Other groups also provided expert assistance and moral support. These include the American Association for the Advancement of Science (AAAS), The Health Foundation of New York (THF), SatelLife of Cambridge, Office of International Affairs of the U.S. National Research Council, and the African Regional Centre for Technology (ARCT). Most important of all resources, however, are the individuals and groups of people who initiated moves to organize these meetings.

Zambia, like any other developing country, has no time to walk—it must run to keep up with the developments of industrialized countries in all fields. In health information provision in particular, the need to focus on the 1978 Declaration of Alma-Alta, which stated that primary health care was the key to attaining health-for-all and the recognition that health-for-all could not be attained without a well coordinated health information system, became critical to Zambia's aspirations to improve health information provision.

PROJECT DESCRIPTION

The AHILA conferences (see Box 2) provided the platform for Zambia to review its performance in the provision of health information. The result was that when the first partners offered to help to solve the problems, the Medical Library

---

BOX 2   The Value of Professional Associations

In certain instances, limitations to accessing health information from neighboring countries were caused by uncompromising political policies that were put in place by the nation towards the pre-independent Zimbabwe and South Africa. What were solvable health information problems became entangled in factors beyond the librarians' boundaries. This situation could easily have lead to professional skills redundancy had it not been checked by the existence of professional meetings at Africa regional level under the Association for Health Information and Libraries in Africa (AHILA) and the Medical Library Association (MLA).

---

took the opportunity and worked to use the resources that were extended to it to increase health information provision. There have been six major developments since 1991 offering solutions aimed at getting Zambia out of the information poverty trap:

- Installation of a HealthNet ground station at the UNZA Computer Centre in April 1991 by SatelLife and the subsequent installation of a Fidonet email point at the Medical Library.
- Installation of the CD-ROM technology by the Health Foundation in 1992.
- Establishment of a Zambia national and Africa regional African Index Medicus (AIM) data base in 1993.
- Initiation of a quarterly publication called the *Zambia Health Information Digest (ZHID).*
- Installation of an Internet connection at the UNZA Computer Centre and the subsequent installation of an Internet point at the Medical Library in January 1995.
- Formation of a National Aids Resource Centre (NARC) in February 1995 (see Box 4).

All the initiatives tell one story: that Zambia wanted to solve her health information poverty problems which dated back to the 1964 pre-independence era. While I have been involved in some way in all of these initiatives and while I see them as very synergistic, for the purpose of this case study I will focus on the Communications for Better Health program, which encompasses the CD-ROM and the *ZHID* projects.

One initiative listed above, the *African Index Medicus,* is important to both me and Helga Patrikios and it has been described in detail on page 45 of this volume. Another initiative, that of bringing Internet connectivity to Zambia, is covered in detail in Neil Robinson's case study on page 191 of this volume.

PROJECT EXPERIENCE AND IMPLEMENTATION

CD-ROM Databases

In 1992, we made major progress in the delivery of health information by installing CD-ROM technologies. The library received a total of 12 CD-ROM databases from THF and AAAS, some of which have full text articles, on such subjects as AIDS. One CD-ROM database, called Popline, is a donation from the John Hopkins University, whereas the Infectious Diseases database was installed by the CAB International. The usage of the databases is illustrated in Tables 1 and 2.

Please note that even though the AIM and Infectious Diseases databases are not CD-ROM databases, their statistics have been included because they are searchable databases. The Popline database was first received after the first quarter of 1995, hence the low statistics. The statistics on the Infectious Diseases database were lower than expected because the contents of the database overlapped with those of the databases that have existed longer in the Library. The database comes with coupons for full text articles donated by the CAB International. Some of the databases were a one-time donation, whereas those that continued to be received periodically were MEDLINE, Popline and AIDS. We update the AIM database regularly.

The University of Florida Health Sciences Center Library continued to provide photocopies of full text articles. Tables 4-8 provide some statistics of the reprints that have been provided with help from THF since the project started in 1992. The statistics are disaggregated by type of request, subject, distribution by

TABLE 1   Literature Search Statistics (1994)

Database	Yearly Total
MEDLINE	273
British Medical Journal	21
Lancet	15
New England Journal of Medicine	21
AIDS	30
Paediatrics	17
Morbidity and Mortality Weekly Report	1
Viral Hepatitis	2
Year Books	1
American Journal of Public Health	12
Family Physician	2
AIM	5
TOTAL ANNUAL STATISTICS	400

TABLE 2   Literature Search Statistics (January–June 1995)

Database	6 Months Statistics
MEDLINE	714
British Medical Journal	88
Lancet	69
New England Journal of Medicine	7
AIDS	95
Paediatrics	13
Morbidity and Mortality Weekly Report	12
Viral Hepatitis	45
Year Books	11
American Journal of Public Health	34
Family Physician	26
AIM	67
POPLINE	36
Infectious Diseases	48

TABLE 3   Categories of Reprints for Medical Library (September 1992–April 1995)

Category of Reprints	Number of Reprints
Topic requests from UNZA Med. Lib.	66
Special requests from UNZA Med. Lib.	159
Clinical information file, UNZA Med. Lib.	947

TABLE 4   Reprints by Broad Subject Category

Subject	Number of Reprints
Cancer	66
Cholera	62
Diabetes	53
Diarrhea	82
Hepatitis	63
HIV/AIDS	35
Hypertension	91
Malaria	36
Maternal & child health/nutrition	43
Measles	85
Meningitis	52
Ophthalmology	42
Sexually transmitted diseases	53
Trauma/wounds	39
Tuberculosis	92

TABLE 5 Distribution of Reprints

User category	Number of Reprints
University of Zambia	586
University Teaching Hospital	703
Health practitioners	762

TABLE 6 Percentage Distribution of Reprints

User category	Percentage distribution
University of Zambia	50%
University Teaching Hospital	60%
Health practitioners	65%

TABLE 7 Health Practitioners Distribution of Reprints

Geographical location	Number of reprints
Within Lusaka	410
Outside Lusaka	352

TABLE 8 Method of Reprint Distribution outside of Lusaka

Method	Number of reprints
Print	176
Email	176

numbers, distribution by percentage, distribution by geographical location, and method of distribution. The total number of reprints received by the Medical Library by April 1995 was 1,172. Another 234 reprints were received in May 1995, bringing the total to 1,406 reprints. In terms of distribution of reprints, there were times when they were distributed multiple times, thereby pushing the statistics high.

The email provided an avenue to request and transmit literature search requests. Furthermore, both the email and post were used to distribute reprints to users outside Lusaka. Our vision is to provide access to the CD-ROM databases to health care workers outside the university by using a leased line. The greatest need for this service is at the periphery health facilities and yet most, if not all, of the databases cannot be networked over a wide area because of the copyright rules that govern them. Serious thought should be given to waiving some copyright regulations to third world countries if information is to be shared equally among all health care workers.

Zambia Health Information Digest (ZHID)

The *ZHID* is a creation of the Medical Library and the Ministry of Health (MOH), with a grant from THF and IBM International Foundation. It is an offspring of the CD-ROM technology component of the Communications for Better Health Project. The first issue was launched on 1 February 1995 at a ceremony held at the Medical Library. Its contents include appropriate and relevant health information designed for all levels of health care workers (presented in the form of abstracts culled from the Ovid MEDLINE and AIM databases), articles on the management of common medical conditions, feature articles on other medical conditions, and institutional profiles.

The digest is produced quarterly and circulated to 1200 health facilities and institutions throughout the country. The MOH plays an important role in the distribution of the digest. The digest is also distributed on the Internet using the ZAMNET gopher. It is our intention to distribute it locally using the local Fidonet email system as well. The launching issue of the digest attracted positive comments from the local readers and from as far away places as Brazzaville, Columbia University, and Geneva. The hardware on which the digest is being produced came from a cooperative grant between THF and IBM International Foundation. The launching attracted dignitaries from Zambia, the United States, the Republic of South Africa and received positive media attention.

The University of Florida Health Sciences Center Library provides full text articles of the Ovid MEDLINE abstracts that are included in each issue of the digest. The provision of the full text articles by the University of Florida is a continuation of the aid which is being given to the UNZA Medical Library.

The CD-ROM project did not start in a vacuum; rather, it built upon the HealthNet project that had just been introduced to the UNZA Medical Library. Part of the technology (a 286 Olystar Computer) had already been installed by SatelLife. THF added on a CD-ROM player, providing one work station for CD-ROM activities. This took place in July, 1992. The pressure on the one computer, which was used for both email and CD-ROM activities, mounted as more and more people became aware of the improved health information services being provided by the UNZA Medical Library.

Efforts to get more equipment from donors met with some hitches as we failed to provide convincing justification for the acquisition of additional equipment. This did not surprise us because statistics maintenance was poor at that time. After a lengthy two years of negotiating with donors, THF working in collaboration with the IBM International Foundation, donated two 486 IBM file servers, each with a 540 megabyte hard disk; one laser printer; one dot matrix printer and color monitors.

With the availability of this equipment, we ventured into publishing the *ZHID*. This project went on smoothly because all that was required to be done was a few lessons in the use of Wordperfect 6.0 and how to use the graphics, both programs that we had acquired with the arrival of the file servers. The project proved a great success and is still running strong. The cooperation from the Ministry of Heath, THF, and the IBM International Foundation motivated us to such an extent that we aimed to do everything as correctly as possible.

THE RESULTS, IMPACT, AND BENEFITS OF THE PROJECT

The reaction of the clientele to both the CD-ROM and the *ZHID* projects was amazing. Initially the Library staff took advantage of the visit of Dr. Leonard Rhine, Medical Librarian at the University of Florida Health Sciences Center Library[1], to market the CD-ROM services. In October 1992, he conducted three half-day seminars on *Automated literature searching* at the Library. The participants in the seminars were drawn from among medical students, the University Teaching Hospital (UTH) health care workers, and research and teaching staff from both the School of Medicine and the University's Great East Campus. The UNZA Medical Library and Main Library staff were also active participants in the seminars.

The publicity leaflets for the seminars were put up before the arrival of Dr. Rhine. From that time onwards, most of the Medical Library clientele became aware of the new technology in the library. They were booked for thirty minutes each to do literature searches, but they complained that time was too short. The time allocation provided for a maximum of 15 searches a day. Some requests for literature searches arrived by email from the periphery hospitals—even though the technology was not adequately marketed outside of Lusaka. However, my involvement in the evaluation of the HealthNet project provided an opportunity to introduce the CD-ROM activities in the Southern Province of Zambia.

The comments from the readers of the digest both from the printed copy and from the Internet were full of praise for the initiative taken and for the quality and

---

BOX 3   Some Comments on the Inaugural Issue of ZHID

The introduction of the *ZHID* is highly welcome and commended in that it will not only keep health workers abreast with new developments in health but will also instill the spirit to do some research.   (Clinical Officer in Kasama)

I was so impressed with your educative material, especially for health workers in remote health centers of the country. Please keep it up. (Environmental Health Technician, Nakonde)

I wish to congratulate you for the introduction of *ZHID*. Surely it will go a long way in changing some attitudes and methods in the manner clients are treated and thereby improve the health standards of Zambian citizens. (Health worker in Samfya)

I wish to congratulate you most warmly on the first issue of *ZHID*. It is most impressive and I particularly like the variety of information included: the institutional profile is an excellent idea, which I hope will be picked up by other countries. (WHO Librarian, Geneva)

---

usefulness of the publication in promoting health information provision. (See Box 3.) Some comments were made against the UNZA Medical Library for excluding some departments of the MOH and other health institutions. Another indicator of the success of the digest was reflected by the number of local and international researchers who brought their reports to be published in the digest. The impact of the digest on the Medical Journal of Zambia is that the editors have been motivated by the progress made on the digest to such an extent that they have regrouped and are working out new strategies for reactivating the publication.

Publicity of the *ZHID* was done in grand style with the Deputy Minister of Health, Dr. Katele Kalumba, officiating at the launching ceremony of the digest. The occasion attracted media coverage that lasted more than one week. The launching was followed by a workshop on Problem Solving For Better Health (PSBH), which took place in Ndola, the Copperbelt Provincial capital. The participants in the workshop came from all over the country, thereby giving an opportunity for the digest to be introduced across the country. The method of disseminating the digest to all health facilities, using the MOH, provided yet another form of publicity. In short, the digest was self-selling.

It has not been easy to measure the impact of the CD-ROM services in the absence of carrying out an impact assessment survey addressed from the point of view of the student performance from the time of the introduction of the service. The other way of measuring impact would be to find out the increase in medical research and publishing activities among health care professionals in the School of Medicine and the UTH. However, the Post Basic Nursing student projects have greatly improved in quality in the past two years. The 1994 projects were even applauded by the Research and Ethics Committee of the School of Medicine after a seminar at which they were presented to the School. As the UNZA Medical Librarian, I give yearly lectures to the Post Basic Nursing students on library services and literature search strategies. Recently, I started to do the same for the School of Nursing students at the UTH.

ANALYSIS OF LESSONS LEARNED

The main constraints we faced in implementing the project were the poor staffing levels at the professional ranks and the lack of appropriately trained persons to manage the projects. I, as coordinator of the project, had to learn computer skills as a matter of urgency in order to get going with the activities. In addition, the support staff were requested to work with me to move the projects forward. This on-the-job training worked for our library but I would suggest that it is better to start with the training before implementing the projects.

One lesson learned from this experience is that it pays to include support staff in traditionally professional projects. We found that many of the medical library staff had a natural instinct for the technology. For instance, the fastest learner we had was a library attendant. Once this person was trained, she then went on to train others, including the library users, to do their own CD-ROM searches.

If I were to start this project again, I would probably not do it much differently. The idea that intrigued me most was the need to be able to build on the existing projects instead of re-inventing the wheel. (See Box 4.) The other thing that I found useful was the use of relatively low budgets in implementing all the projects. In some cases, the projects were parasitic in the sense that they had no budgets at all, but relied totally on the existence of the other projects. An example of this is the AIM project which has no budget of its own and is dependent on the CD-ROM project for sustainability.

BOX 4   National AIDS Resource Centre (NARC)

This latest project is still in its infancy. In spite of the fact that the proposal is still under consideration by donors, some local HIV/AIDS literature was pulled from the UNZA Medical Library and UNICEF databases and put on the ZAMNET gopher. The Tropical Disease Research Centre (TDRC) Library has also prepared some abstracts that are still to be installed. The NARC coordinating center is the UNZA Medical Library and the TDRC Library is a satellite center. The participating centers are the HIV/AIDS information producing institutions which are on the email. Data collection will be done by email, whereas the AIDS database will be resident at the UNZA Medical Library. The ZAMNET gopher will be updated regularly.

We were also able to build on the electronic communications initiatives of the University's Computer Center. In 1991, through the Computer Centre, we got hooked to a Fidonet system and installed a HealthNet satellite ground station. We started using electronic communications for the following purposes:

Library Partnership Program

The first use we made of email was to request literature searches. To do this, we found a partner in the United States —the University of Florida Health Sciences Center Library—to carry out the searches on our behalf. SatelLife facilitated the partnership. In June 1991, the first request (for information on meningitis) was sent to Florida late one afternoon. By the following morning, we had received a long list of citations, complete with abstracts. Dean Kopano Mukelabai of the School of Medicine at the University of Zambia acknowledged this giant breakthrough in the provision of health information by inviting me to address a meeting of the Eastern and Southern African Chairmen of Paediatrics Departments, in August 1991.

HealthNet News

SatelLife introduced an electronic newsletter that we disseminated to health care workers linked to the Fidonet system. A snap survey on the impact of the *HealthNet News* in 1993 showed that it was not widely read by users largely because of the busy schedules of the health care workers at whom the publication was targeted.

Literature Searches

We used the HealthNet communication system to receive and transmit literature search requests from the health care workers within the country. This aspect of SatelLife's information services was slow to be fully used because the health care workers were not fully aware of the information facilities that were at the Library. By 1994, SatelLife paid for a Grateful Med account to the National Library of Medicine with access to Toxinet, Cancerlit, AIDS, and Alert.

The HealthNet Communication Service

At the national level, the Library was linked to the Fidonet system but, at global level, communication was limited by Healthsat to those collaborators who were hooked to the HealthNet communications system. Most of the communication was centered on literature searches and to a lesser extent on other non-specific consultations with health care workers and medical librarians.

In January 1995, we received an Internet account from ZAMNET (see Neil Robinson's case study in this volume.) This development further enhanced access to and provision of our health information services. Some of the things we are able to do with the Internet are listed below:

Access to Health Information Databases

Through the Internet, the Library can access many unrestricted databases, such as the WHO Library database in Geneva. Because a subscription is needed to access some databases, the Medical Library still needs some assistance to support these charges.

Access to the ZAMNET Gopher

We have installed the *AIDS Bibliography* on the ZAMNET gopher. A pointer to *ZHID* was opened on the Zambia's Worldwide Web homepage in November 1995, and it is accessible to all Internet users around the world. We have plans to have more health information on the Internet as more is generated.

Access to Other Databases

The world of information both related and unrelated to health opened to the Medical Library users with the installation of our Internet node. We have access to multidisciplinary information through the Internet.

CONCLUSIONS AND RECOMMENDATIONS

Good programs have been brought to the Medical Library and implemented to the best of our ability. What we have been doing is just the beginning of a long road to providing health information for problem solving. Although HealthNet became a household name in health information transmission, the project failed because it failed to attract funding after the pilot phase. There is no more health information being transmitted by Healthsat because the ground station was moved from Zambia to a more needy site.

In another vein, the Fidonet system which spread all over the country is, in some cases, being replaced by the interactive Internet. Progress and technology are playing a major role in the development of a better health information system. Neil Robinson's case study describes this progression from Fidonet to Internet and explains how ZAMNET is providing service to all levels of users in Zambia.

Although CD-ROM usage statistics have shown a steady increase since 1992, the use of the databases outside Lusaka has not improved much. The most frequently used databases continue to attract more and more users, while the less popular databases continue to be underused. The Popline database is proving to be very popular.

The AIM database is regularly consulted, too. The collection of data outside the School of Medicine and the UTH has proved to be slow because of the time and personnel factors. The first NARC HIV/AIDS bibliographies were culled from the AIM database. Since the database is accessible on the Internet, it has a wide circulation, but we have not yet devised a method to monitor usage at the national level. The only statistics available are collected from users who use the database from the library. On average, there are eleven clients who use the AIM database per week, and seven of these requests are made by readers of the digest.

Although only two issues of the digest have been released, the feedback from the readers in form of comments and requests for full text articles has been good. The usage and comments on the usefulness of the digest will be monitored continuously through a feedback mechanism built into the publication.

The Medical Library will continue to need support from partners to develop these programs that improve information provision to health care workers. The devastating effects of the structural adjustment program on the development of health information and literature can only be alleviated through the sort of assistance we have received and hopefully will continue to receive until the national economy strengthens. In view of the above concerns, I suggest the following:

- We need to network the CD-ROM for greater accessibility to databases by health care workers who cannot easily come to the library.
- We need to subscribe to key CD-ROM databases not only for the Medical Library clientele but for other health care workers who depend on us for information services.
- There are eight other health sciences libraries in Zambia that should be linked to Zambia's Internet service.
- We need to market CD-ROM databases and other health information services outside Lusaka.
- We need to purchase a portable CD-ROM workstation that we can use for demonstrations.
- In order to confer on issues relating to health information provision, Zambian medical librarians should meet at least once a year.
- We need to continue to improve the coverage and frequency of publication of the *ZHID*.
- We need to send medical librarians to all AHILA meetings where much of the professional sharing takes place.
- We need to subscribe to more databases on the Internet, for example, MEDLINE.

The issues that haunt the UNZA Medical Library hinge on whether health information and literature provision will develop at the same pace as health provision—which is attracting reasonable funding from both the government and donors. Or will these efforts collapse soon after the current crop of Library staff disappear from the institution?

I would like to wrap up this story with the following: partnership, intelligent use of available resources, marketing of health information, and willingness not to give up are very important factors in the provision of health information. Better health information leads to better health care. Lastly, our philosophy has been to access information—not to OWN it. Collaboration with others, regardless of geographical or political boundaries, and acceptance of the changing information and communication technologies is the way forward.

NOTE

1. The Florida Health Sciences Library has a twinning arrangement with the University of Zambia Medical Library.

CASE STUDIES ON DESKTOP PUBLISHING

The concept of desktop publishing (DTP) synthesizes the capabilities of typesetting, graphic design, book production, and platemaking in one integrated, cost effective hardware and software configuration. It allows the computer user to combine text and image files into a single document and then design a page that looks like a page in a book or journal. The operator can select different typefaces and type sizes, can format the text in several columns, or can run text around graphic images. The page can then be sent to a laser printer for inexpensive page proofs or to a typesetting device for final printing.

DTP can help to invigorate Africa's struggling publishing houses. Editors and publishers can use DTP to convert manuscripts into final form and to locally produce textbooks and journals. Scientific communities can use DTP to publish and disseminate the results of their research.

As these authors show, the skills required to operate this software at a professional level are not always easy to learn. The difficulties of obtaining good design, typography, and layout are not at all diminished by desktop publishing software. Further, the authors found they needed more than a basic personal computer: they also needed high-resolution monitors; scanners for the input of text and images; a mouse (which makes manipulation of the text and graphics much easier); and laser printers. They also required special software for printing chemical formulae and scientific figures.

Most importantly, they demonstrate that a DTP press needs to operate on the same professional basis as a regular, commercial publisher. These authors describe how they have instituted the peer review process, good accounting practices, and high standards for timeliness and quality.

The authors have used DTP to publish newsletters and journals, scholarly books and proceedings, and such materials as flyers, invitations, and announcements. Thus have they increased publishing opportunities for African scientists and created new and innovative means of disseminating scientific and technological information to a broader audience.

Desktop Publishing at the University of Zimbabwe

by Dr. Xavier F. Carelse

Xavier F. Carelse lectures in the Department of Physics, University of Zimbabwe and is in charge of the Faculty of Science DTP Facility. He is a graduate of Fort Hare, South Africa, and has a special interest in the development of science and technology education in Africa. He has written two books that address problems relating to the construction and improvisation of science equipment in secondary schools in developing countries.

BACKGROUND AND CONTEXT OF THE PROJECT

Historical Background

After a period of settler rule that had lasted about 100 years, Zimbabwe attained national independence and majority rule in 1980. Before that date only 40 percent of our children entered primary school and usually stayed at school for only three years. Today 70 percent of our children stay at school for at least 11 years and graduate after completing the General Certificate of Education at the Ordinary Level, the examinations for which are set in the United Kingdom.

Education in Zimbabwe

The increase in the secondary school population, rising over twelvefold from 74,000 in 1979 to 871,000 in 1989, is a particular indication of the heightened aspirations of our citizens since independence. In that same period the primary school enrollment rose from 819,000 to 2,103,000. The rate of transfer of children from Grade 7 to Form One is now about 76 percent.

Over the same period the national expenditure on education has risen from $200 million to $500 million. With the total population of Zimbabwe being estimated as 12 million, 30 percent of our population are now pursuing full-time education. With 25 percent of the national budget being spent on education, Zimbabwe is becoming the country in Africa with the most highly educated population and the demand for education is still growing. Education in Zimbabwe is therefore a multi-million dollar growth industry. This captive market has served to support a variety of services which have benefited from this growth. The largest growth has been in the manufacture of school uniforms and in book sales.

Book Production in Zimbabwe

Another area of information transfer lies, of course, in the supply and availability of information in the printed form. This includes not only textbooks, but also the form of information transfer that deals with the updating of our immediately available information. This is achieved through the publication of newspapers, journals, magazines, from which the general public usually benefits. Of equal importance in the academic world is the publication of bulletins and newsletters targeting a specialist group and that disseminate information that has a direct impact on our immediate professional knowledge.

Zimbabwe has a good publishing infrastructure and is able to produce good quality books at a very low cost. With the formation of the Southern African Development Conference (SADC), Zimbabwe was chosen to be the publishing center of the group and has remained relatively unchallenged in this respect. An appreciable number of books are being written and published for schools and are usually directed at the local primary and lower secondary school syllabi and curricula, that is, up to the 11-year-old age group.

A shortage of locally produced books continues to exist at the upper secondary level with a pupil population of only about 20,000. The syllabi, at this level, are drawn up by the Cambridge Examinations Board, for which a very great number and variety of books are available overseas. But, because of recurring devaluation of the Zimbabwe currency, these are becoming increasingly expensive. In the last five years, the cost of imported textbooks have increased by a factor of 5, while the cost of locally produced books have risen by a factor of 2.5. There is, therefore, a good case for reducing our dependence on imported text-books.

The situation at university and polytechnic level is even more acute. Virtually all undergraduate textbooks are imported and the cost of all such books has increased seven or eight times in the same period. Although the University of Zimbabwe Press (UZP) has been in existence for decades, very few textbooks are produced in Zimbabwe. The publications they produce are usually extended reports of research findings in the humanities and are adopted as textbooks for specialized courses. In the science disciplines, the Department of Biochemistry has produced some books that were published by the UZP.

Information Technology in Zimbabwe

In 1990, the Posts and Telecommunications Corporation (PTC) launched ZimNet, which is based on the X.25 package switching protocol. Many financial concerns, such as banks (including the Post Office Savings Bank), building societies and insurance companies, are using it on a nationwide basis. In 1991, the University of Zimbabwe acquired its first link with the Internet via the UNINET gateway in Grahamstown, South Africa and, in 1992, a second link under the host-name of MANGO, Microcomputer Access for Non-Government Organizations, was established via ESANet, the Eastern and Southern African Network. It is hoped that, before the end of 1995, the University would have acquired our own gateway to the Internet. In fact, such a gateway already exists in the commercial sector but is too expensive for most academic users.

PROJECT DESCRIPTION

Origin and History

The Information Systems Project at the University of Zimbabwe has two phases. In the first phase, the Faculty of Science purchased desktop publishing equipment because we believed it would be a sound investment that, in the long run, would show benefits in two important areas: the local production of text books and the establishment of a facility for publicizing, to the public, the programs presented in the Faculty of Science. The second phase, for which funds are now being sought, concerns the creation of a campus computer network.

In 1990, Professor C.J. Chetsanga, then the Dean of Science, and now Director of the Scientific and Industrial Research and Development Center, obtained a Carnegie Corporation grant with which he purchased for the Faculty the basics of a powerful desktop publishing system. The purpose of this facility is to encourage the publication of textbooks by the academic staff. The move was seen as an attempt to address some of the problems outlined above.

Dr. N. Dune, Chairman of the Department of Computer Science, who happened to be on sabbatical leave in the United States at that time, was asked to make a suggestion for a suitable basic system for our DTP facility. He submitted a list of Macintosh-based equipment. This system was deemed to be too expensive and Mr. R. Braithwaite, the proprietor of Software Engineering, Portland, Oregon, who had spent some time as a guest lecturer in the University's Department of Computer Science, was invited to recommend an alternative system. He presented us with an IBM system based on the Intel 80386 microprocessor. This provided us with DTP equipment at a remarkably low cost and this allowed us to acquire some accessories such as a tape streamer, the full-page scanner, a surge protector, mathematics and graphics software, and other facilities without exceeding our budget. (See Box 1.)

BOX 1   IBM versus Macintosh

In addition to the advantage of having a lower cost, the IBM-system was preferred because, in 1989, a decision had been made at the University to standardize all purchases of computer equipment. It was decided that the university's Computer Resource Committee should only authorize the purchase of IBM-compatible computers, including clones, and also the BBC Micro, because of the impact the latter was making on the educational market at that time. The BBC Micro was a 6502-based computer commissioned by the British Broadcasting Corporation for use in a computer education series for television. It had a number of input-output ports which made it unique as an educational tool. This decision was taken to avoid the proliferation of too great a variety of computers at U.Z. as great difficulty was being experienced in servicing the wide range of computers that were appearing. Thus, at the time that the DTP system was being considered, the Macintosh was not considered to be a possible option. As almost all purchases of new computers already complied with this decision, the Mac would not have been very useful to the Faculty.

General and Particular Objectives

The main purpose of the new equipment was to assist the academic staff to produce textbooks or, alternatively, to compile their lecture notes in a form which could serve as a textbook. Over the last five years, a number of lecturers have used this facility for either one or the other purpose. The present Dean of Science, a mathematician, was one of the first to produce a textbook using the Faculty of Science DTP Facility.

A second objective was to produce a newsletter to publicize some of the activities of the Faculty such as the research interests of the staff, new degree programs that were being offered, the announcement of conferences, workshops and seminars that were of general or specific interest, and many others. This was the first aspect of DTP that was implemented and that eventually served to popularize the service that the facility offered.

The DTP equipment has been in use since January 1992, when a newsletter, entitled *Integrator*, was launched, under an editorial board appointed by the Board of the Faculty of Science. I was invited to be member of this board because of my previous experience in computerized type-setting and publishing. A DTP operator was also appointed and designated for training.

The chief success of the program has been in the production of textbooks. Although little was accomplished in the first year—mainly because of lack of familiarity with the use of the facilities—an article that appeared in *Integrator*, Volume 1, No. 2, alerted the faculty to its potential. Since then, a number of publications have been produced using the equipment. Though these were compilations of lecture notes, a few are already in the process of being rewritten into textbooks.

Products, Technologies, and Services Delivered

The Hardware

The system was specified and delivered in 1991 and reflects, in a modest way, the status of personal computers at that time. The heart of the system is a 30 MHz 80386-based computer, with 8 megabytes of RAM, installed in a tower case. It has four disk drives, as follows:

- Drive A is a 1.2 megabyte 5-inch floppy drive;
- Drive B is a 360 kilobyte 5-inch floppy drive;
- Drive C is a 1.4 megabyte 3-inch floppy drive; and
- Drive D is an 80 megabyte hard drive.

We felt that two floppy drives, one high density and one double density, were needed to allow for the fact that many university departments do not have computers with high-density drives and an occasional incompatibility occurred. With the present trend towards the exclusive use of high density media, this is no longer a problem. Data security is supported with a tape unit for backing-up the contents of the hard disk. Total back-up is not usually necessary as it is seldom that user files will be stored on the hard disk. Application files can normally be reloaded if necessary.

The user input-output devices include a visual display unit (VDU) that is a 14-inch (35-cm) video graphics array (VGA) color monitor with the high resolution essential for desktop publishing. A Dexxa serial mouse and an enhanced keyboard were also included.

The semi-commercial, heavy-duty Hewlett-Packard LaserJet Series III printer prints at the rate of eight pages per minute. It is equipped with Hewlett-Packard's resolution enhancement feature which gives high quality, professionally acceptable typeset-quality printing of text and graphics. It has 5 megabyte of installed memory, built-in PostScript features but, more importantly, it also has built-in a wide range of mathematical and Greek symbols used by many scientists, especially physicists, mathematicians and engineers.

The scanning of documents and photographs is undertaken with the Chinon Model N-207 DS-3000 overhead scanner that is capable of digitizing an A4 size page of text and graphics by using a charge-coupled device (CCD) image sensor with a camera-type flat surface scanning method. It is used for scanning the photographs and line graphics used in the newsletter.

The Software

The original operating system was MS-DOS, version 4, but this has now been upgraded to version 6. The main environment is Microsoft's Windows 3.1, which is a very popular GUI (graphics user interface) and is rapidly becoming the industry standard environmental software for IBM-compatible computers.

Microsoft's Word for Windows, originally version 1.1, and now upgraded to version 2, was probably the most powerful word processor for the personal computer and dwarfed that of almost all dedicated word-processing machines. Its capabilities overlapped considerably with some of the sophisticated DTP programs and inclined us to the view that it would be more than sufficient for the purpose of producing our newsletter. This program was able to handle tables, graphics and mathematical formulae. It was a simple matter to insert these into the document file and to position them relative to the text.

A fonts software package, Adobe Type Manager, increases the range of fonts and symbols available under Windows 3. To broaden the scope of mathematical typesetting, we have several auxiliary programs such as MathEdit (described below) and Hewlett-Packard's Type Director to assist the esoteric user.

The scanner is operated through a graphics program called Paintbrush. The operation is done at various resolutions—300, 200, 150 or 75 dots per inch—and produces files with the .PCX extension. A single resolution on the printer is adopted for printing the graphic. For example, 300 dots per inch (dpi) scanned files will print out a picture that is the exact size of the original while, correspondingly, a 200 dpi scan would print out with two-thirds of the linear dimensions. We are using the latter in the newsletter. In almost all cases we have found that this resolution is suitable for our purposes and so avoids the need for shrinking the picture before printing.

Graphics files consume large amounts of storage space. Typically, a 200 mm by 150 mm photograph will, at 200 dpi resolution, produce a .PCX (a graphics file format) file of 400 kilobytes. Because of this large size, these files are normally stored on the hard disk only, although back-ups of the .PCX files are kept on 1.2 megabyte floppy disks for our archives. Word for Windows requires graphics in the tagged image file format (TIFF). The .PCX files produced by Paintbrush therefore have to be converted to .TIF files before they can be loaded into the newsletter. The above .PCX file would be converted to a .TIF file of 800 kilobytes. The latter are not normally stored on floppy disks. They are invoked when an image of the picture is to be displayed on the screen or when the document is to be printed with the picture in place.

When a TIFF graphic is inserted into a Word for Windows file, only references to the graphic are actually inserted. The Word file, containing references, such as the dimensions, clipping and scaling information of a 600 kilobyte TIFF file may therefore only occupy 20 kilobytes when saved on disk. The disk holding the TIFF file itself must be inserted in the drive if it is necessary to inspect the graphic on-screen or to print a document containing the references.

The desktop publishing equipment includes a variety of quite sophisticated software accessories specifically directed to the needs of the academic staff of the Faculty of Science. A brief description of the facilities is enough to engage the interest and respect of a serious scientific author.

PageMaker

This package was rated by *BYTE,* the computer magazine, to be the best of the crop of DTP programs that appeared in 1991. It is considerably more powerful as a DTP tool than Word-for-Windows, which is, first and foremost, a word processor. PageMaker is a tool for preparing a newspaper and has facilities far beyond what we require for a newsletter.

MathEdit

As a formula-editing utility this program is heaven-sent for mathematicians. It incorporates a selection of 220 mathematical symbols and is essential for our DTP support. Word-for-Windows handles about 120 mathematical and Greek symbols, which may be enough for some but hopelessly inadequate for others. Like Word, it displays WYSIWYG (what you see is what you get). This is a major advance over other type-setting programs such as PC-TEX. It produces TIFF files that can be imported into Word.

DERIVE, Version 2

Described as a Mathematical Assistant, DERIVE is used for simplifying, solving, and plotting mathematical expressions. It is capable of handling derivatives, integrals, vectors, and matrices, as well as algebraic tasks such as factorization and expansion of expressions.

Fractool

The inexpensive but powerful program generates splendid fractals that can be used for enhancing presentations.

CSS

This is a time-series program module that contains a wide range of descriptive, modeling, and forecasting methods for both time and frequency domain models. Besides incorporating transformations, modeling, and plotting program, it also includes ARIMA, the Autoregressive Moving Average Model for estimating seasonal and non-seasonal parameters for the autoregressive and moving average process and for forecasting.

PROJECT EXPERIENCE AND IMPLEMENTATION

Through *Integrator,* the DTP has had an impact that was not originally envisaged. Although it is only produced at six-monthly intervals, each issue contains important information on the working and development of the Faculty of Science.

In most developing countries, the Faculty is often underrated as being only a means of producing science teachers. The articles on careers in science and on the roles of scientists as consultants to industry, to parastatals and to the government are used to publicize the Faculty and have served to create a new image that is not often seen in other developing countries.

The Newsletter

The first Editorial Committee was appointed by the Dean, Professor Chetsanga. The Editorial Committee chose the title *Integrator* for the newsletter. They felt that it had a scientific nuance and, at the same time, reflected the spirit of unity within the Faculty. The formulation of the contents of the *Integrator* makes an interesting story:

Without specifying the type of articles required, the editorial committee invited the departments to submit one article, relevant to each, that they would like to see published in the first edition of the faculty newsletter. A somewhat disjointed collection of articles was presented to the committee. There was an article on each of the following:

- the research interests of the chemists;
- a new research venture by the geologists;
- a new M.Sc. program by the biochemists;
- a report on a recent colloquium from the biologists;
- an essay on careers for physicists; and
- a report on the launching of the new Department of Statistics.

After reading the articles, I realized that the departments had unknowingly laid down the structure of the newsletter. A newsletter is a continuing exercise with regular features as well as special one-off features. The collection of articles that we had received reflected the needs that the departments wished to express and so could be used to reflect the needs of the faculty. It was therefore appropriate that we should use this as a starting point from which to decide the nature of the articles that we would request in each regular or special feature.

The editorial board agreed that the following regular features would be requested from each department in sequence:

- Meet the . . . . A description of the research interests of individuals in a chosen department and of the consultancy services they could offer to industry or to the parastatals.
- Master of Science in . . . . A description of a postgraduate program offered by the featured department.
- Careers in . . . . An article directed at high school pupils and describing the career opportunities existing in the featured department.

- Announcements. An announcement of conferences, workshops and seminars due to be held in the Faculty of Science.
- Student Science Societies. Reports from the students on the science societies that they operate.

Special features that any individual, not necessarily from within the Faculty, could produce include:

- New research ventures in the Faculty;
- New resources and developments in the Faculty;
- Reports on conferences held in the Faculty;
- Reports on international conferences that have a bearing on the Faculty and the University; and
- Reports of donor agencies and sources of funds from which the Faculty could benefit.

The DTP Software

A general purpose WYSIWYG word processor operating in a GUI (graphic user interface) is, in our opinion, highly recommended for a small DTP facility. In addition to Word-for-Windows, most typists in Zimbabwe are familiar with WordPerfect 5.0 or 5.1. Such word processing programs may not be very useful for the production of newspapers or other materials with more than four columns, but for the purpose of producing textbooks and newsletters, it cannot be excelled by any of the more advanced DTP programs such as PageMaker or Ventura. Efforts to master PageMaker, which we had also acquired, were abandoned very early in this program. It was found that a great deal of time was required for the training of the operator and other users.

The decision to use Word-for-Windows Version 1.1 almost exclusively for our DTP activity was found to be an excellent choice because of the following reasons:

1. The ease of use once the general Windows environment was understood.
2. The power and versatility of this program.
3. The ability to handle and manipulate the graphics images produced by the scanner, without any additional software.

We acquired it in 1993 and it has been the only program that we had used for the production of the *Integrator*. Other workers preferred WordPerfect Version 5.1, which was also installed, and since then WordPerfect Version 6 has appeared and seems to have become a strong rival to Word-for-Windows. Nevertheless, it is my opinion that the even newer Word-for-Windows Version 6 would prove to an excellent successor to Version 2 and I cannot envisage any foreseeable intention of moving away from this word processor. In truth, there is much evidence that use of Word-for-Windows is increasing world-wide while the use of WordPerfect may have reached a plateau.

The Layout of the Newsletter

After a series of experimental sessions during the training of the DTP operator, the present layout was chosen as being the most presentable while keeping the cost of production down to a minimum. The newsletter consists of 16 A4 pages and is printed on A3 paper. The presentation is in three columns, except for the last page which carries the table of contents. For ease of reading 8-point Helvetica print is used but all headlines are in Times font of various sizes. The use of Microsoft Word Art, which comes packaged with Word-for-Windows Version 2 has been used extensively in Volume 3 to enhance the presentation.

The Scanner

In spite of its low cost, this scanner produces quite adequate copies and has served very well for the production of the first volumes of *Integrator*. It has also been used by lecturers and research students to reproduce graphs and diagrams for insertion into their papers. It is still serving us well but, since its purchase, many new scanners have appeared at a reasonable price and with more facilities. We believe that the time has come to upgrade the scanner. For Volume 3, published in 1994, we used an Apple flatbed scanner belonging to the University Publications Office. This scanner allowed very smooth sizing of the graphics without a change in resolution.

The Reprographic Facility

The Hewlett Packard Laserjet III has proved to be an excellent choice for a printer of the master copies. The fact that the printer was made easily accessible to all users may have been a mistake because it has led to considerable abuse and overuse and the expense of excessive replacement of toner cartridges. Many would have preferred that its use was strictly monitored and a nominal charge levied for use, but in retrospect there is evidence that the "free use" policy played a principal role in the instant acceptance of the DTP Facility.

During the first year of production of *Integrator*, the masters were submitted to the University of Zimbabwe Reprographic Unit. After that initial period, it was felt that the production could be streamlined if we had our own reprographic facility. In 1992 we successfully applied to Carnegie Corporation of New York for funds for a heavy duty photocopier that could be used for the relatively low bulk production of the *Integrator*. A Konica photocopier was purchased and this has made the faculty completely independent of the University's Reprographic Unit and so has reduced the cost of production. Volume 2, No 1, January 1993, and

> **BOX 2   Benefits of the *Integrator***
>
> The publicity that we have received through *Integrator* and through the M.Sc. in Applied Physics program has opened the door to a number of consultancy projects for the lecturers and has served to enhance the reputation of the department in the industrial sector.

subsequent editions of *Integrator*, were produced in this way.

RESULTS, IMPACT, AND BENEFITS OF THE PROJECT

Once the DTP facility was in place, the early launching of the *Integrator* was very well conceived. The very first issue contained an article on the DTP project and the equipment that was available for prospective authors. Without the *Integrator*, it is unlikely that DTP would have been accepted so soon by the Faculty.

There can be no doubt that the original purpose of the DTP facility, namely, the production of compiled lecture notes and textbooks, has been realized. Compilations of lecture notes have been produced in the Departments of Physics, Chemistry, Biochemistry and Mathematics. This reflects a general trend in the University and has been confirmed by the Director of the University of Zimbabwe Press, where a plan to produce more textbooks is already under way, with three books having been approved for publication in July 1995 alone.

The DTP facility may be used in the production of masters that can be submitted to the University Reprographic Unit for printing. The advantage of this is gained through the ability of the Reprographic Unit to use cheaper paper for their printing process and also being able to produce large quantities without imposing a strain on their equipment. They have a copy printer and other standard printing equipment. As they are able to produce color layouts, they may be invited to produce our front and rear pages in color at a later stage in our development.

Benefits

The increase in publicity that was generated by the *Integrator* for the Faculty of Science cannot be overstated. (See Box 2.) It had an effect among both students and staff. A few examples relating to the Department of Physics will suffice to illustrate this point.

In the period 1986 to 1989, the intake into the Department of Physics dropped progressively from 132 in 1986 to 77 in 1989. This was partly due to the launching of the B.Tech. program that was heavily science-oriented and, among others, offered two new areas into which school-leavers with physics grades could be absorbed, namely, Applied Physics and Electrical Technology. The article on Careers in Physics that appeared in the first issue of *Integrator* created a new interest in mainstream physics and our intake has reached and stayed at about 100 students since then.

The publication of the questionnaire on the proposed Master of Science in Applied Physics program created a new interest in physics. The response from industry and from the graduates was gratifying. In our first year (1993), we received over 30 applicants but were only able to accept 8. Although we had intended to accept candidates only in alternate years, we decided to admit 8 new students again in 1994. This Masters program required candidates to spend 6 months attached to an industrial firm in order to become acquainted with industrial practice in Zimbabwe. After this period, the students are required to work on a research project. We invite the firm to suggest a suitable project that can be completed with the firm and that will allow the student to continue working with them. In every case where the firm was approached, a project was found.

Many of the courses that were offered in this program were newly conceived and it was difficult to find suitable textbooks. One of the first products was derived from lecture notes on Atmospheric Physics. The present Dean of Science, a mathematician, was one of the first to produce a textbook using the Faculty of Science DTP Facility. Textbooks on Microprocessor Applications and a Laboratory Manual are being planned.

ANALYSIS OF LESSONS LEARNED

Training of DTP Operator

In 1990, a typist with computer experience was appointed specifically for training as a DTP operator. At that time such typists were a rare commodity in Zimbabwe and the DTP operator acquired a rather special status. Within a year she was promoted to the level of a senior secretary and was attached to the Dean's office. Although ostensibly she was still the DTP operator for the *Integrator*, she found it increasingly difficult to fulfill all the tasks required of her.

Meanwhile, with her limited assistance, I found myself almost solely responsible for the publication of the newsletter. With hindsight, it is clear to see now that there should have been more than just one person trained for operating the typesetting facility and to produce the *Integrator*. That I did not do so was due to the fact that I had been appointed Chairman of the Department of Physics in 1989 and had very little opportunity to run such a training program. It was, in fact, easier for me to browbeat other chairpersons into producing the soft copy and, with the assistance of the DTP operator and my own departmental typists, to devote one week of intensive work to the production of the newsletter. What is learned from this experience is that the publisher of the newsletter must be someone with clout and who has clerical help beyond what was officially designated to the editorial board. I was able to extract information and cooperation from important agencies such as the Information Office, the Reprographic Unit, the Publications Office and the Dean's Office that may have been more difficult for others to obtain.

Computers became more plentiful soon after 1993 when ESAP, the economic structural adjustment program, allowed the relatively free importation of such seemingly luxury items. More typists are now familiar with the use of computers and this has allowed more departments to benefit from the Facility. The typists can produce the manuscripts to disks and these can be quickly typeset and included in the newsletter. A training program for at least one typist per department would now be indicated. In this way the articles could have been near-"camera-ready" without much intervention by the DTP operator. The departments themselves would have benefited through the typists' improved ability to prepare highly attractive documents and manuscripts and also to assist the research programs in the preparation of camera-ready copy for professional journals.

Training of Academic Users

The DTP Facility proved to be quite popular with the academics who wished to produce books or compile lecture notes, and with research students who were preparing their theses or dissertations. The enhanced presentation of graphical material was particularly favored. Within this framework, these users were able to receive assistance from myself or from the DTP operator. But, on the whole, they tended to acquire the rudiments of typesetting without any difficulty. (See Box 3.)

The Hardware

When the search for a suitable system for DTP was first launched, there were two choices: use an IBM-compatible system or adopt the more user-friendly Macintosh systems. The most important consideration is cost. We can concede that the Macintosh is seductively user-friendly but this comes at a cost that is not only financial but also found in its restrictiveness—in most cases only software specific to the Mac may be used.

Although all Mac machines today are capable of running DOS-type applications, this additional capability costs extra money. It is significant that Mac users wish to use DOS applications but IBM users do not wish to use Mac applications on their machines. We were able to purchase an IBM clone for less than half the

---

BOX 3   Need for a Training Program

The consequence of the deficiency of trained persons was vividly illustrated this year when a new publication coordinator was appointed while I was on sabbatical leave. As he did not specify that copy had to be received on disk in the recommended formats, he received hard copy and had to retype everything himself. This seriously hindered the continuity of publication of the *Integrator.*

price of an equivalent Macintosh. The savings enabled us to purchase accessories such as the scanner, additional supplies of toner cartridges, and a wide selection of software for scientific typesetting which we would not otherwise have been able to afford. Recently the price of Macintosh computers has come down but accessories are still expensive because of the lack of cheaper clone products. For users in poor countries low cost must take precedence over user-friendliness.

For us, the wisdom of purchasing a Macintosh was questionable and we are pleased with the decision to use an IBM-compatible computer. Indeed, there were, at that time, dozens of IBM clones in use on the campus and only one Macintosh. Our purchase of the latter would have disadvantaged almost everyone on the campus and thus would have seriously delayed the acceptance, and undermined the usefulness, of the DTP Facility.

When it was purchased it was, because of its specifications, the most powerful computer in the Faculty at that time and many wished to use it. Today there is a proliferation of much more powerful computers in all departments and, sadly, the 80836 computer has become nearly obsolete. If the system was purchased today, a 32-bit computer with an Intel 486i or a Pentium microprocessor would be at top of the shopping list. There are many advantages of having such powerful computers, the most important of which is the remarkable versatility of graphics and other applications software that is associated with them. Software supported by Windows 3.1 or Windows 95 now offers a degree of sophistication that demands such high quality graphics and it is well worth the investment.

The purchase of a CD-ROM drive is also recommended because of the low-cost of the software available on it and of the high capacity and reliability of this storage medium. The average CD-ROM holds 600 megabytes of data, the equivalent of over 400 high density 3.5-inch disks. Quite impressive clip-art and fonts are now available on CD-ROM and this will greatly enhance the appearance of documents and books.

The Need for a Network

The day-to-day use of the DTP Facility is restricted by the fact that is only accessible to one person at a time. If we want it to be more widely used, we must incorporate networking, which today is the single most important hardware-related advantage in computer usage. This will give all DTP users access to all the desirable components of the network without the need to leave the office. This includes access to the laser printer, the clip-art, the word processor, graphic packages and the typesetting packages.

The would-be author could stay in the office, surrounded by personal texts and references and, if connection to the Internet with World Wide Web is available, to the wealth of information that is now almost freely accessible on this medium. The DTP Facility then becomes one of the other services available on the network and using it becomes less dependent on special trips to the Faculty of Science DTP room where you may find that someone has already beaten you to the computer.

The Laser Printer

One of the principal attractions of the DTP Facility was the fact that the laser printer was used at no charge. There are arguments for and against such free use of an expensive piece of equipment but a levy on the use of the laser printer would have discouraged the use of the DTP equipment as a whole. Fortunately, sufficient funds were available to purchase a considerable stock of cartridges. Some savings were made by the purchase of recycled cartridges. Because of the now heavy use of the printer, it may now be advisable to impose a levy to offset the running costs.

The administration of the Facility then becomes a task which has to be added to the other tasks of those guarding it. It was decided in 1992 that the running costs of the Facility should be shared by the departments in the Faculty and that the Dean, before allocating funds to the "Consumable" account of the departments, would withhold a levy for the use of the Facility. This was readily agreed to by the departments. The use of the Facility thus continued to be "free" to individual users.

Upgrading the printer facility has mainly taken the form of ensuring that software drivers for the implementation of a laser printer were available for all applications. Because of the relative isolation of Zimbabwe at that time, this was not easy for some of the relatively more esoteric applications, but gradually the goal was achieved. Nevertheless after four years of heavy use, it is now time to consider replacing the printer. At the time of purchase, the Hewlett Packard LaserJet III was at the top end of the DTP accessory market. Since then there have been many improvements in the specifications of printers from which we now have to choose.

Although laser printers are more reliable and still produce the best quality output, we now have ink-jet printers which, simply by changing the ink cartridges, produce hard copy in color. As they generally cost about half the price of laser printers, it may be advantageous to keep an ink-jet printer as a stand-by for special purposes such as the production of covers and brochures which are best done in color. Textbooks are often produced in two colors—black and a second softer color, usually dark orange or dark blue. This improves the readability of the text and has found wide acceptance in school and freshman texts. This improvement is recommended for developing countries where the medium of instruction is not necessarily the language of the home and readability is important.

Flat Bed Scanner

Although the Chinon DS-3000 overhead scanner was relatively unsophisticated at the time of purchase, it was, to the best of my knowledge, the only full-page scanner available on the campus. The Computer Science Department had a video frame-grabber which was jealously guarded and unavailable to staff from other departments. This relatively inexpensive scanner was useful for the insertion of photographs and hand-drawn graphics into the documents and produced bitmapped files in a variety of formats. After the printer, it was the second most important accessory to the DTP system and, though still serving well, it is starting to show its age and limitations against the newer products which are now available at affordable prices.

Today we would have purchased a flat-bed full-page scanner with an ability to shrink and expand the graphics without undermining the resolution. Perhaps, for economy, we would still select a black and white scanner, but for enhanced presentation, a color scanner would be recommended. It would serve well for the production of book covers, pamphlets, brochures, and posters. Many modern scanners are packaged with OCR (optical character recognition) software with various degrees of reliability and usefulness. The scanned image is converted by the software to a binary file which can be imported into a text editor or a word processor. This is very convenient for editing pre-printed matter.

Upgrading the Software

Although PageMaker was included in the original purchase and attempts were made to bring it into use, it soon became clear that it was too powerful and demanding for our purposes. Initially we did feel the need to use it but by 1992, word-processors such as Word-for-Windows and WordPerfect had already provided the power that made them more than adequate for the production of newsletters and text books. Since the establishment of the Facility, we have used only Word-for-Windows as the medium of typesetting. This has proved to be quite sufficient for our needs.

Most of the Departments in the Faculty of Science have adopted the use of this word-processor, although many are still using WordPerfect Version 5.1 or ChiWriter Version 4.1 because of their ability to run directly under MS-DOS. The Microsoft drawing program, PaintBrush, supplied with the original setup is also popular and many use Lotus-123 for the production of graphs. There seems to be a sizable lag in the use of more sophisticated programs, such as Excel in its many versions.

There is a need to have a continuous review of the software used for DTP. The original Word-for-Windows has been upgraded from Version 1.1 to Version 2, and includes Word Art, a package used to enhance the presentation of the *Integrator*. The effect of using this package may be seen by comparing the front page of *Integrator* Vol. 1, No. 1, January 1992, with the front page of *Integrator* Vol. 3, No. 2, July 1994. We are considering an upgrade to Version 6, which has even more advanced features which are useful for DTP. WordPerfect Version 6 is now also run in the Windows environment. It allows:

- Easy switching to full screen viewing of page. This is useful when wishing to see the full effect of page presentation.

- Autoformatting. This allows a set of styles associated with a template to be assigned instantly to a document. Unformatted draft copy can be converted to a new camera-ready form with a single command, instead of applying each style paragraph by paragraph.
- The creation of unequally sized columns. This provide more flexibility in layout design and more easily allows the incorporation of different sizes of graphics.

Reprographics by Copy Printer

The integrated system, consisting of the 30 MHz 386 with an 80 megabyte hard drive, Chinon scanner, HP laser printer, and Konica photocopier, worked very well till this year, 1995. The extent to which the facility is being used has increased to a level that was not foreseen five years ago when it was first conceived. The shortcomings of the system are now beginning to show. The photocopier is emerging as the weak link in the chain mainly because of the heavy usage to which it is being put, especially with regards to the lecture-notes and other hand-outs. It is also being used as a stand-by when other photocopiers in the Faculty have broken down.

Under normal circumstances, a photocopier would be expected to serve for five years and, as the Konica was one of the most reliable and resilient of the machines we had identified, we thought that this would be the case even with heavy use. This has not been true and, in the last six months, it has begun to show the strain. The officer in charge of the Faculty of Science Reprographic Room, now feels that the time has come to move one step higher and to replace the photocopier with a copy printer. He has identified a suitable machine: the Risograph Digital Printer GR 3750. The machine is available in Zimbabwe through an outlet in South Africa. We believe that the addition of this copy printer to the system would greatly enhance its effectiveness.

Some time ago it was discovered that photocopiers need more frequent servicing when a certain type of cheap paper is used. This paper is characterized by the high degree of fluff (loose fibers) generated by the paper. These fibers clog up the gears and other moving parts of the printer. It therefore became imperative that we use only high quality bond paper for the photocopier and printer. The fact that a copy printer can use cheaper paper for publication is a further incentive for purchasing one.

The Photographic Library

A good newsletter must be well illustrated, preferably with a number of photographs of the faculty staff, both academic and non-academic. The service of the Reprographic Services photographer was used initially but was found to be expensive and it was difficult for him to coordinate with the movements of the subjects he was to photograph. As publisher I knew quite well the type of photographs that I required for each article. So after the first year of publication, I decided to take my own photographs. During the short period that we have been in existence, we have acquired a sizable photographic library and so it is generally easy to find suitable pictures for use in the newsletter. The scanned images of the photographs are kept on disk and may be used instantly when required.

CONCLUSION AND RECOMMENDATIONS

Conclusions and Plans for Future Development

There is no doubt that the DTP Facility is fulfilling a need in the Faculty of Science. Its use has only been restricted by the fact that we do not have a network with multi-user capability. It has served the purpose for which it was purchased, namely, the production of compiled lecture notes and textbooks. A newsletter, *Integrator*, is published at six monthly intervals. Our plans for future developments include:

- The placing of the DTP Facility at the disposal of all staff in a multi-user environment such as a network. We have already made much headway on the campus in this direction so we hope that this goal will be speedily achieved.
- The purchase of the following:
  — a more powerful computer to host the DTP Facility;
  — a high resolution flat-bed scanner possibly with the capability of scanning in color;
  — an ink jet color printer; and
  — a copy printer with the capability of sorting and collating large volumes.

Recommendations

The following recommendations are made in relation to the acquisition of a new facility.

The Newsletter

For any group who wishes to popularize its DTP facility, a well-produced newsletter is a mandatory starting point. The readers are immediately made aware of the facilities and possibilities available to the user. You should insist that all articles for inclusion in the newsletter be submitted on disk with as little previous formatting as is consistent with clarity and readability.

Training

Many academics are able to master even the most complicated of the computer processes quite quickly. This is less easy for clerical staff who certainly need to attend a training program with at least 8 hours of hands-on practice. It is recommended that a workshop be run annually during the long (summer) vacation to train as many typists as possible in the use of the word-processor for typesetting.

Personnel for the Newsletter

The publications work force should consist of one publisher and an assistant—both possessing sound computer experience. With practice, many are able to master the art of laying out a newsletter if the intricacies of manipulating the text are understood. They should not have to type any articles except their own. They should be assisted by a good secretary who is thoroughly trained in the use of the word-processor for typesetting applications. The secretary should be able to produce accurate drafts that have been subjected to thorough spelling checks.

Planned and Regular Upgrading of Hardware and Software

There should be built into the proposal for a DTP Facility, plans for regularly upgrading the hardware and software. Funds should be sought for the replacement of outdated equipment and application programs well in advance of their becoming obsolete. This includes the replacement and upgrading of the word processor, graphics and clip-art, and the supplementation of the available fonts.

Printer and Collator

The laser printer and the copy printer, if available, would incur almost all of the running costs of the facility. It has been found that the free use of the laser printer could lead to abuse but, in terms of the purpose for which the facility was acquired, it is probably the best policy. The recurrent cost should be borne by the Faculty of Science through levies imposed by the Dean. This levy becomes an incentive for the departments to make full use of the facility. Attempts to exact levies direct from individual users will be counter-productive and complicated to administer and should be discouraged. The benefits to the students and to the Faculty as a whole should always be considered foremost.

Color Presentations

The use of color may be considered to be a luxury—which it probably is—but it has its advantages in terms of the quality of the work that would be produced. If funds can be found, the acquisition of a color scanner and a color printer is recommended.

Networking

Many universities in developing countries are working towards the establishment of a campus computer network. If this is available, the DTP Facility should be made accessible to the network users. If necessary, prohibitions could be made against users from outside the Faculty of Science, but it is preferred that some financial arrangement could be made with such users.

Desktop Publishing at the Tanzania Commission for Science and Technology

by Albina Kasango

When she wrote this case study, Albina Kasango was the Scientific Editor at the Tanzania Commission for Science and Technology (COSTECH), where she was also the assistant editor of Tanzania S&T News. She is currently the Editor, Publications and Publicity Officer for the Economic and Social Research Foundation, an NGO that carries out research on social and economic pssues and offers policy options to the government, international organizations, and the public. She is still actively involved in desktop publishing and in producing works that contribute to scientific literacy.

BACKGROUND AND CONTEXT OF THE PROJECT

Background Information on Tanzania

Tanganyika (now Tanzania) attained its independence in 1961. It was then that the efforts of "Mwalimu" (Teacher) Julius Kambarage Nyerere at the United Nations resulted in the granting of self rule. Before that, Tanzania had been a British Protectorate and had been under German colonial rule before the econd World War. After two years of independence, on 26 April 1964, Tanganyika formed a union with Zanzibar and became what we now know as Tanzania. Accordingly, the President of Tanganyika became the President of the United Republic of Tanzania and the President of Zanzibar became the Second Vice-President and retained the Presidency of Zanzibar. The First Vice-President of Tanzania was to come from mainland Tanzania.

Tanzania emberked on a Socialist path to development in 1976, with President Nyerere's "Azimio la Arusha" (Arusha Declaration). This period saw the nationalization of the major means of production. Banks, post and telecommunication, and electricity-generating systems became public property.

The early 1990s brought great changes. Following the wave of democratization around the world, the fall of the Eastern Bloc countries, and the end of the

Cold War among the superpowers as the former Soviet Union collapsed, the political climate changed and the Tanzanian people felt they too were ready to take the maturity test. The Constitution of the country was amended in 1992 to allow multiparty politics. Today there are 13 registered political parties, with General Elections due in October 1995.

Tanzania has an estimated population of 26 million, with people coming from more than one hundred and twenty ethnic groups or tribes.

Institutional Information

The Tanzania Commission for Science and Technology (COSTECH) was established by Parliamentary Act No. 7 of 1986. It is a parastatal organization whose parent Ministry is the Ministry for Science, Technology and Higher Education (MSTHE). Being a service-oriented institution, it runs its activities by Government subvention, which it receives through the MSTHE.

COSTECH deals with the popularization, promotion, and coordination of science and technology activities in the country. The Director General of COSTECH recently reiterated the principal functions of the Commission (COSTECH) as stated in the enabling Act. These are to:

- formulate policy on the development of science and technology and recommend its implementation by the government;
- monitor and co-ordinate all activities relating to scientific research and technology development of all persons or body of persons concerned with such activities;
- acquire, store and disseminate scientific and technology information, and for that purpose hold or sponsor conferences, symposia, meetings, seminars or workshops or publish any newspaper, periodical or do any other act or thing designed to promote interest in science and technology development;
- advise the government on:
  — priorities in scientific research;
  — the allocation and utilization of research funds according to priorities referred to above;
  — regional and international cooperation in scientific research and transfer of technology;
  — matters relating to the training and recruitment of research personnel;
  — instruction on scientific subjects in educational institutions within the United Republic;
  — the initiation, formulation and implementation of research policies and programs;
  — the establishment and maintenance of national scientific standards; and

— science and technology policy.
- provide researchers with funds for conducting research in areas given priority by the government upon the advice of the Research and Development (R&D) Advisory Committees; and
- provide users with the information to make appropriate choices in the kind of foreign technologies suitable for importation and assimilation.

COSTECH is governed by a Chairman (a Presidential appointee) and Commissioners who are nominated by the Minister, with the Director General in the capacity of Secretary to the Commission. The Director General is also a Presidential appointee. COSTECH has four directorates: Information and Documentation; Research Promotion and Coordination; Centre for the Development and Transfer of Technology (CDTT); and Administration and Finance.

The CDTT provides the public with the information and expertise to make the right, pertinent, or appropriate technological choices when, say, importing machinery from abroad. The Centre, of course maintains close liaison with Trade Attachés of diplomatic missions and other relevant personnel in the country and international agencies abroad dealing with the same.

The Directorate of Information and Documentation—where I worked—is actively involved and committed to providing information to all members of society. The Directorate of Information and Documentation COSTECH has several sub-units as described below:

- The Documentation Centre includes a library collection in the fields of science and technology that serves an indiscriminate group of clientele from the Tanzanian public.
- The Publications unit has the DTP facilities under its jurisdiction and produces documents for publication.
- The Popularization Unit produces radio programs in conjunction with the parent Ministry that are in Kiswahili and serves to popularize science and technology at the grassroots level.
- The Training and Communications Unit organizes and holds training courses for various groups of the Tanzanian community (women scientists, technologists and researchers, librarians); provides electronic mail and fax facilities to an increasing number of scientists; and also takes care of the computer maintenance at the Commission.

PROJECT DESCRIPTION

Origin and History of DTP at COSTECH

The Desktop Publishing (DTP) unit is a new phenomenon: COSTECH's initial plan was to have a Printing Press Unit, complete with all of the now-old technologies that would have occupied an entire room. But, before we could proceed with this plan, we were swept up in the printing revolution known as desktop publishing. DTP software became available in COSTECH through the UNESCO-funded database project that aimed at producing a directory of scientists. The DTP equipment and software was "borrowed" from this project when it was not being used to input data. This marked the beginning of the DTP Unit at COSTECH.

In 1990, COSTECH secured funds from the International Development Research Centre (IDRC) of Canada to produce a directory of scientific personnel in the country. The project, called the Tanzania National Information System on Science and Technology (TANISSAT), was to be achieved with a database management system that incorporated the use of DTP software, called Pagemaker. At the same time, there was an urgent need for COSTECH to produce a newsletter on science and technology in a bid to popularize the same within the country.

Theophilus Mlaki, the Director for Information and Documentation, was charged with this responsibility and, at first, he thought that WordPerfect 5.0 would suffice. It had all the facilities for producing camera-ready copy ready for publication. The only snag was that WP 5.0 lacked the ability to "cut and paste" photographs and other graphics (from programs other than WP)—a capability found in more sophisticated software. This facility allows the user to use photographs, emblems, or illustrations from other sources and to place them with the text. The user can rotate, size, and edit the graphics involved. So COSTECH decided to use PageMaker on the equipment that was provided by UNESCO. Of course, this was to be done only when the computer was not being used for data entry. Mr. Mlaki designed the first newsletter, selected the typefaces and fonts, and wrote most of the articles.

Initially the DTP Unit produced one main publication: the *Tanzania S&T News,* a newsletter aimed at popularizing science and technology in Tanzania. Over the years, the number of publications has increased with the expansion of the Commission and the activities it performs. Five years after its inception, the DTP Unit has produced camera-ready copy for public lectures; the *Proceedings of the Annual Scientific Seminars;* the Act of Parliament for COSTECH; three annual reports; books of abstracts for the Medical Association of Tanzania, the International Centre for Industrial Technology and Environmental Sciences, and the National Fund for the Advancement of Science and Technology (in both English and Swahili); and other smaller publications, such as birthday cards and wedding and party invitations.

General and Particular Objectives of DTP at COSTECH

The function of the DTP unit at COSTECH falls squarely under the division that deals with the dissemination, popularization, and storage of scientific and technological information. Specifically, the project's objectives are to:

- produce articles for publication in the daily newspapers in a bid to disseminate technologies or generate interest in the need to change production processes where necessary;
- publish proceedings of the annual scientific Seminar and thus create a means for our indigenous scientists to draw national and world attention to their findings and get the acknowledgement they need;
- disseminate the latest news of national interest on pertinent science and technology issues to members of the scientific communities, the National Assembly, and government to enable them make pertinent choices/decisions; and
- inform the scientific communities and the general public on the latest developments in the activities of the Commission

PROJECT EXPERIENCE AND IMPLEMENTATION

When I first moved into COSTECH, I spent long hours sitting alongside Mr. Mlaki and Mr. Andrew Dachi, COSTECH's Computer Specialist and the typesetter. Together, we would work on producing what were the overdue back issues of the newsletter. Because I was not well-versed in this new line of work, I worked first as a "gopher." Mostly, I remember, I would be sent upstairs to collect the original documents that I had used to compile the articles—as I invariably did not have all the pertinent information incorporated into my text. Slowly, though, I learned the trade and was even able to typeset the 1993 issue of the Newsletter unaided—but still under Mr. Dachi's supervision.

In 1993, COSTECH embarked on an ambitious project to popularize science and technology by holding fora where scientists, technologists, industrialists and members of the general public could meet to discuss pertinent issues in the realm of science and technology. The first of these COSTECH Scientific Public Lecture Series was given by Keto Elitabu Mshigeni, Professor of Botany at the University of Dar es Salaam who is on attachment at the University of Namibia. His talk was entitled "The Seaweed Farming Story along the Western Indian Ocean Coast: Past, Present and Future." Using its DTP facilities, COSTECH has been able to produce the camera ready version of the lecture.

In 1993, COSTECH also secured funds from UNESCO's Intergovernmental Informatics Programme (IIP) to conduct a computer training course for Tanzanian women scientists, technologists and researchers. This was undertaken in a bid to empower women in the workplace and make them more competitive with their male counterparts. Women graduates were indeed found to possess very few computer skills. Out of the 250 course applicants, 42 percent of the women with Masters Degrees had no computer knowledge! COSTECH provided the technical aspect of the training with a few trainers coming from affiliated institutions. And of course the "Course Manuals" were prepared using the DTP facilities. One such manual is for the Advanced Computer Course.

BOX 1   Dedication
Typesetting other smaller documents is not hard in itself. Most difficult perhaps are the odd hours in which typesetting is not only required but becomes a priority! An emergency invariably arises just as one is about to leave for the day or, worse, for the weekend. Dedication and altruism are required for this job.

We have also produced posters, brochures, certificates, and other documents to advertise the Tanzania Awards for Scientific and Technological Innovation Achievement (TASTA). These are given to people and institutions who make discoveries likely to promote and accelerate the social and economic progress of Tanzania.

On 1 July 1995, the National Fund for the Advancement of Science and Technology (NFAST) was launched by the Honorable Dr. Salmin Amour, the Second Vice-President of the United Republic of Tanzania and President of Zanzibar. NFAST motivates inventors and innovators as well as the general public. Through NFAST, we hope that Tanzania will make a quantum leap in its ability to apply new technologies, especially in such frontier areas as biotechnology, solar/ biogas energy, new materials technology, and electronics. The NFAST program, information brochure, invitation cards, and charity walk cards were produced using the DTP facilities at COSTECH.

Perhaps our most important product (and the most time consuming!) is the *Tanzania S&T News*, a quarterly newsletter that is mailed to over 500 prominent individuals and institutions worldwide. In Tanzania, the mailing list includes ministers, heads of research and development institutions, and the private sector. Internationally, the newsletter is mailed to UN bodies involved in the development of science and technology, Tanzanian embassies abroad, the American Library of Congress, and others.

Then there are the annual reports which represent the activities that have been undertaken by the Commission each year. This report includes the audited financial statements of the Commission. These are prepared up to the camera-ready version using the DTP facilities available at COSTECH.

We also compile articles of interest to the Tanzanian science and technology situation from the annual seminars, international newspapers, or other sources and send them to the top leadership and the scientific community. Some of these articles get published by the local newspapers. We have published over 30 newspaper articles under this program.

Finally, there are the "Greenwire" files that COSTECH produces from electronic mail messages written by an international group of experts on environmental concerns. COSTECH staff within the Directorate of Information and Documentation scan these and select some for dissemination. This ideally should be accomplished using email (with COSTECH as the node and other institutions/ bodies being the points). However, due to the fact that not many institutions and scientists are connected to email, these messages are first downloaded onto a diskette, printed out, photocopied, and then compiled into files that are mailed to research and development institutions affiliated with COSTECH and other interested parties known to us.

It may have been difficult but now I am reaping some of the fruits of that hard labor. Besides, when I did the typesetting myself, at least I was sure that I corrected all the mistakes that I noticed. There is still a need for proofreaders—there will always be some mistakes if only one person is assigned to the entire production cycle. Nevertheless, there is one publication that makes me very proud—the *Tanzania S&T News* of December 1993 marked my début into typesetting. (See Box 1.)

THE RESULTS, IMPACTS, AND BENEFITS OF THE PROJECT

The project has received much positive feedback. Some of the comments we have received include the following:

A prominent member of Parliament said that the *Tanzania S&T News* is "extremely informative and useful."

The Embassy of Tanzania in Stockholm wrote and said that it found the "contents interesting and varied."

A medical doctor wrote to say how impressed he was with the quality of the articles in the newsletter.

A university professor told me that he especially like the newsletter column on scientific tidbits.

A secondary school teacher told us that he finds information that he can use to teach and stimulate his class.

A number of local newspaper editors have printed some of our articles.

I can say that it is very gratifying when you receive requests from people who want to be included on the mailing list. It is also very rewarding to hear that news of the contents in the newsletter is getting around. For example, Mr. Sam Baker, who worked for the Cooperative College in Moshi and is now a Computer Consultant at Coopers and Lybrand, made a survey on information technology with funding he received from COSTECH. As part of our usual news compilation, we included a brief review of his findings in our September 1994 issue of *Tanzania S&T News*. Later, we heard that he wanted a copy of that Newsletter because "people had been telling him about it." So we are certain that the news we write gets across even though we do not always get direct feedback from the readers.

We usually send articles on a weekly basis to one of the local newspapers, including the bi-weekly *Express*. Interestingly, when we are running against our own deadlines and miss sending the articles, the *Express* Editor notes our absence and sends a message to the effect of "Where is this week's article. . . ." Obviously, if the readers did not find our articles useful and worth reading, he would not show such enthusiasm.

More recently, we did an article on one of the prominent woman scientists who, incidentally, was later nominated to be a member of the Commission of COSTECH. As usual we sent her a single copy of the newsletter. We were happy to get her request for a few more copies.

Authors of papers accepted for the annual scientific seminars have used our products to obtain promotions in their workplace.

We are now certain that there are more readers who appreciate our efforts than the actual number of letters of appreciation would imply. Also since we attempt to write on issues that will interest the target group, we are optimistic that, in the long run, the long weekends spent producing the newsletters, newspaper articles, press releases proceedings and the like will produce positive results.

Scientific and technological awareness is slowly gaining a foothold—through the continued efforts of the Commission to keep information flowing to the leadership of Tanzania. The launching of NFAST, mentioned above, is proof of this progress. So far, 13 million Tanzanian shillings have been pledged to NFAST. Other pledges and contributions are being collected and we hope to have a total of 100 million Tanzanian shillings (US $166,666) by the end of December 1995.

ANALYSIS OF LESSONS LEARNED

The project has taught me several lessons. First, I know it is important to have a synergistic group of people working together in DTP (as in any other working group) for the best results. This group must be dedicated to the improvement of the press as there are always long hours of concentration and hard work required to complete a publication. Being able to do this kind of work—writing, editing, proofreading, typesetting, mailing—necessitates a supportive supervisor who believes in the staff, gives it room to grow, and also guides it through the various steps.

I have also learned that, for the best results, the basic tools and personnel are needed. For instance, if I could start the project over again, I would hire a clerk to assist in typing and addressing/mailing the newsletters so that I could concentrate on the tasks of writing good articles.

I would also make sure that the DTP unit had the proper equipment available to it on a full-time basis. This includes a dedicated 386 or 486 computer with a laser printer and a scanner for more effective compilation of camera-ready copy and for importation of graphics.

Finally, I would institute a proper training program for DTP staff. I think that people with backgrounds in mass communications, publishing, or linguistics might naturally have a better understanding of how a scientific press needs to operate but, as we have seen in our project, the aptitude for editing, design, and management can come from a variety of disciplines. Whatever the backgrounds, however, special training in the use of the DTP hardware and software is essential.

CONCLUSIONS AND RECOMMENDATIONS

Seeing that information is the determinant of which nations succeed and which do not, I think those African countries that see the importance of cooperation should do all they can to elevate their scientific and technological information (research and development) projects and activities to the highest possible level. A network of STI systems in Tanzania, Africa, and indeed the world should gradually be built through cooperative ventures (learning from each other through other case study follow-up projects).

Jacques Delors, the former President of the European Union, has said that without confidence, no people can be united to work for a common cause. So the first objective should be to build people's confidence. And how does one do that exactly? By helping people to help themselves so that they do not "live on hand-outs" and by giving people a sound education and letting them make their own (rational) decisions. This may take longer to achieve but gives the best results in the long run.

ACKNOWLEDGEMENTS

I am very grateful to Theophilus Mlaki for all his support and guidance. . .and his demand for excellence! Also at COSTECH, I would like to thank Mr. Yonazi, Senior Scientific Officer and the Desk Officer in charge of TANISSAT, who has been very understanding when I use his equipment. I have worn his patience rather thin as there are so many documents to produce.

I am also grateful to my husband and children for their understanding every time I came home late or worked on Sundays.

Environmental Publishing Network—
ENVIRONET at ICIPE Science Press
by Agnes Katama

Agnes Katama is Manager of ICIPE Science Press and project leader of the Environmental Publishing Network (ENVIRONET)—a network linking seven institutions in the Eastern Africa Region. She is also a volunteer lecturer for women undergraduate students at the University of Nairobi, where she coordinates programs for gender-equity. Her main focus of research in book production is on market orientation within the scholarly publishing world and on the search for alternative human resource formulae to enhance cost efficiency. She is a journalist by profession. She has been appointed Coordinator of the African Forum for Children's Literacy in Science and Technology, an activity of the Rockefeller Foundation.

BACKGROUND AND CONTEXT OF THE PROJECT

The International Centre of Insect Physiology and Ecology (ICIPE) was established in Kenya's capital, Nairobi, in 1970. It was given the twin mandate to:

a) undertake basic research in integrated control methodologies for arthropod pest management and
b) to strengthen, through training and collaboration, the scientific and technological capacities of developing countries.

In 1988, ICIPE created the ICIPE Science Press (ISP), as its own, internal publishing house. I joined ISP in 1991 as the Marketing and Information Executive; I am now the Manager of ISP. In March 1992, ICIPE undertook a thorough study of the literature and realized that there was little or no coordination of the development of self-sustaining and significant scholarly publishing ventures in

Africa. There was limited up-to-date information on establishing well-managed subscription services or on the mailing and marketing of environment-related publications.

Also in 1992, I carried out a study for the Association of African Universities in which I investigated the merits and the demerits of the management and organization regarding the marketing of scholarly publishing activities in Western and Central Africa. I recommended the creation of a specialized sub-regional publishing network in order to meet local needs in a coherent fashion.

Since both studies identified such pressing needs for the publication and marketing of scholarly works, the ISP decided to pool its resources with those of other institutions to create the Environmental Publishing Network (ENVIRONET).

The purpose of ENVIRONET, which was founded in 1993, is to develop means for the more efficient dissemination of research findings. For instance, many scholarly works can be redesigned into effective university course work material. ICIPE's own authorship had traditionally covered environment-related issues and the enriching combination of publishable material from the ENVIRONET participating institutions made it possible for us to launch other publications in areas such as desertification, food security, and crop sciences. ENVIRONET also facilitated the publishing of print-worthy material from peer research institutions, the sharing of information resources, and the quest for formulae to effectively commercialize the printed results according to market rules.

A key contributor to the design and implementation of the first phase of the project was the International Development Research Centre (IDRC) in Canada. IDRC has played a significant role in the development and strengthening of scholarly publishing throughout the African region. Recently, in partnership with the Association of African Universities, the Council for the Development of Economic and Social Research in Africa (CODESRIA), and several research institutions in the region, it created opportunities for inter-institutional cooperation, the sharing of resources, and dissemination of vital information. It also provided funding to establish ENVIRONET.

PROJECT DESCRIPTION

I am the ENVIRONET Project Leader. ENVIRONET is housed at the ICIPE Science Press offices in Nairobi. Since ISP had already proven to be a self-financing publishing operation, ENVIRONET benefited from staff expertise in this area and its location at ISP fostered cooperation between ENVIRONET and ICIPE Science Press. There is a very symbiotic relationship between ENVIRONET and ISP.

The first phase of the project was initiated in June 1994 as an 18-month experiment. Its main objectives are to create a credible, market-oriented, and self-sustaining network for the provision of information on environmental publishing activities and to train adequate human resources in the areas of book production, management, and marketing. Specifically, the first phase of the project was established in order to:

- Create a network of publishers and research institutions specialized in environmental matters with an adequate institutional framework;
- Conduct a marketing study with the aim of garnering support for innovative methods of self-sustaining scholarly publishing;
- Develop a database comprising an author and subject roster on environmental materials published in the region. This will include the development of linkages with other organizations pursuing similar goals; and
- Foster the capacity-building potential of participating institutions, especially in the area of training and publications marketing.

Phase I has concentrated on establishing lasting self-sustaining methods of managing the funds available for this activity. A key concern of the project is to identify collaborating institutions and activities whose needs are similar enough to seek common methods to ensure efficient production, distribution, and marketing capabilities. Phase II, to be launched in June 1996, will focus on the establishment of a well-managed and efficient Publishing and Information Center.

The establishment of a training program was a key accomplishment of Phase I and this program is described in more detail later in this case study. The training of ENVIRONET members benefited directly from the publishing systems and services used by ICIPE Science Press. For example, ISP uses an Apple Macintosh system for its desktop publishing (DTP). The software we use includes Aldus Pagemaker, Microsoft Word, Adobe Illustrator, and Excel. These are the same packages we use to train ENVIRONET members and the ones trainees will use on their own work stations, which the Network provides.

Participating Institutions

ENVIRONET seeks to revitalize the authorship capability among a selected number of research institutions in Eastern and Southern Africa, while stimulating a healthy diversity of environment related publications. The participating institutions are:

IDRC	International Development Research Centre, Nairobi
ICIPE	The International Centre of Insect Physiology and Ecology, Nairobi
ACSS	African Crop Science Society, Kampala
OSSREA	Organization for Social Science Research in Eastern Africa, Addis Ababa
ICRAF	International Centre for Research in Agroforestry, Nairobi
ELCI	The Environmental Liaison Centre International, Nairobi
ITFC	The Institute for Tropical Forestry Conservation, Mbarara University, Uganda

---

BOX 1   Finding a Business Balance

We still need to strike a fair balance between the purely business-driven considerations on the one hand and, on the other, our academic commitment to attaining
the goals for which the Project was initially designed. We still need to make environmental information readily and easily available and affordable to our tertiary
educative and research constituencies.

Our main source of publishable material is the research results obtained from
all collaborating, international, and regional organizations with related aims. ISP
was selected to host this experiment because of its current ability to self-finance
all its activities. Having achieved financial autonomy, the next logical step forward is to present an up-market strategy to wean the publishing program off the
donor support needed at its inception. This will truly be the main achievement of
the project. (See Box 1.)

The self-sustainability of ISP has taken four years to design and implement.
Naturally, there were the real advantages in having beautiful premises on the science campus of the University of Nairobi. Furthermore, the first Director of ICIPE,
Professor Thomas Odhiambo, allowed flexibility of cost recovery mechanisms with
the concerted support of the financial system of the whole institution. He encouraged me to formulate and consolidate the measures needed to allow ISP to recover
costs and, ultimately, to break even.

The sale of our expertise has been the key element of our sustainability. ISP
has a policy of 10 percent returns on all consultancies—whether in cash or in
time—and staff are encouraged to open out to the other institutions in the area.
Indeed, our first contacts with the other members of the Network have been as a
result of our help in starting up the publications unit. In the case of the African
Crop Science Society, ISP published the first issues and coordinated a colorful
launch of their journal in Kampala. These are assignments that are carefully budgeted and afford ISP substantial benefit.

Another area of expertise has been the publishing of conference proceedings
on behalf of institutions in the region. A powerful marketing edge has been the
ability of ISP to see these important assignments to completion within the year.
Recently, ISP has been commissioned to edit (myself), design (ISP team), and
layout papers for a major meeting on Equity and Social Considerations Related to
Climate Change. With assignments such as these, ISP has been able to move into
high quality publishing for a consolidated group of institutional clients. Needless
to say, the possibility of having attachment students (described below) greatly cuts
down on the cost of initial start-up of the different assignments since these need
considerable negotiation, supply of information, and other staff-intensive inputs.

The marketability of the published material, as well as the services made available at the start of the Project—training, workshop coordination, high technology computer graphics, and so on—are being used to generate independent funding that can then be plowed back into publishing or related activities. Interestingly, during this 18-month launch period, we have made the best use of our new desktop publishing facilities by fulfilling donor-funded assignments from collaborating institutions or by completing direct consultancies from the donors themselves.

PROJECT EXPERIENCE AND IMPLEMENTATION

The project and its implementation schedule were beset with multiple problems. The worst of these was the restructuring of ICIPE, the host institution, which lasted a full six months. During this time I had neither the necessary resources nor the time to dedicate to the project.

To analyze the positive and the negative points of our project implementation after the first ten months, we made use of a management tool, called SWOT. SWOT helps identify the Strengths, Weaknesses, Opportunities, and Threats facing a project. We placed particular emphasis on the DTP training component since, to date, it is the only one that has been completed as proposed at the outset.

We used the information received from the SWOT analysis to evaluate project's impact on the users, the host organization, and the collaborating institutions. It also brought to light the aspects of the project that were not well done or that could have been done better. It therefore gives us a basis for the further development of the project. The results of the SWOT analysis are given below.

Strengths

- ENVIRONET Phase 1 has established a training ground for future trainees. Four professionals have been trained and this training has served as valuable blue-print material to involve the trainable officers in important information generating institutions.
- Local and international collaboration with scientific and environmental organizations has provided a reference base from which ENVIRONET has spread its initiative since it is getting recognition among interested and upcoming projects.
- All staff and trainers have been encouraged and challenged through the project to engage in administrative tasks. Computer knowledge and exposure acquired by the trainees from different organizations serve as gateways to promoting skills present at the project. This in itself has boosted the credibility and name of ISP at both a local and an international level.

Weaknesses

- Training—This four-month course included elements of theory classes and practical computer training. We altered the course after the trainees had arrived and fell short in properly formalizing the time tables outlining the activities.
- Trips and Visits—We should have foreseen the need to plan trips, social activities, and talks by various guests.
- Evaluation—We should have conducted an ongoing activity evaluation to keep track of the quality of the entire training component. For instance, we could have sent questionnaires to trainees, the Board of Directors and trainers before, after, and during the training.
- Finance / ICIPE Headquarters—We faced heavy bureaucratic constraints.
- Interaction—The Project Leader, trainees, and consultants faced limited and difficult interaction and interpersonal communication due to external and internal pressures surrounding the restructuring exercise.
- Trainees' had limited participation in and attendance at the training because their publishing projects had not been discussed and distributed in advance.
- We should have documented complaints and disappointments to improve inter-party communication for subsequent courses.

Opportunities

- We could train trainers and colleagues from collaborating institutions in the use of the DTP equipment. We can train ICIPE and other research staff at the project premises through the help of a full time computer instructor. Our existing expertise in scientific writing and editing can also be shared with network members and others.
- Due to the gradual credibility status achieved by the project, an increasing number of institutions wish to belong to and support the project.
- Increasing the number of trainees attending each subsequent DTP course will increase the desired cost-efficiency level for each institution and will help the project participants generate their own revenue.
- The greatest hindrance to the sale of scholarly titles is the relative lack of information, reviews, and follow-up on behalf of individual and institutional authors. We could formulate further courses on marketing, pricing, and dissemination strategies.
- Email is promoting the status of ENVIRONET and in itself provides a base for marketing various publications. Access to the Internet is desirable and could help improve the flow of news about African scholarly activity. Of particular interest are possible author/subject indices, book reviews, and author profiles. Such guides will include the accomplish-

ments of experts in the areas of environment and natural science and would help libraries and others keep current bibliographies of published and unpublished literature written by Africans.

- Email has much potential as a method for curbing the costs associated with editing, peer review, and author changes. Electronic publishing of journals, proceedings of meetings, and bulletins is another possibility that we must explore. The results we achieve in ENVIRONET can be replicated by ISP to benefit other non-scientific institutions in the ISP *Tertio* program.[1]
- ISP has initiated and finalized the work plans for *Enviroburos* which, though not a part of ENVIRONET, will be supervised by ISP as commercially running document production centers at the service of the environmental and conservation communities. To ensure financial viability, we have increased our in-take capacity by the creation of these bureaus. We are now carefully documenting the results of the pilot study and will use this to rationalize the replication of these all over the continent.

Threats

- The heavy dependence and linkage to the ICIPE headquarters slackens work progress. Red tape and personal office set-ups are an obstacle to flexible market-oriented responses necessary for the project's smooth running in the financial and administrative spheres.
- Unless we undertake an organized evaluation, the Project may receive a negative image leading to a reduction in regional supporters and international collaborators.

THE RESULTS, IMPACT, AND BENEFITS OF THE PROJECT

The main activities at ICIPE Science Press include discovering new marketing angles for scholarly publishing, training publishing staff, and creating a network of collaborators to the benefit of effective scholarly material being produced. The ENVIRONET project is just over one-year old and I will discuss some of the results in this section.

The experimental marketing of the books to be produced within the network has not yet taken place because the member institutions do not yet have suitable titles ready. The publishing of manuscripts supplied by ISP is now under way, however. Some of the titles that have been discovered and whose authors are now being guided include manuscripts ranging from conservation and biodiversity to the keeping of commercial insects.

For the marketing of products and services, ENVIRONET has made use of bookfairs and forums that bring together publishers as well as persons or institutions involved in the development and distribution of environment related literature. Several institutions have made inquiries on the possibility of collaborating in this venture. I have been asked to speak at numerous symposia and conferences.

Benefits of the Project

The benefits of the project include:

a) enhanced project management as a service to ICIPE as well as to several institutions with similar aims and objectives;
b) infrastructure enhancement for the publishing division of the ISP;
c) human resource development for both trainees and women university students on attachment;
d) training manuals for successive courses to be hosted for the DTP of scientific manuscripts;
e) published material; and
f) email catalogs of grey literature to be accessed online.

The University Students Attachment Programme (USAP)

The USAP is in many ways an integral part of ENVIRONET because it has helped contribute to its success. This program was first established as a means of helping the ISP program break even. Since its inception, we have made the study and consolidation of USAP and other innovative, up-marketing strategies a priority aspect in management, time, and resources allocation. I will, thus, take some time to describe the details of this attachment program. We plan to help publishing houses in the region create similar programs to cut down on the prohibitive overhead costs of running a publishing house.

The USAP is one of my ideas to make administrative work more cost-effective. Some of ISP's services are only possible because of this attachment program of university women. Yes, but why women? Women count for only one of every six of the university population. Job seeking for women can be agonizing, given the strict requirement of prior working experience. It was to respond to this need in the student community that USAP was born. (See Box 2.)

Operation

We select university students from diverse faculties who can contribute to the general working of the press. They are then attached to the various ISP de-

---

BOX 2   Training Program for Women

USAP is a Women Empowerment Project that I helped form in 1993 to serve the dual purpose of training on the job while reducing the number of permanent administrative staff of ISP. This program takes, for a duration rarely exceeding six months, university students who are on vacation.

partments after intensive on-the-job training by the proceeding group of USAPers. The students are involved in marketing, soliciting, distribution, production liaison, mailing, and subscription activities. We have prepared comprehensive procedural manuals to help smooth the flow of work. Students work free of any supervision, although I am available for guidance. Weekly meetings allow feedback on tasks assigned to each person.

Professional development classes are offered to all USAPers. USAP organizes its own activities to help other students participate in professional enrichment activities. So far, the major outlet has been to annual rural promotion projects. They have proved to be very resourceful and often prepare the educational material on their own.

USAP Benefits

There have been many benefits of the USAP. Women in Management (WIM) and Women in Science (WIS) are two new projects geared toward the professional promotion of undergraduates. Both projects fall under the USAP umbrella. These grew out of the great diversity of training and orientation needs of the various USAPers. We saw a clear need to help students develop in their own fields of specialization. There exists an eagerness to attend extra-curricular professional sessions since these always offer increased job prospects.

Women in Management was formed for students who hope to specialize in commerce and business administration. Women in Science is for students looking for careers in the sciences. In addition to university students, these projects also target students in middle level colleges and young professionals.

The USAP Alumni

Every three months, there is a new USAP group at ISP. A total of over 60 women have benefited directly from the hands-on training program, while up to 250 have benefited from off-shoot activities. Bulletins and regular get-togethers of the USAP Alumni are two major methods of exchanging ideas and giving new information and feedback on tasks accomplished. Also since many women obtain good jobs on completion of their undergraduate studies, there is the rewarding opportunity of listening to their expectations and desire to excel.

Future Prospects : The USAP Resource Centre (URC)

The establishment of a URC will be a major step forward. We are approaching donors to help equip a resource centre that will link women from countries in the region. Given that these students are already trained and are resourceful, such a center could help in the provision of support for this activity as its popularity spreads among collaborating institutions. These activities include the preparation of educational material for rural promotion projects, coordination of USAP pro-

fessional classes, and planning the activities of WIM and WIS. We are fast form-
ing links with other university students in the world in order to facilitate better
communication. A first stop will be Makerere University, Kampala, Uganda where
a WIM program has already been simulated.

ANALYSIS OF LESSONS LEARNED

I know that ICIPE itself has contributed to the success of ISP and the
ENVIRONET project. Unlike many international research institutions, ICIPE has
encouraged and permitted creative system design that stretches beyond ISP's traditional mandate. Experimenting with different cost-recovery mechanisms and being innovative in the use of staff has allowed ISP to attain self-sufficiency. Beyond
this broad lesson, we have learned a number of specific things.

For example, following their program, the trainees reported to the Board members. The issues they raised in their joint report were also discussed at ICIPE's own
ENVIRONET training post-mortem meeting with ICIPE's senior-most staff. The
resolutions taken by ICIPE as a result are discussed below.

Training Organization

The administration of the training clearly demonstrated shortcomings. Most
of these emanated from a lack of foresight as to the viability of such an activity,
when both ISP and headquarters staff were working in a low efficiency mode. As
we discovered, training should never have started during the restructuring of the
host institution. In the future, any training carried out will be entrusted to the
training division of ICIPE, while all technical aspects will be the responsibility of
ISP. ICIPE's training division will then take charge of the preliminary notification
and will establish the training needs of all participants and the correct modus oper-
andi during the program. This will lead to a closer working relationship between
myself, the Head of Training at ICIPE, and the ENVIRONET Board members.

Finances, Trainee Per Diem, and Travel

The trainees should know, prior to the start of training, the details of their
travel arrangements, allowances, and the full nature of their program, including
time off, recreation, other travel opportunities, and so on. We are in the process of
circulating such rules and regulations to the Board for its approval.

Organization

The restructuring of ICIPE has moved ICIPE Science Press and all of its
various projects from the management to the research arm of the institution. This
will ensure that the project's own research content, objectives, and goals are being

evaluated as a research assignment and that they continue to fit within the broader picture of ICIPE's research mandate and interests.

ENVIRONET - Training Objectives

The training program was overly ambitious and there existed a clear mismatch between targeted achievement and real attainment. Smooth communication was either difficult or less effective than desired. The resulting working atmosphere was sometimes tense both between the institution and the project, as well as among the project management and trainees.

Advocacy

A number of institutions and professionals in the relevant fields have shown interest in participating in the project and in learning more about plans for expanded collaboration and professional capacity building. Furthermore, the professionals trained in the project will need additional monitoring, support, and networking. A simple one sheet newsletter is being sent out to all interested parties and collaborating institutions of the project. Emphasis on clarity of reporting is paramount to establishing links as the project faces the challenges of fund-raising for its successive phases.

Electronic Publishing

Electronic publishing is now the focus of my efforts as well as those of the collaborating institutions. The links have now been set up. ENVIRONET will have a dedicated telephone line and switchboard independent from the ISP main lines. Email facilities are now available for trainees' needs. We have designed a home page on the Internet via The University of Edinburgh and we have installed systems for online publishing and documentation transfer. Start-up funding is a real problem since the initial hooking up is the most costly in terms of design and equipment.

Evaluation

The project has been evaluated by an expert selected by IDRC with specific terms of reference, as is critical within the framework of sustainability of the proposed activities.

Author's Roster

An important component of the research in ENVIRONET is the compilation of a marketing tool. This will consist of a database of two types:

a. *Books in press and in print.* In conjunction with the Library of Congress, the African Publishers Network (APNET), and others, this project will study ways to harmonize information on authors and titles to meet a North-South online demand. This research is vital and could be a great service to the region since most existing databases are not online. I have started discussions with interested parties so as to harmonize input from the beginning. I estimate that we will start this project in about three months.

b. *Grey literature.* ENVIRONET's mandate is to publicize existing grey literature by the continent's specialized authors. Availability of information about market, slant, and constituency are the mainstay of the project and we are seeking funds for serious research of this sort.

Publications

ENVIRONET is to publish or cover the cost (including the marketing) of five publications. Although originally to be prepared by the trainees while in the training program, only two of the institutions had ready material. Also it was not possible to complete these given the lack of time. Authors for the five manuscripts are now being guided. The possibility of their marketing via the online system is a critical aspect of the research component.

ENVIRONET Phase II

ENVIRONET will have to compete for scarce funding for its successive stages and group financing of activities will be the foreseeable scenario. Despite the difficult launch period during the restructuring of the host institution, there is considerable interest within the region in the activities and the objectives of the project. A number of institutions have asked to be affiliated with it particularly given the specificity of its training. This clearly presents financial challenges. Through considerable donor contact, I am now coordinating fund-raising for the second phase.

CONCLUSIONS AND RECOMMENDATIONS

ENVIRONET Phase I now comes to a close to pave the way for ENVIRONET Phase II. In Phase II we hope to seek funding for the expansion of the Information and Publishing Center. Through the center, ISP will be able to source work from various organizations in the region and publish it for them. We will continue to publish material included within the broad paradigm of environmental studies analysis.

The mainstay of the project will continue to be the satisfaction of information related demands in the region. Via the ENVIRONET Information Center, ISP will continue to assist in the marketing of scholarly publications and to study the factors that continue to determine real publication development for the university and other tertiary readers.

Querying the information center will be possible via the email facilities of the user nodes, even though providing connectivity and access is probably the single most expensive activity that the project has identified. Quick access to existing information on particular areas of interest could be a marketable service to offer the Northern scholar at a differential costing and pricing. The profit will then fall as a subsidy for the Southern researcher.

Training will be another important aspect of the second phase. A critical mass of information providers will be built upon the already existing loose network of the ENVIRONET family of institutions. By the end of 1997, 20 prime research and development organizations will benefit from this training and will thus become information disseminators in their own right.

The ENVIRONET hub will try to speed up the publication process. What is now apparent is that the scholarly world will not publish in Africa unless there evolves a real commitment to sharing the cost of the manuscript processing. We are proposing that authors be able to submit manuscripts via the network to ISP where general editors help assemble the document. Thus the usually frustrating review process could be facilitated by putting the reviewers online with ISP. Authors will only need to go to a network point to approve manuscripts. Likewise the service of forwarding manuscripts to foreign journals could be handled for a gradually growing constituency.

The USAP project, now officially featured in ICIPE's Annual Reports, has no doubt presented exciting findings in the world of information packaging in the region. We will properly quantify their role and the service they can market to collaborating institutions. The importance of reducing overhead is critical to the survival of a scholarly publishing press. To add to the exposure these students will derive from their association with ISP, first as undergraduates and later as colleagues in collaborating institutions, we now propose to set up exchange programs where these women will gain personally from interaction with work places and information packaging concerns in the more developed parts of the world. These attachments will be coordinated by ENVIRONET to ensure that undergraduates acquire relevant work experience to the region's needs. This project is worthy of enhancing and its experience used as a pilot for gender equity concerns, particularly regarding the concern of a greater female representation in science and technology.

ISP has often seen the need to expand its collection points within the region. Thus we came up with the idea of the Enviroburos. The concept, which had to be nurtured and promoted among the non-commercial environment that typifies the scholarly publishing world, is now evolving. These will be market-oriented information packaging units in strategic cities in the region. Their marketing and procedures will derive from ISP's own rich experience in beating the cost-efficiency crunch. They will be put under the care of the members of the ENVIRONET

Board. They will serve moreover as further arms for the publishing of worthy grey literature.

Today, we can consider the creation of an audiovisual laboratory because the costs are falling so rapidly. Publishing in Africa must keep abreast of technological advances elsewhere. We propose to create a pool of resources available for the use of the collaborating institutions to enable the documentation of research findings and events by video. A facility of this nature could easily reside in ISP given its ample premises within the university campus. Also the running of such a project is justifiable and easier to fund when the positive impact will be felt by so many users.

ENVIRONET proposes to provide to a wide public the results of the indexing of grey literature. The publishing of all material on CD-ROM is now an eventuality that ISP would like to spearhead. Of particular interest is the archiving of information on discs. This, though clearly important, will require careful planning by a number of interested donors and partners, since the task calls for substantial funding.

The launch of the project has had its own teething problems and the challenge ahead entails parallel commitment from all. As regional initiatives progress, the task is now at hand to safely conduct ENVIRONET past its infancy into the dynamics of growth.

NOTE

1. *Tertio* is a series that ISP launched in 1993 for non-scientific and technical readers—it includes mostly social science monographs. One Tertio publication, entitled *Africa Development's Last Frontier,* by Sadig Rasheed, will have a considerable impact for the inter-disciplinary scholarly publishing system continent-wide. One main title is being published under the Tertio program every year.

ACKNOWLEDGEMENTS

As Project Leader, I would particularly wish to thank the four trainees in the pioneer course, who mastered publication development skills offered by ENVIRONET. Their final report will go a long way to help chart out a more efficient plan for the successive training/orientation sessions the project may host in the future. Special commendation from the senior management of ICIPE goes to the IDRC Programme Officer, Dr. Habib Sy. Through his active and knowing guidance the project has now become an experiment the positive results of which are awaited by a significant number of future collaborators and information facilitators the world over.

Innovations in Desktop Publishing at the African Academy of Sciences, 1989-1992
by Dr. Alex R. Tindimubona

Alex Tindimubona is now Chairman of ASTEX—the African Science and Technology Exchange—based in Kampala, Uganda. From 1989 to 1992, he was program officer and associate editor at the African Academy of Sciences in Nairobi. There, he was involved in introducing desktop publishing in support of scientific communication. At ASTEX, he continues to promote science and technology for development and is now working on the networking of African scientists. Dr. Tindimubona has a PhD in quantum chemistry and previously taught at the University of Nairobi.

BACKGROUND AND CONTEXT OF THE PROJECT

This case study describes the introduction of desktop publishing (DTP) at the African Academy of Sciences (AAS), which was a pioneer in using such technology for scholarly publishing in Africa. The AAS is a continent-wide, non-governmental organization of senior scientists, science managers, and policy experts dedicated to the promotion of science and technology for development in Africa. It is the brainchild of 22 leading African scientists who met in Trieste, Italy in July 1985 at the Third World Academy of Sciences. A task force under the chairmanship of Professor Thomas R. Odhiambo of Kenya presented the constitution of the AAS within six months. In December 1985, it was ratified at a second meeting in Trieste and the Academy was born with 33 Founding Fellows. It began operation at its headquarters at the International Center for Insect Physiology and Ecology (ICIPE) in Nairobi, in June 1986.

The AAS is an honorific society that promotes excellence in science and technology by recognizing outstanding individual accomplishments through election to the membership (Fellowship) of the Academy. Admitting new Fellows at the rate of about ten per year, the membership now stands at just over 100. It has also developed a series of prizes to reward excellence, the most notable being the AAS/Ciba-Geigy Prize for Agricultural Biosciences.

BOX 1 External Leadership of African Science

Until the founding of the AAS, the leadership for organization and management of science in Africa lay in externally-based institutions such as the United Nations family (UNESCO, UNECA, UNIDO, etc.) or in the former colonial powers, which worked through African government bureaucracies, such as the French ORSTOM; the British Commonwealth Science Council; or the United States Agency for International Development. Thus, final decisions were taken in Paris, London, or Washington, D.C. African scientists had not yet organized themselves into a community that could articulate its potential and needs, or its usefulness to society. Science was still marginalized.

From the beginning, the AAS decided to be an active, practical organization whose members would address the daunting problems of the continent. For the AAS was formed at a time of deep crisis for Africa: the continent faced major famines, external debts, declining economies, social conflicts, and a growing questioning of the political leadership. (See Box 1.)

The AAS vowed to take the lead in reversing Africa's decline through science-led development. It decided to tackle the problems that transcend national and ideological boundaries: drought, desertification, and food deficit. Finally, its members rallied around the theme of "bridging the gap between the scientists, industrialists, and policy makers in Africa." The AAS chose a core program covering four areas:

- Mobilization and strengthening of the African scientific community;
- Publication and dissemination of scientific materials;
- Research, development, and public policy; and
- Capacity building in science and technology.

Early on, the AAS realized that publications would be a major instrument for building the African scientific community, for making it aware of itself and its mission, and for interaction with its constituency. This constituency was very well defined: it included the scientific community itself, the policy makers, the entrepreneurs, and the general public. The publication program thus started as soon as the first staff member, Professor Peter Anyang' Nyong'o, came on board in July 1987 as Head of Programs. Using outside typesetters, he immediately started publishing *Whydah*, the quarterly newsletter of the AAS and working on the first book, *Hope Born Out of Despair*. He also helped develop the publication strategy of AAS: they would publish a newsletter, a journal, books and monographs, as well as other products. The publishing arm of the AAS was called Academy Science Publishers, or ASP.

PROJECT DESCRIPTION

The ASP initially took on desktop publishing to underpin the publication of the AAS's *Discovery and Innovation (D&I)*, which was a quarterly, approximately 100 page per issue, peer-reviewed, multi-disciplinary journal of research and policy discourse. The feasibility study performed prior to establishing the journal involved over 80 scholars, scientists, and professional consultants from Africa, Europe, and America and unearthed many problems facing publishing in Africa. The study found that of the 70,000 or so journals published worldwide, only about 150 were from Africa. Many of these were of dubious quality, frequency, and duration. The main problems were prioritized as lack of resources, but more significantly, there were managerial problems, such as the:

- Low professional capacity in editing, typesetting, printing, marketing, and distribution; and
- Management of the intellectual processes: peer review, content-quality assurance, timeliness; and inclusion in the world's secondary (abstracting, indexing, and citation) literature.

Many African scientists were worried about publishing their best work in an "obscure journal" whose results might not be seen by their peers. This might possibly result in duplication of research or, worse, competitors might claim they got the results first. There were also doubts in some foreign quarters as to whether Africa was doing enough high-calibre science to support such an advanced journal. The leadership of the AAS, who had much experience on the African scene, insisted that the time was ripe for such a journal. All in all, the study came up with conflicting predictions that could only be tested in the field through praxis.

It is a tribute to the resilience, persistence, vision, and managerial acumen of the leadership of the AAS that the journal not only started, but has survived and has become a regular, well recognized beacon of scholarly publishing in Africa. The tribute equally goes to the donors of the journal, particularly the Carnegie Corporation of New York and the Kuwait Foundation for the Advancement of Science. But thirdly, and significantly, the tribute must be shared by a technological innovation—desktop publishing—which is at the base of the success of this journal and indeed of the AAS's entire program of publication and dissemination of scientific materials.

In May 1988, Professor Turner T. Isoun arrived from Nigeria to take his post as the Editor of *Discovery and Innovation*, plus other AAS publications. On assuming duty, he immediately took steps to ensure the acquisition of good quality manuscripts for consideration for publication in the journal. He developed and sent out announcements of the new journal, instructions to contributors, and personal invitations to contribute articles to key scientists inside and outside Africa (including all Fellows of AAS). He was rewarded with an encouraging response to his campaign. Over 100 scientists indicated a willingness to contribute articles and, by the time he produced the first issue in March 1989, he already had over 60 papers undergoing the peer review process—enough to fill the first four issues of *D&I*.

PROJECT EXPERIENCE AND IMPLEMENTATION

The feasibility study had recommended the introduction of desktop publishing for the journal. Accordingly, the AAS acquired a Macintosh IIci computer, with a laser printer and back-up dot matrix printer. It had advanced word processing (Microsoft Word) and DTP (Aldus Pagemaker) software. The AAS already had three IBM-compatible personal computers with dot-matrix printers that were used mainly for word processing. A database management program (Dbase III) was used for the project on *Profiles and Databank of African Scientists and Scientific Institutions*. The AAS newsletter, *Whydah*, had been published since 1987, using outside typesetting service. Three books and other several other products of the AAS had also been published using outside services.

The new equipment was ready when the next editorial staff member joined in October 1988. Gillian Ngola had broad experience in publishing and quickly became proficient on the equipment, mainly using her familiarity with the printing terminology that had been incorporated into the DTP software (e.g., fonts and point sizes, bromides, camera-ready copy, etc.). Arriving in January 1989, as an Assistant Program Officer, I brought my experience as a physical scientist familiar with computers, science writing, and publication generally. I began to troubleshoot simple problems, conduct in-house training on computer literacy, undertake technical editing of scientific articles, and plan for expansion on the DTP path. I actively participated in the thrill and agony of putting together the first issue of *D&I*. When it finally came out in its purple splendor in March 1989, we celebrated!

Two major issues were identified and dealt with at that time. One was the whole area of typesetting mathematical expressions, which was extremely tedious with the conventional programs then available. It was eventually solved to some extent with the Expressionist software, a shareware program supplied by Miriam Balaban of Israel. The second was a more fundamental one, dealing with refereeing of papers through a peer review process. The system of peer review designed for *D&I* was extremely innovative, rigorous, and uncompromising regarding what would be accepted for publication. It was based on the principle of pure peer review as applied by the best journals of the world.

As 1989 ended, it was clear that *D&I* was succeeding beyond the expectations of its initiators. We had managed to bring out four issues of high quality material, every issue on time (in the month shown on the cover). We had received some 314 manuscripts and had processed enough of these to keep two issues ahead in terms of articles ready for production. Also, we had received 236 paid subscriptions.

Innovations related to computers were becoming very useful, for instance:

- some authors were submitting their articles on diskette, thus obviating error-prone re-entering of text;
- we had the manuscript tracking system computerized; and
- we had introduced and mastered a mathematical typesetting software (Expressionist) that improved our handling of physical science papers.

After one year of operation, we could better understand and deal with our business environment. The information technology environment within which DTP grew at the AAS was auspicious in some respects, but terrible in others, though each of these facets had to be recognized and managed by doing. Nairobi, and particularly the ICIPE campus at which the AAS was housed until 1992, was full of microcomputers, but not DTP. A good proportion of the secretaries could operate a word processor but had not been trained in the more complicated aspects of page layout or importing graphic files. Technical support was available but insufficient, especially when it came time to dealing with hardware problems.

In terms of scientific content for our publications, the supply was good, as nearly all scientific and technical disciplines were well represented in Nairobi—in professional societies, universities, libraries, government agencies, research institutions, international organizations, and NGOs. The AAS, through its project on *Profiles and Databank of African Scientists and Scientific Institutions,* the Fellowship of the Academy, and the Network of African Scientific Organizations (NASO), was already in touch with much expertise Africa-wide and indeed world-wide. (See Box 2.) ICIPE itself represented a multidisciplinary scientific and technological milieu. Its scientific programs and activities kept the AAS replete with new visitors, contacts, information, and advice. Nairobi was (and still is) the hub of trade, communication, and commerce for Eastern and Central Africa and attracts much equipment and trade information. Telecommunication within Nairobi and outside is easy, but not cheap. Thus the ASP Editor had no major problem originating publications ready for the printers. He could mobilize peer-review and technical editing, and consult other experts and libraries for scientific and techni-

---

BOX 2   Complementary Projects

The peer review process reinforced the AAS's desire to develop a deep and broad knowledge of the African scientific community. This is why the *Profiles and Databank of African Scientists and Scientific Institutions* project was so useful. Often the *D&I* Editor came to my office and said: "Alex, could you look in your database and find me an expert to review this paper—preferably not from the following country(s)." Most of the time I would succeed, and also take the opportunity to add the authors to the database, if they qualified.

cal publishing minutiae (e.g., the current convention for depicting vectors and matrices in print).

The printing industry in Nairobi responded well and turned out to be up to the task of printing a sophisticated publication like *Discovery and Innovation*—at reasonable prices and with acceptable timing. Although most printing had previously been taken outside (mostly to London), this was traced to the colonial legacy of Kenya and the perceived editorial shortcomings of African editors. Thus, it was actually editorial expertise that was sought. Once that editorial confidence was built—and the ASP/DTP did a lot to build it in Nairobi—there was no looking back. In other words, while the environment affected AAS, AAS did much to affect the STI environment too!

The one clear negative aspect of the STI environment for the international scholarly publisher in Kenya was the prohibitively expensive international postage demanded by the government-run Kenya Posts and Telecommunications Corporation (KPTC). High prices forced the AAS to ship its publications, in bulk, to a cheaper distributor in the United Kingdom or Amsterdam. While saving us money this also led to horrible delays in fulfillment of subscriptions and orders. Telephone and fax, also managed by the KPTC, were at least four times higher than in neighboring Uganda. The other barrier in Kenya was the lack of full liberalization of foreign exchange markets (unlike Uganda) and high duty on computer equipment.

Departure of Professor Isoun

The first major challenge to the DTP program at the African Academy of Science came in early 1990 when Professor Isoun returned to Nigeria. He retained his post as non-resident Editor and the office in Nairobi was reorganized. I was appointed Associate Editor and was to assist him in ensuring the editorial quality, scientific content, and general sustainability of the journal. Specifically, I was to deal with:

- the editorial acceptance process: referee selection and manuscript traffic monitoring;
- technical editing for scientific content, especially in the physical sciences; and
- overall program development for AAS publications.

I did this along with my duties as Assistant Program Officer in charge of several other projects. (See Box 3.) Mrs. Ngola, in turn, took on more responsibility for managing the journal's technical editing, production, publication, and marketing. We were lucky in October 1989 to hire, as a graduate secretary, Mrs. Nancy Amulyoto, who grew to be invaluable in running the manuscript tracking system and generally running the office. She was the *de facto* Assistant to the

---

BOX 3 Profiles of African Scientists

I was asked to publish *Profiles of African Scientists*, from my computerized databank. I was initially appalled because I thought it a retrogressive step to go from electronic to paper-based data. Later, it dawned on me that most of the world was still "paper-bound" and could not access our data anyway. But computers would still help, via DTP. There followed one of my most nightmarish exercises—converting my IBM Dbase files into Microsoft Word files ready for DTP on a Macintosh! We published the book, complete with photographs, in March 1990. It had about 400 entries. The book was an immediate hit, and generated a lot of interest and heated discussions, particularly by those who had been left out. The photos were included because, apparently, there were some people who still doubted that there actually *are* African scientists. This book put those doubts to rest. The second edition, revised and expanded, was published in March 1991, with over 600 entries.

Editor while Mrs. Ngola became, in essence, the Production Editor.

The Peer Review Process at the AAS

I want to provide some detailed information about the peer review system that we used at ASP. If a journal is to be taken seriously by the international scientific community, it must follow a rigorous peer review process. The system established for the peer review of *Discovery and Innovation* was among the first in Africa.

After preliminary assessment of a paper by the editor, we mailed copies to two or three independent referees. We first removed any information about the author—name, country of origin, and current institution—so that the reviewer would not be unduly influenced by such particulars. We looked for reviewers who were not from the same country as the authors. In order to continuously recalibrate our standards, we also chose reviewers from outside Africa. Depending on referees' comments, the editor would:

1) accept for publication;
2) send referees' comments (anonymously) back to author for revision/ response;
3) send copy to other referee(s) for further opinion; or
4) reject and return the manuscript to author.

The revised manuscript could be accepted or sent back to referees. Clearly the peer review process often resulted in extended cycles of interaction between authors and referees, mediated by the editor. Though expensive and time-consuming (given Africa's poor postal communications), we found this process extremely important in safeguarding the quality, credibility, and integrity of the journal. Never during the first four years of publishing *D&I* did the AAS receive any feedback challenging the intellectual content of the journal. Indeed, potentially embarrassing submissions were caught before damaging our reputation. Some of the exchanges generated a lot of heat. We also learned that the matter of confidentiality is often a managerial formality to protect the concerned parties: active experts worth their salt can usually guess the identity of the author or at least the institution from which a given paper originated. As long as this formality is respected by all, however, the process can obviate any suspicions of bias, plagiarism, blockage, and unfair competition in the scientific community.

Another unique feature of the *D&I* peer review system was that it was purely voluntary. We correctly believed that if our journal was excellent, then reviewers would find it an honor to be associated with it and contribute to its success.

As 1990 ended, it was clear that *D&I* was well established. We had fully mastered the intricacies of originating and producing a high quality, peer reviewed journal on African soil. However, *D&I* was now pushing the human resources to the limit, particularly at the post-production, business end: marketing, distribution, subscription fulfillment, and so on. This became the focus of our struggle: to convince our donors to support the hiring of a marketing officer. This was finally accomplished in June 1992. With this position filled, the AAS controlled all the basic functions of DTP, and ASP became, at last, a full (but still small) DTP-based publishing house.

Other Publications

As soon as ASP proved the viability of DTP for scholarly publishing in Africa with the release of *D&I* in March 1989, the managers of AAS were emboldened to widen the DTP scope to include books, monographs, and reports. The editorial office already had four manuscripts on hand, coming out of other AAS programs or through outside collaboration. These quickly became pioneer DTP books under the ASP imprint. Their titles were:

- *Science for Development in Africa;*
- *Soil and Water Management in Africa;*
- *Directory of Scholarly Journals Published in Africa;* and
- *Regional Integration in Africa: an Unfinished Agenda.*

By November 1989, we had produced the African Academy of Sciences' *Strategic Plan 1989-1992*, much acclaimed for its design excellence and quality production in green, cream and gold, which became a major selling point among the AAS's donors and clientele. Production of equally well-designed Annual Reports became a tradition at this time.

In 1992, another milestone was passed when *Whydah*, the AAS newsletter, was finally produced inhouse by DTP. This was a major achievement, because it was accomplished through internal capacity building, without expanding the staff. Our Administrative Secretary, Miss Margaret Anaminyi, taught herself DTP basically by watching and doing over the years, until she challenged us to let her do it all. Her pioneering effort allowed us to produce the newsletter more efficiently. She also spread the skills and confidence she gained to the other staff members and other AAS projects. This caused a quantum leap in the efficiency of our secretariat and the quality of our products as we became almost 100 percent computer-literate.

As 1992 ended, problems remained at the post-production, business end but these were being addressed by the new marketing officer. The biggest problem threatening the DTP operation was that many of its pioneering staff began to leave for a variety of reasons. After Professor Isoun left in mid-1990, we managed to cover for his absence through sheer energy and hard work. But when, at the end of 1991, Professor Nyong'o left to join the multiparty politics of Kenya, the pressure became unbearable. At the same time, I was making plans to return home to Uganda and decided to stay only one more year as Head of Programs and Associate Editor. Under this pressure, we still managed to produce all of our serials on time every time in 1992, but the book publishing slowed down.

In the meantime, it appears that the impetus for dynamic use of DTP has been picked up by the ICIPE Science Press, which is covered by Ms. Agnes Katama's case study (included in this volume). Her study shows the development of the market-oriented, potentially sustainable strategy that we were planning at the AAS but had not yet begun to develop and implement.

RESULTS, IMPACTS, AND BENEFITS OF THE PROJECT

By the end of 1992, DTP was well established at the AAS. The result was that all programs could confidently produce camera-ready copy: books, journals, newsletters, brochures, and reports on time and to consistently high levels of quality. Our flagship publication, *D&I,* had broken all records by coming out regularly, on time, for four volumes (16 issues).

Its high quality content, favorably reviewed in *Nature,* helped us break through a thick barrier into the international science citation system. It was abstracted and indexed in the secondary literature by *Chemical Abstracts* and *Current Contents.* It was also carried in the catalogue of the African Book Collective in London, signalling its entry into worldwide promotion, marketing, and distribution. The number of papers submitted had risen to 780. *Discovery and Innovation* was quickly establishing itself as the principal forum for scholarly and policy discourse in Africa.

ASP books and periodicals were displayed at international conferences and book fairs worldwide, and could be found in many libraries. Our books were hitting the market at a prolific rate, with 11 titles in our catalogue, plus thousands of brochures, pamphlets, flyers, catalogs, indexes, and promotional materials. Academy Science Publishers became one of the fastest growing scholarly publishing houses on the African scene. A new AAS staff member confessed that he had been misled before joining, by the number of publications reaching his institution, into thinking that AAS was a large organization with a hundred employees. He found about ten. We worked hard, and we worked smart, mostly through DTP. (See Box 4.)

The AAS is pinning great hopes on ASP to become the main pillar of its quest for self-reliance and reduced donor dependence.

Impacts of DTP rapidly spread throughout the organization. The dot-matrix printer was abandoned suddenly for the laser when our Director started refusing to sign non-laser printed letters. Suddenly, everyone wanted a Macintosh with laser printer. Timeliness, quality, and financial prudence became AAS management goals. DTP could ensure delivery of the required results most of the time.

AAS's pioneering spirit created a mini freelance industry in DTP, mainly composed of expatriates who were unemployed because of Kenya's strict employment regulations. They set up DTP facilities in their houses and serviced the high-pressure demands of the AAS, through their spouses and friends. Miriam Isoun worked in this way to publish *Science for Development in Africa,* taking a great weight off Gill Ngola's shoulders; she also stepped in for an issue or two of *D&I* when Mrs. Ngola was away. Laura Tindimubona designed almost all the books, the *Strategic Plan,* and Annual Reports. She used DTP to publish *Inventions of African Scientists,* which was printed by ICIPE Science Press in 1992. These entrepreneurs were soon joined by others, including ICIPE secretaries and graduate students at the University of Nairobi. And so DTP spread in Nairobi.

Here are some other examples of the impact of the desktop publishing program at the AAS:

- One industrialist saw a new food formulation reported in an AAS publication and started a new production line in his factory;
- An article from *D&I* was repackaged for the popular media and got carried by several news agencies in Africa;
- I won the 1992 UNESCO Swraj Paul award for work on development of

---

BOX 4   Impact of ASP

A colleague visited a foreign organization based in Nairobi with the mandate of collecting and disseminating African literature. He asked them whether they had any books on science in Africa. They said, "Sure." So he said: "Can I see some so as to acquire them for the AAS library?" They brought out the books they had, and lo and behold, they were all from the AAS.

a science culture in Africa, an article first published as a guest editorial in *D&I* in 1990;

- My analysis of the characteristics of the African scientific community, published in the *Profiles* book, led to a better understanding of the same and helped in design of new AAS programs, such as the Education of Girls and Women; and

- Experts who received papers to referee for *D&I* ended up submitting papers or getting involved in other AAS projects.

Finally, I believe that *D&I* and other AAS publications went a long way in building the African scientific community, and perhaps, ultimately, an African science. Any journal is an expression of the scientific community that surrounds it. The famous "internationally recognized" journals that the African scientists were clamoring to publish in, e.g., *Journal of the American Chemical Society (JACS)*, are actually quite parochial in their core, because they have to be relevant to the needs and aspirations of American chemistry. For these reasons, African papers reporting on African problems would not be easily deemed relevant to such journals. *D&I*, if it could overcome the problems it faced, could be such a mouthpiece, and yet be internationally recognized. This program in turn has had a great impact in making the AAS a highly visible authoritative leader of science in Africa.

ANALYSIS OF LESSONS LEARNED

The main lesson we learned is that DTP should not be confused with simply typesetting or design on a computer—which is what most laymen think. It should be understood as *publishing*, first and foremost: this means managing the entire process or chain by which raw manuscripts are transformed and delivered to the consumer in the most appropriate fashion. This entails managing the origination, printing, marketing, and distribution—and ideally doing all of this profitably and in a self-sustaining way. The computer can play a role anywhere along this chain.

Seen in this way, DTP as most people see it, is only a small part of the entire process. In our time, the AAS certainly mastered the origination process and we depended heavily on the mature printing industry of Nairobi, but we had yet to come to grips with the post-production or business end. There is still lots of room for innovation and capacity building in these areas in Africa. Otherwise, why do we still have so few reliable, sustainable scholarly journals in Africa? The key aspect we mastered was the technology of DTP—at a time when few others had much experience with its application.

Another key to our rapid expansion in this period is traceable not only to the internal training of secretaries but to the more fundamental trick of strategic recruitment of a cadre of several young university-trained graduate secretaries. They had the basic knowledge, skills, and aptitude to scale the heights demanded by the high standards set by the AAS in all its work. Tribute must be paid to this cadre for many of the achievements of DTP at ASP. Most of them have since grown professionally to even higher levels and many are training their other colleagues. Marketing and distribution of scholarly materials in Africa is still tough, and more training and capacity building is needed in this area. But the imminent creation of an African market, since South Africa became free, evidenced by more free movement and the vibrant Book Fairs at Nairobi and Harare, may all improve matters in the near future.

In scholarly publishing, it pays to have a good, marketable product to work on. The AAS itself, its mission of excellence, its Fellows, and programs could be sold to a good extent, inside and, more particularly, outside Africa. We had no problem getting materials to work on. But spotting and working on these took interest, vision, talent, and devotion.

CONCLUSIONS AND RECOMMENDATIONS

This report has highlighted the experiences of an emerging scientific organization whose dynamism and leadership was spearheaded by DTP. In the period 1989-1992, we initiated and firmly established DTP at the African Academy of Sciences through a series of creative innovations. The AAS can now embark on the post-publication activities such as promotion, marketing, and distribution. The results today (1995) give cause for looking at the future with confidence.

At the end of the reported period, ASP was also looking to consolidate and expand its scholarly publishing business. Consolidation means putting in place all the basic parts (people, funds, and equipment) of the publication chain, so as to make it market-driven and self-sustaining. This process has continued. The ASP can expand into tertiary level textbooks and other scholarly materials, while maintaining the journal and newsletter. This door remains open for ASP, since the market is still underserved. Other prospects lay in strengthening the role of the Fellows and their ownership of the Academy.

The commitment of the donors, especially the Carnegie Corporation of New York and the Kuwait Foundation for the Advancement of Science, was crucial at a time when we had to build up the credibility to attract a revenue base from subscriptions and advertisements. They had the vision and patience to nurture, over a long period, what was clearly a promising idea, while keeping the pressure high for quick maturity and independence. The challenge was how to support the basic parts of the process so that donor withdrawal would not lead to collapse and thus wasted effort. Clearly, more quantitative and diverse funding and promotion are needed to sustain scholarly publishing and we look to any innovations in this regard. The challenge to Africa's supporters remains.

CASE STUDIES ON
ELECTRONIC NETWORKING

Perhaps no information technology generates as much interest as networking. Bringing electronic networking and Internet capability to a country opens avenues of communications that create hundreds of other opportunities. Computer-based communications provides a means to bridge time and distance to facilitate interpersonal communication. People who have the need or desire to communicate about a particular subject can do so without being either physically present in the same location (as in a conventional meeting), or even available at the same time (as in a telephone conference call or a video teleconference).

Electronic communication is in everyday use in many organizations in Africa; however, getting it into place in a new environment poses many challenges. Complex economic, social, political, and legal factors affect the use of the technology and present barriers to its successful implementation. The telecommunications systems in many African countries are suffering from deteriorating equipment and inadequate investment. Telecommunications costs are high in relation to other costs, and participation in some computer-based communication activities can require scarce foreign exchange.

Still progress is being made. In the last year or two several African countries have gained full Internet connectivity. Others are creating local networks and adding users one by one until they build a user base large enough to sustain an Internet connection. In the meantime, the users and the system operators are learning valuable skills.

The case studies in this section describe the difficult processes that five system operators have gone through in order to build the networking capability in their countries. These five projects are interconnected since the project managers were introduced to the technology by many of the same people and through many of the same megaprojects. Their individual stories are unique, however, because each author overcame different technological, managerial, and infrastructural constraints.

As one author wrote, networking tends to sell itself. The more users you have online, the more users you have waiting to be connected. So, almost one user at a time, these authors are helping to build Africa's information highway.

Electronic Networking for the Research Community in Ethopia

by Lishan Adam

Lishan Adam has a B.Sc. in Electrical Engineering and a M.Sc. in Computer Information Systems. He is working towards his Ph.D at the University of Sheffield, United Kingdom. He has worked in the information field for the last six years, focusing mainly on technology for accessing information, which includes electronic communication networks. Currently, he is the coordinator for the Capacity Building for Electronic Communications in Africa (CABECA) project. His research interests include electronic communications for grassroots institutions, networking technologies, and techniques for building qualitative information systems and networks.

BACKGROUND AND CONTEXT OF THE PROJECT

This case study describes the challenges faced in setting up a research communication network in Ethiopia. It covers the activities I undertook and the constraints I faced while expanding electronic connectivity to a research community. It also discusses the lessons I learned in the process.

Ethiopia is located in the horn of Africa and shares borders with Sudan, Kenya, Somalia, Eritrea, and Djibouti. Addis Ababa, the capital city, is often called "a city for Africa" because it hosts two major organizations: the United Nations Economic Commission for Africa (UNECA) and the Organization of African Unity (OAU). UNECA is the African regional arm of the United Nations Economic and Social Council. UNECA has established and sponsors a number of African institutions to promote all aspects of socioeconomic development of the region.

The Pan African Development Information System (PADIS), one such regional institution under UNECA, was created to build both information and networking capability in African countries. PADIS was instrumental in setting up a national electronic network in Ethiopia and in connecting members of the research community to each other locally and with colleagues worldwide.

| BOX 1   Under-use of Equipment | There are only a few advanced research institutions and two major universities in Ethiopia. Addis Ababa University, the country's largest university, administers most of the colleges. The Agriculture University of Alemaya, in Harar Province 500 kilometers east of Addis Ababa, is the next largest research center. Health research is undertaken by the medical faculty of Addis Ababa University and at two other research colleges in Gondor and |

A recent survey conducted prior to linking colleges outside of the capital city with the network showed that one college received a few modems in 1993 and did not know what to do with them. The modems were locked up in cupboards for two years!

Jimma. The country has several teacher training schools and research centers.

The level of scientific and technological information (STI) and infrastructure in these research centers varies. Some colleges lack the most essential resources, such as paper and ink. Others use computers and connect to the local electronic networking host. The need for STI and communication is great, especially by colleges outside of Addis Ababa.

The Current STI Environment in Ethiopia

Ethiopia is the second poorest country in Africa, having been devastated by long-lasting war, drought, and mismanagement. The national STI environment is generally weak, reflecting the poor economic situation in the country. The transition[1] economy is too weak to support the population, which is growing at an annual rate of 3.1 percent, with the fertility rate mounting to 7.5 percent. The STI environment has suffered from the poor economic performance during the last twenty years.

All STI centers, including university libraries, have been unable to expand and keep up with demands. There were hardly any books coming to the country during the previous socialist government. According to the head of the Addis Ababa University libraries "most collections are those of the 1960s." Those were the "golden years" of library collection development—when resources were made available to support new acquisitions.

Most colleges are not equipped with computers and other information technology tools. The more remote the college from the capital city, the less it is exposed to computing technology. (See Box 1.) Under-use of existing equipment due to lack of training and low quality of maintenance is also common. Lack of knowledge about different hardware contributes to the under-use of computer accessories.

Computer equipment is generally expensive. A non-error correcting, 2400 bps modem that costs $40.00 in the United States costs the equivalent of $200 in Ethiopia. The local price of accessories is between 400 percent to 1500 percent more than the original cost. A bureaucracy for clearing equipment through customs exasperates most possibilities of getting it through mail order or from friends residing in foreign countries.

One additional problem, unique to the country, is related to the use of Ethiopian script. Ethiopia is one of the oldest countries using its own script. The shortage of good, easy-to-use software that is adaptable to local script is a major problem. Generic native-language software interfaces that allow easier storage and retrieval of textual information in local languages and scripts are not well developed. Modern tools, such as Windows [Byte, 1994], that have features for processing data in all languages simultaneously are not readily available in Ethiopia.

A lack of good training schools and colleges in computing technology has created a chronic shortage of trained personnel in advanced networking, although Addis Ababa University now offers courses in computer applications and system design. Due to the lack of incentives and of an enabling environment, one seldom finds dedicated computer "gurus." The culture for competition and independent effort to solve complex computing problems is not well developed.

Several small computer companies were set up during the transition period but they have not become a source of objective advice in computing technology. Most companies focused on generating quick income through computer applications training. Qualitative and advanced services in networking and local area network (LAN) management are not available at these companies. Due to the lack of a good professional background, techniques such as application development, system integration, and networking are not practiced.

The telecommunication sector is another underdeveloped area in the country. National telecommunication service in Ethiopia is owned by the government. Analog telephone[2], digital leased lines, and radio links to rural areas are major services of the national operator. There is no modern communication technology. Rural telecommunications is still operator assisted. Packet switching and ISDN (Integrated Services Digital Network) are under consideration.

A three to five year queue is usually the case for individual households that wish to install a telephone. Business and international organizations may get telephone lines within one to three months when lines are available. Some institutions have to wait for months to get direct lines.

The above national STI environment dictated the type of network technologies we chose to use, as well as the pace at which we could install and apply them. Policy, regulatory, management, and cultural problems were by far the most challenging—even when compared to the technical bottlenecks faced in setting up electronic mail links to the research community. All the same, electronic networking in Ethiopia was started during one of the most rigid governments in Africa.[3]

PROJECT DESCRIPTION

Networking activity in the country began under a project funded by International Development Research Centre (IDRC) entitled "Computer Networking in Africa." The aim of the project was to assess the viability of networking between

African institutions. The specific objectives of the project in Ethiopia were to:

- improve the exchange of scientific information within Ethiopia by establishing a working, efficient, and reliable electronic network that brings contact with other networks locally, regionally, and internationally;
- develop human resources in electronic networking through training, transfer of skills, and university teaching;
- develop corps of skilled users in the country through training, troubleshooting, and ongoing technical support;
- establish a national scientific network that supports all levels of technologies (Fidonet, UUCP, and TCP/IP, which stands for transmission control protocol/Internet protocol and connotes a full, interactive Internet connection) for various categories of colleges and users under different situations; and
- set up an Internet link through development of the user base that justifies the cost of a TCP/IP connection.

PROJECT EXPERIENCE AND IMPLEMENTATION

The first activity of the project in Ethiopia was initiated in September 1991, when the Ethiopian Science and Technology Commission, which coordinates the national STI networks, participated in the first African workshop on low cost networking. The workshop provided training on low cost communications technology and charted connectivity strategies among research institutions in Africa and those in Ethiopia. Subsequently other academic institutions (universities, colleges and faculties) began to link to the main national host.[4]

To date the main national host serves over 1,000 users drawn from NGOs, research institutions, government, business, and others. Researchers evolved from network-"hesitant" to power users. For example, a connection was made to the chemistry department of Addis Ababa University at the beginning of 1993. At that time, a professor said openly "this is a waste of time and of computer resources." In 1995, the department became the top user of the national hub and a center for network support to Addis Ababa University users.

Network usage and development activity at the university intensified in October 1993, immediately after a workshop was organized for participants drawn from various departments of the Addis Ababa University. The workshop created conditions for setting up a steering committee to promote networking within the university. The steering committee evolved from a few actors to a full fledged university-wide networking group. It established a networking committee to promote networking in the country and develop connectivity to the Internet.

The research community became the second largest user of the national network (See Table 1.) It constitutes 14 percent of PADIS installed sites and 26.2 percent of total local users.

TABLE 1   Composition of PADISnet Users (April[5] 1995)

User Category	Number of installed sites	Percent of total sites	Average number of users	Total number of users	Percent
Research and academic	39	14	7	273	26.2
NGO	91	32.7	4	364	35
Government	11	4	4	44	4.2
Business	16	5.75	3	48	4.6
Individuals	48	17.25	2	96	9.1
International	72	25.9	3	216	20.7
Media	1	0.4	2	2	0.2
TOTAL	278	100	-	1043	100

Source: PADISnet registration forms.

In addition to developing a sound user base that would eventually justify the upgrade to a full Internet connection, one of the major activities of the project at the beginning involved experimenting with a mix of technologies to select the hardware that was most appropriate for working with poor telephone lines. We conducted the experiments using a mix of technologies to arrive at appropriate solutions. We evaluated the following four connection techniques during the process:

• long distance dial-in to UNIX hosts in North America;
• UUCP[6] link through a leased line by running a gateway software;
• packet-radio connection to health institutions; and
• Fidonet[7] based mail connection to Internet using GnFido gateway in London.

Our first attempt to link researchers in the country used long distance dial-in to UNIX hosts in Canada and the United States. Access to large academic networks such as BITNET was the main interest at the time. A direct dial-in to a UNIX server at Carleton University in Canada was made every day to collect and send messages to the research community. Rudimentary terminal access programs such as Procomm were used to link to the Carleton server. This turned out to be one of the most frustrating means of making connections as the lines broke at almost every trial. Successful connections were so rare that the connection was discontinued after a few months. The cost of telecommunications mounted every month. The cost was made up of:

• long distance telephone charges;
• low speed connections (successful connections were at 300 bps); and
• additional procedures required as a result of long distance dialing and

line breaks (i.e., transferring files several times after line breaks; login procedures to packet switching network in the U.S.).

Paying enormous bills every month for long distance connections forced PADISnet to switch to a more cost effective site. While exploring sites, a link using the United Nations Alternate Voice and Data (AVD) leased line to the Institute of Global Communications (IGC) became cheaper and more attractive. The IGC link enabled us to convert local Fidonet messages into UUCP format before leaving the PADIS host via a gateway software. This created conditions for developing local expertise in running gateway software and in experimenting with UUCP packets. However, since the line was devoted to UN communications (voice and fax), it became slow and inadequate for data communications. PADISnet was given only a 15 minute window to send and receive UUCP messages. This was an inconvenience and resulted in the final suspension of the connection after ten months of operation.

Another technology used for STI connectivity in Ethiopia was a HealthNet link. PADIS helped to establish this link and to secure its ground station license. The HealthNet ground station, which links to a low earth-orbiting (LEO) satellite operated by SatelLife, was licensed in April 1994—after 18 months of negotiation with the national telecommunications operator. The ground station was installed at a teaching hospital, one of the largest in the country. This connection was not used as effectively as hoped due to the following difficulties:

- Unreliable power supply. Fluctuation in electric current at the site of the ground station led the system to crash from time to time.
- Very complex software. A home-written Fidonet software made configuration difficult. Lack of documentation and troubleshooting tools heightened the problem.
- Synchronization of systems. The HealthNet system is composed of a receiver, transmitter, modem, antenna, microcomputer, satellite, and software. Failure in one or more of these systems resulted in a complete crash of the node from time to time.
- Lack of an overall plan for user support. The national HealthNet node did not come up with a plan for introducing the technology, connectivity, or regular user support.
- Low bandwidth. The uplink and downlink speed of the modem and satellite pass time was limited. With growing user demand for bandwidth-intensive documents, such as reports with graphics or images, the system became inadequate.
- Marketing. The failure to develop an expansion plan and lack of marketing of the services limited its use in the country.

A direct Fidonet connection to the Association for Progressive Communications (see description on page 189) in London using public telephone lines remained the most attractive of all the above techniques. This connection is currently our main link to the global networks and provides all store-and-forward Internet services. Due to a lack of knowledge about the potential of store-and-forward technology, researchers mainly use the email and bulletin board services of the linkage. Some students and a few researchers are exploring other potential services such as:

- searching the PADIS database using email query;
- accessing the Hornet bulletin board system (BBS);
- batch Internet services such as ftp, gopher, and archie through mail; and
- conferences and Fidonet echo mail.

The Hornet BBS is perhaps the most unique application of low cost technology in Ethiopia for information exchange. Hornet offers an introduction to the potentials of electronic information systems and provides a reservoir of background information and discussion on the Horn of Africa. [Parker, 1994] The bulletin board offers:

- Fidonet conferences (or echoes) to as wide an audience as possible, with no on-site software set-up necessary;
- a mechanism to exchange information and skills among users of the PADIS system; and
- a central store of information, files, help, useful Internet addresses, and so on.

Simplicity and minimum hardware requirements on the users' side make the BBS more popular. Prompted by this offering, a number of research institutions, including the Addis Ababa University and the Ethiopian Science and Technology Commission, are setting up a scientific bulletin board system. Local bulletin board systems connected to information reservoirs, such as databases and tools on CD-ROM, are found to be the most useful tools for STI networking under the local infrastructure.

During the last two years, increasing user demands for real time connections, the need for joining the Global Information Infrastructure (GII), and congestion of the host telephone line forced the national node to look for a better technology. At the time of this writing, the node is exploring full Internet connectivity and/or other intermediate solutions. The effort to get a full Internet (TCP/IP) connectivity is hampered by three major problems:

- high cost of leased lines;
- institutional and national constraints; and

• financial resources to cover implementation and running costs.

Leased Line Costs

The national telecom operator provides leased lines at a very high tariff. Table 2 shows approximate monthly charges for international leased lines to the United States and South Africa.[8]

TABLE 2   Cost of Leased Line from Ethiopia to Selected Countries

Type of circuit	Country	Cost/month
19.2 kbits analog	USA	$4,700
19.2 kbits analog	South Africa	$6,200
64 kbits digital	USA	$11,700
64 kbits digital	South Africa	$15,500

Source: Action plan document of a committee for Bringing Internet To Ethiopia (BITE).

National Infrastructure and Political Constraints

The low level of infrastructure as well as policy-specific problems continue to hamper the progress of setting up full connectivity to global networks in Ethiopia. Changing the attitude of the government and of the PT&T (the national telecommunication provider) remains one of the most challenging tasks. Some of the national infrastructure and political constraints we face include:

• competition and unwillingness of the national telecom operator to endorse operation of national cooperative or private nodes;
• low participation of government institutions in overall network implementation;
• lack of knowledge of electronic communication by government officials that results in delays to approve research network (see Box 2);
• education structure and low value accorded to information management, transmission, exchange and use; and
• lack of a critical mass of trained UNIX experts or "gurus."

Despite the above problems, the project continued to work towards improving network access to researchers. The bottom-up approach for building a network (starting from users, soliciting institutional support, and then approaching the government) helped us bypass an often difficult bureaucratic structure in the country. Eventually, the increase in the availability of local "hand holders" and troubleshooters encouraged expansion of the network. The local troubleshooters created

---

BOX 2   HealthNet in Ethiopia

Often government policies work against the introduction of new technologies. Lack of understanding can lead to delays and other frustrations. For example, it was a painful process to secure a HealthNet ground station license for Ethiopia. The process took over 18 months. Simply clearing the ground station equipment from customs took over a month. An engineer from SatelLife, who could have been used for training and set-up, ended up running between the national telecom operator's office and the Ministry of Health. The license was approved with a traffic compensation fee of $350 per month. The ground station, which was donated as national asset to aid in the transmission of health information, was instead treated as a CNN hub. The word "ground station" was found to be misleading for technicians who did not bother to know what a packet radio connection to low earth orbit satellite was. The traffic compensation fee was waived six months later.

---

institutional champions and then the institutional champions helped users get around configuration problems. In time, we motivated others to get connected.

Reliability of the network has also contributed towards the diffusion of networking technology in Ethiopia. Network reliability is a function of good systems operators (sysops) running the node, advanced computing technology tools, and reliable telecommunication infrastructure. PADIS' effort to make the system reliable by hiring additional system operators[9] and acquiring the latest technologies favored the situation.

Other factors that contribute to further network expansion include:

- the availability of dedicated local champions and
- the availability of simple network learning tools, such as the Hornet Bulletin Board System.

PADIS management played a major role in leading and supporting networking in the country. The availability of information[10] at PADIS provided incentive for several users to seek connection to the network. PADIS made its resources available via the network to satisfy users who wanted to go beyond electronic mail.

Individual willingness—especially from top government officials—to embrace existing technology and their demand for better services are perhaps the major motivating factors for expansion to a full TCP/IP. Influenced by their former contacts (usually at universities or NGOs in developed countries) researchers who are not connected demand quicker and better connectivity. Contact requirements and realization of benefits of networking compelled several users to demand email services even under difficult circumstances. What are the major benefits that prompted researchers to look for electronic networking?

RESULTS, IMPACT, AND BENEFITS OF THE PROJECT

Reduced Communication Costs

The most outstanding benefit of electronic networking to the research community in Ethiopia was that of bringing a new tool for reducing high communications costs. Ethiopia is a country with one of the lowest pay scales in the world. The following vital figures shows the situation.

Professor or researcher salary per month $162.00

Cost of:
1 page fax to UK	7.20
5 page fax to UK	16.10
3 minute telephone call to UK	8.20
5 minute telephone call to UK	13.70

Electronic networking brought a considerable amount of communications cost savings compared to fax, telex, telephone, and courier service. Though email costs are complex and difficult to quantify, we do know that networking offers a far cheaper option to all existing transmission media. (See Table 3.) The following tables and computations show a considerable comparative advantage of email over a fax—without involving costs of other elements such as hardware, or training.

Using compression tools, such as PKZIP, an average document can be compressed 2.5 times. The amount of bytes per minute after compression would be:
Compression factor 2.5
Total bytes per minute $2.5 \times 103342 = 258357$
High speed modems, with good error correction, synchronized to the receiving modem, can also increase the amount of bytes transmitted per minute. Using 28.8 Kbps modem the amount of bytes per minute would be: bytes per minute of 28.8 kbps modem $(1.5 \times 285357 = 387535)$
Using the above figures, we can calculate the cost per kilobyte of different means of communication.

TABLE 3   Raw data used in computation

Date and Time	Number of bytes transferred	Time taken	Bytes/minute
10 July at 6:00	565,583	5:25	104,737
11 July at 6:00	728,410	6:53	105,873
11 July at 1:00	353,496	3:30	100,998
11 July at 5:24	562,256	5:24	104,121

Source: Log files of the PADISnet host July 1995.

In addition to the reduction of communications costs, email made the following contributions to the research community in Ethiopia [Adam, 1994]:

- It facilitated the organization of international seminars, joint authorship, and the execution of joint projects that otherwise would have been expensive and time consuming. According to the Director of the Institute of Ethiopian Studies, Dr. Bahru Zewde, "Global conferences in Ethiopia and those on Ethiopia in 1994 were cost effective and successful because of email connections."
- It inspired the introduction of standard computing operating systems such as UNIX. Recently the School of Information Science for Africa (SISA) purchased a UNIX server as a networking backbone. The Mathematics Department of Addis Ababa University received a UNIX computer in connection with its networking effort from Ethiopians residing in North America. Deans and department chairs were forced to plan to "wire" their offices and create local area networks (LANs) to cope with an increasing demand from researchers to have independent accounts on work stations.
- It facilitated a switch from the hierarchical model of organizational procedures to the informal interaction among researchers in the country and those worldwide. User feedback indicates that delays in signing regular correspondence were eliminated upon arrival of email. (See Table 4.)

Email also brought about the reunification of the research communities in Ethiopia with those elsewhere. It improved family and informal ties between Ethiopians residing overseas and those at home.[11]

Improved Training Options

Electronic networking facilitated the availability of more national and institutional trainers. It created the expansion of knowledge on the use and benefits of

TABLE 4 Cost Comparison Between Fax Message and Electronic Mail Between Addis Ababa and London

Medium	Average kilobytes/per minute	Cost/KB	Cost ratio to a fax
Fax[12]	40	0.18	1:1
Email using 14.4 modem	237	0.0093	1:19
Email using 28.8 modem[13]	355	0.0062	1:29

networking and TCP/IP connectivity. The methodology used in training contributed to improved skills in the country. The national host uses the following techniques to train users.

Introduction

Users are introduced to key features of networking. This covers basics of local networking, what it involves, cost, and types of services.

Site configuration and training

Site training is meant to connect researchers to the network. It involves configuring the hardware, setting up telephone lines, providing hands-on training on system usage, and training in basics of troubleshooting.

Ongoing assistance

The host provides continuous online assistance to improve users skills in dealing with different utilities and to work on improved and cost efficient techniques.

Workshop

This is used both as marketing tool for the national node and for advanced training. Experience indicated that initial introductory workshops overload users with new concepts. Successful workshops could only be held after usage of the networks. Advanced workshops were found to be useful in promoting connectivity.

Improved Skills

Another considerable impact of the network was an increase and improvement of the skills at the main national node. We developed skills in managing networks, dealing with administrative problems, developing techniques to respond to users' problems, managing system malfunctions, developing tools and guidelines, and gathering data. The experience we gained was immense.

Improved Access from Rural Areas

The spread of the network to the rural area is one of the most significant achievements of the project. Despite technical problems, such as unreliable connections and more focus on the capital city, a number of users were able to link to the PADISnet from outside of Addis Ababa. NGOs with field offices outside of the capital found networking a convenient tool for sending logistical information and data on field situations.

Doctors with no telephone connections were able to use networking. Medical doctors from *Medicins Sans Frontiers*, headquartered in Belgium, who were working 800 kilometers from Addis Ababa were able to send messages and data to their correspondents all over the world. Lacking telephones at their field site, they send messages via small airplane to Addis Ababa for uploading to their host to resend to PADIS. All international messages received are sent back by the same plane the following day. Other mobile field researchers from the same location were able to link their modems to the nearest city where phones are available.

A number of colleges outside of Addis Ababa are discovering the value of networking. They face double isolation—from both the developed world and the country's capital where most of the activities and decisions take place. Everything in the country is hierarchical and centralized. Decisions at higher levels (at the capital) take a long time to reach institutions in remote areas. Networking can reduce the isolation and make communication more efficient.

Connectivity to the rural areas facilitated the coordination of resources and the diffusion of technology. Connectivity at the Mekelle College (710 kilometers from Addis) recently stimulated the establishment of a LAN for connecting individual professors to the global network. A project run by the Ethiopian Science and Technology Commission to link over thirty-six colleges outside of the capital stimulated further international cooperation between the colleges and other universities worldwide. The Commission intends to "wire" all colleges and high schools in the country while working on a full TCP/IP connection at the capital.

ANALYSIS OF LESSONS LEARNED

Lesson 1

The resources required for achieving access to knowledge and wider national coverage are a fraction of the benefits gained by building networks. Coordinating activities at a national level assists in realizing cost effectiveness and efficiency. Networks can subsidize themselves. Lack of an infrastructure should not be seen as a major bottleneck to networking.

There are two major goals of electronic networking of the research community:

- wider coverage of users by reaching many scientists, researchers, students etc.; and
- improving access to knowledge by bringing global information resources closer to the scientific community.

Attaining these two goals needed institutional and infrastructure readiness from the outset. When these two goals were first proposed to managers and policy makers their initial reaction was that "there are no resources" and "we can not do it under our telecommunications situation"!

Lesson 2

Training is the main element in infrastructure development. Do not start training on DOS based networking at universities, start with UNIX, which I believe to be the multi-user system of choice for networking universities.

Wider national coverage requires local infrastructure development. Local infrastructure means not only the physical set-up of machines and software, but also building a sense of awareness and increasing the participation of users. Training should cover a wide range of groups at different levels and should introduce all standard technologies such as UNIX to the academic community from the very beginning. Starting training in the DOS environment limits universities' capacity to move quickly on to sophisticated techniques. Using DOS for networking universities instead of UNIX is like using typewriters instead of word processing. Good documentation saves time.

Lesson 3

Build as many local area networks as possible. A LAN is a building block for Internet connectivity.

Capacity building in universities requires setting up of a university-wide network for inter-connecting many LANs, serving individual departments, libraries, and administrative offices, and offering the connections to the Internet through gateways. LANs are building blocks for good research networks.

Lesson 4

Good network management practices should begin when the number of users is very small. Good network administration can prevent user and donor frustration.

The professional management and administration of a network should begin as soon as you have two users. A well-run network needs a good billing structure, well developed methods for gathering data on the type and nature of users, and mechanisms to backup log files, document problems, and track progress. Put these systems in place before the number of users grows to an unmanageable size.

Lesson 5

Networks should be interactive on both an inbound and outbound basis.

Interactive sysops are the best assets of good networks. Inbound interaction with local users and outbound links to other networkers worldwide assist in sharing knowledge, resources, and time. Documenting tips and passing them on to users helps networks to expand.

Lesson 6

Using software with simpler user interface is important.

One of the major components in infrastructure building is the provision of simple tools to users. Users should get uncomplicated tools. Using software with good user interfaces reduces frustration and improves users' interests in networks. The community of Macintosh users should not be neglected.

Lesson 7

Do not focus only on global information sources. Assist in building local capacity in STI exchange.

Improved knowledge access can be achieved by creating a collaborative atmosphere within a country and by connecting to global networks. National STI sources should be strengthened to enable local exchange of information and collaboration. Networking should be built with maximum participation of local STI providers and users.

Lesson 8

Do not promote the concept of subsidy. Promote the concept of "pay a small amount to keep your network healthy."

Networks should sustain themselves. Income-generating should start at the beginning. Users should be told to pay for services. Subsidizing researchers is important; researchers should, however, know the costs and participate in paying for services from the beginning. The payment could come from university budgets or projects.

CONCLUSION AND RECOMMENDATIONS

Scientific and technological information in Africa needs to be strengthened. African input to global information resources emerges from the local STI institutions. Databases and low cost networks will ultimately serve African information needs. This is especially true for local loops where telecommunications and other infrastructure continue to be problematic. The international link itself is also inadequate. Except in South Africa, the other eleven African countries with Internet connectivity have a maximum speed of (usually) 19.2 Kbps. Reaching the global community and providing African STI to global users need efforts in strengthening the local capabilities both in networking and in information generation, management and dissemination, while upgrading the bandwidth for international connectivity.

Quality, reliability, and sustainability of African STI and networks is becoming another critical focus. Surveys and experience indicate that databases on STI lack good quality and are mostly unreliable. Database and information systems development in the region need to build quality tools and strategies for sustainability of African STI databases. The quality and sustainability of low cost electronic networks serving STI in Africa should also be improved.

Electronic communication will become a major tool for distributing global information to Africa. This does not mean African researchers need and can afford full TCP/IP connectivity. The key questions become: Is the African STI environment ready for full Internet connectivity? Will communication be two-way (from Africa to developed world and vice versa)? What will be the overall implications of Internet for a few in the capital cities versus those who are isolated due to a poor infrastructure and who need to break the isolation?

The answers to these questions remain a challenge to STI providers in Africa. African STI institutions need Internet connectivity. Internet connectivity means full participation of local providers and STI institutions in information generation and usage on the global networks. The current trend in most African countries focuses on Internet "proximity": bringing Internet closer to the users with no expansion plans for wider connectivity using low bandwidth links. Encouraging STI institutions to participate in information exchange will become the next challenge after bringing an Internet link to a country.

The situation in Ethiopia, which is often similar to that in other countries in Africa, indicates that careful analysis of the national STI environment should be made to design the most appropriate solution to improve overall research capacity in a country.

Efforts should begin by building the capacity of national science and technology institutions, such as research institutions, colleges, and small STI service providers. They should be encouraged and trained to manage information and use global information sources. Interim innovative services, such as connections to major databases or Internet services via local Bulletin Board Systems, should be available. Users should be made fully aware of the services available to them even through existing low-cost, store-and-forward technologies.

One of the major tasks facing African STI networks is a lack of knowledge of what is happening in the same region, the same country, or even the same institution. We should develop directories, dissemination tools, and guides on STI networking efforts. We should disseminate via our networks STI meta-information (information on scientific and technology information). Without a solid regional STI base, connectivity alone cannot serve its purpose.

NOTES

1. Ethiopia's longest crisis and war years were between 1974 and 1991. During the transition period (1991-1995) the government attempted to eliminate centralized and rigid policies to make favorable conditions for economic growth.

2. International telephone linkage to major cities in the world is relatively good. Users can connect with up to 28 Kbps to London without difficulty. A 300 to 900 CPS connection can be achieved using error-correcting modems. It is often easier to telephone internationally than across regional cities. The call from Addis to Mekelle is often compared to that of Addis to London. Cost of international communication is also high. The tariff was raised by 75% in May 1994.

3. The Ethiopian socialist government which had fallen apart in 1991 promoted strict policies on communications. Modems were not allowed due to reasons related to national security. Any move towards opening up communication was looked upon as a "war against socialism."

4. The national host was set up at PADIS and the network is called PADISnet. It is open to all categories of users on a fee-for-use basis.

5. Since April 1995, the number of installed sites has increased by an average of 5 per week, thereby nearly doubling since that time.

6. UUCP is a UNIX based store-and-forward technology. Developments were fast and based on international cooperation between programmers. It is a suitable start up technology for the academic community.

7. Fidonet is a store-and-forward networking technology by which computers poll each other to exchange email and conference messages. Ability to work over poor telephone lines and software that enables off-line working make Fidonet attractive to NGOs and African institutions with small budgets.

8. Leased line costs to South Africa are almost 1.5 times those of links to the United States. There is double hop to reach South Africa.

9. In June 1995, PADIS used an intern—an Ethiopian PhD student from Columbia University— to look at university-wide networking and to improve the reliability of local systems.

10. The PADIS information system consists of bibliographic databases on African socioeconomic development, databases on African experts, on-going research projects in Africa, research institutions in Africa, and other numerous complementary and specific databases on Africa.

11. The author received numerous requests from Ethiopians studying abroad to link to their families at home. Families separated during the war and those who fled economic problems are beginning to use networking to reunite with their families. Ethiopian researchers abroad who discovered the existence of the linkage are connecting back with their former teachers and institutions.

12. Fax costs vary based on text type. Graphics can be 100K or more. Regular fax message can be 10 to 70K in size. An average size was taken for this calculation.

13. A 28.8 Kbps was taken to be 1.5 times faster than a 14.4 Kbps modem.

BIBLIOGRAPHY

Adam, Lishan. (1994) Sustainable Academic Networking in Africa: System Operator's Perspective, paper published by American Association for Advancement of Science, Accra, Ghana.

Beyond Windows: Globalization of Windows. *Byte* June 1994, pp. 177-183.

International Association of Universities (1991) *University Based Critical Mass System for Information Technology.*

National Research Council (1991) *Status of Scientific and Technological Information Systems and Services in Selected African Countries.* National Academy Press, Washington, D.C.

Parker, Ben. (1994) The Hornet: The Horn of Africa's Electronic Information Exchange. Addis Ababa, Ethiopia

Networking in West Africa

by Moussa Fall

Moussa Fall is network manager for ENDA-Dakar node in Dakar, Senegal. He also works for the CABECA project and through that project has installed electronic mail nodes in Morocco, Chad, and Mali. He has plans for working in Mauritania, the Gambia, Guinea, Guinea-Bissau, Niger, Togo, and Benin. He was an administrative assistant at ENDA before getting into the networking field in 1991. He asks that his case study be dedicated to "Pape, gone so early, and to Touti and the whole tribe for their help and support."

"Networking means connecting people to people and people to information; it does not mean connecting computers to computers."

> *Wendy D. White—Growing the Internet in Africa,*
> *Internet Society News, 1994, Vol. 3, No. 2, p. 28.*

BACKGROUND AND CONTEXT OF THE PROJECT

I work for an organization called Environment and Development Action in the Third World (ENDA). It was founded in 1972 in order to:

- work with grassroots groups on the basis of their needs and objectives;
- contribute to the search for alternative development possibilities at all levels as well as to the various kinds of training programs that will make this development possible; and
- contribute to intellectuals' and trained personnel's involvement in the setting up and implementation of development programs in the service of the largest number of people possible.

ENDA has also had a leading role in various global networks dedicated to habitat, energy, street youth, pesticides, and other issues that have an environmental component. ENDA works in all parts of the Third World but the headquarters, where I work, is in Dakar, Senegal, in West Africa. Senegal is a francophone country.

Since 1975, my role at ENDA, among other administrative tasks, has consisted of organizing seminars, conferences, and training sessions. These outreach tasks have helped to put me in contact with many people and I believe that I started networking from there.

I first met Doug Rigby[1] in 1991, at an Interdoc meeting in Epe (Netherlands), at which there was an introduction to electronic networking. He spent considerable time talking to me about Fidonet technology and the NGOnet project. (See Box 1.) Back in Dakar, I pushed my boss to get an email account with a European private email provider. We accessed this account through the Senegalese PTT X.25 and we extensively used it for email and for the fax service.

PROJECT DESCRIPTION

In June 1992, the NGOnet project organized a one week workshop in Dakar to introduce Fidonet to the non-governmental organization (NGO) community. Doug Rigby was the organizer and, of course, I was among the participants. To encourage NGO networking, the project donated one PC 386 for the node and four modems. ENDA was chosen to host the node because of its commitment to immediately acquire a dedicated phone line and to allow me to give part of my time to the networking project.

BOX 1   The NGOnet Project

The NGOnet project was instrumental in bringing networking to Africa. It started as a project of the Environment Liaison Centre International (ELCI) in Nairobi where a Fidonet bulletin board system had been set up to provide a conduit for electronic mail traffic in the region and to NGOs worldwide. This was done using a high-speed modem to make daily calls to the GreenNet Fidonet (GnFido) gateway in London.

The project was based on a survey that found that there were significant numbers of non-governmental organizations that had computers but were not using them for electronic mail. To provide NGOs with the cheapest access, emphasis was placed on establishing a series of hosts with high speed modems distributed throughout Africa. These then provided NGOs with local support and a local call to connect to the global electronic network. Four prototype hosts were set up, one for each region of Africa - ELCI in Nairobi, MANGO in Harare, ENDA in Dakar, and ENDA-Arabe in Tunis.

Here, I have to confess that I had no DOS skills—ENDA only used Macs. But, because I was really interested in this new technology, I bought books on DOS and computing in general and started learning. When you are very motivated you can "move mountains". . .

For three months, the four NGOs that had received training and modems started communicating just among themselves. There was no international traffic! Then, in August 1992, the network received another donation from the NGOnet project— a high speed modem (Telebit Trailblazer 2500)—which made us ready to connect to the rest of the world.

Fidonet—A Grassroots Network

My introduction to Fidonet was so important that I should take time here to describe this form of networking in more detail. Fidonet is a grassroots electronic communications community that has been hard at work for over a decade devising ever cheaper and increasingly sophisticated tools to serve its needs through dial-up, store-and-forward, and modem-based connections. Fidonet technology has proven to be a powerful do-it-yourself tool for establishing initial footholds into the world of electronic communications. It offers users an affordable option even if they lack institutional affiliations, financial resources, or are located in a country where the nearest electronic communications link requires an expensive dial-up call over international phone lines.

Because Fidonet technology emerged in an environment where individuals operated each system independently and covered their own costs for phone calls and equipment, it had to be very flexible, decentralized, and designed to operate inexpensively with standard modems and microcomputers connected over ordinary phone lines. The "handshaking" and file transfer protocols built into all Fidonet-compatible software incorporate compression, error correction, and error recovery capabilities that squeeze as much data as possible into the shortest transmission time that the hardware will allow. Instead of using packet-switching, these independent systems establish gateways with larger, international electronic mail systems using high speed modems. At regular intervals, the independent systems dial into the larger systems to swap incoming and outgoing messages. This approach keeps down the cost of international calls without requiring sophisticated computer equipment.

Fidonet messages are sent along a hierarchy. At the top are five very broad geographic zones. Africa is Zone number 5. The zones are divided into regions, then into hosts, then into hubs, and then into nodes. Just like all the levels above them in the chain, nodes offer local email, pass new messages to and from the hub, and collect messages to and from the *point*—the lowest level of the Fidonet hierarchy. Point operators have systems that are configured with all the software necessary to call (or poll) the node and upload and download messages and files whenever it is convenient. The computer can do all the work automatically, making the calls

---

BOX 2   Internet Navigational Tools

TELNET - Telnet, the Internet standard protocol for remote terminal connections, is used for logging into and searching other computers connected to the Internet.

FTP - FTP stands for File Transfer Protocol and allows users to exchange files between their workstations and remote computers connected to the Internet.

GOPHER - Gopher, a software program for browsing and information retrieval, provides a menu-driven interface that shows what is available on a server. The user burrows through a set of "nested" menus to get closer and closer to a specific topic. Gopher collects information scattered across many computers and presents it on the same menu.

VERONICA - Veronica is an indexer that can query every gopher on the gopher system to search for a keyword or phrase in a menu title. It then gives the address of all the menus with those key words.

WAIS - WAIS, Wide Area Information Server, searches the full text of a document to look for specified key words. WAIS accepts commands in plain English, processes them at the user level, and relays the processed information from the user to the selected databases.

WORLD WIDE WEB (WWW) - WWW is a tool for working with collections of data, or databases. It is a *hypertext* based system that provides access to a variety of files and information. Hypertext allows a user doing research on one document to jump to a related item in another document through hypertext links. In WWW, each document contains highlighted items for which additional information is available. The additional information is contained in another document that is displayed when the user selects the highlighted item. With appropriate software, such as *Netscape*, the user can view not just text but pictures, sound files, and video.

---

into the central system at a time when the lines may have less traffic or the costs may be lower.

Fidonet is a communications technology that many consider to be less advanced and, therefore, less useful than other technologies. It does not offer all of the sophistication that other, more costly systems do. However, as you have electronic mail capabilities, you can access important Internet tools like file transfer protocol (FTP), Gophermail, World Wide Web (WWW), Veronica, Wide-Area Information Servers (WAIS), and listservs—even if you do not get the results immediately as in a direct Internet connection. (See Box 2.) Fidonet technology has limited expansion capabilities, insofar as it will always remain a store-and-forward, modem-based network. It lacks the capability for online information retrieval, database searches, remote-login, and remote-execution that other systems offer. However, while the expansion of more advanced computer networking technologies is often constrained by prohibitively high costs and inadequate telecommunications infrastructure, Fidonet technology is not.

The Association for Progressive Communications (APC), a global network dedicated to NGOs, was involved in the NGOnet project.[2] The APC was our natural partner. Through the APC London-based member, GreenNet, we connect through their Fidonet gateway (GnFido) to the rest of the world. GnFido serves as a gateway for small Fidonet hosts not only from Africa, but also from Asia and Latin America.

Through this system we have been able to use email, download conferences, and use the GreenNet fax service, which costs very little compared to the national PTT charges. The computer conferences received were on various topics: environment, development, health, AIDS, and so on. We also followed the United Nations Environment Programme's preparatory conferences and the NGO discussions regarding these conferences. ENDA now runs a private conference for its own use, linking its various offices around the world.

PROJECT EXPERIENCE AND IMPLEMENTATION

How Users Are Trained

Users are trained either on an individual or group basis. After only one hour, the trainees are able to send messages and check their mailboxes. Usually training is done gradually. It is better to have three sessions of one hour each than just one session of three hours. During the second session, users are shown how to encode files to be sent and how to decode the received ones. The last session teaches them how to subscribe to conferences, how to contribute to a conference, and how to quit a conference.

Because the point software we use is user-friendly, after the training sessions, users need very little help. This they can request by sending a message to the postmaster who will respond to them as simply as possible.

For organizations using desktop computers, training is organized on site. For individuals or organizations using laptops, we ask them to come to the ENDA offices where things will be easier in case there is a problem.

Development of the Network and Perspectives

Accessing our network is relatively cheap[3]. Since the host is a non-profit, non-governmental organization, it does not intend to make a profit from providing networking services.

Our active users are our best advertisers! They help us "sell" the benefits of networking. Presently the ENDA-DAK node has over 110 users—coming from national and international organizations, individuals, government agencies, universities, and even the private sector. Our users come not only from Senegal, but also from other neighboring countries, including the Gambia, Mali, and Burkina Faso. The demand is increasing locally and also in all the neighboring countries.

Connecting Problems

During the period of April-May-June 1995, we experienced problems in our connections with GnFido in London. The Senegalese phone system was not working properly and users complained that their mail had not been delivered in time. We tried several modems and, paradoxically, the modem with the worst reputation behaved better than all those of a supposed higher quality. Now the situation is better and we are presently using a Zyxel modem.

Regional Networking

In 1994, I was a consultant to the United Nations Environment Programme, Global Environment Facility Project, which consisted of linking national teams doing research on greenhouse gases in Senegal, the Gambia, Morocco, Uganda, Tanzania, Nigeria, and Kenya. My part of the work consisted of developing teaching tools for national teams in Senegal, Gambia, and Morocco. I also did system installation, provided training, and helped link these teams to the conference set up for them. They were thus able to exchange data on their research, exchange views on methodology and software used, and share experiences. It should be noted that this conference was bilingual and I did most of the translation into French.

Since 1994, I have also been involved in the PADIS/IDRC CABECA project (see Box 3), which tries to give access to countries where there is no connectivity at all or where the existing infrastructure is too expensive for the NGO community to afford. An agreement between the ENDA Executive Secretary and Nancy Hafkin, who is the head of PADIS and the CABECA project, allowed me to work full time in electronic networking.

This agreement was easier to reach than might be expected. I should point out here that first our two institutions shared a common goal: to give electronic access to communities at the grassroots level. This facilitated the collaboration. I should also note that Nancy Hafkin's devotion to African networking and her confidence in this continent and its human resources made this institutional collaboration possible.

Through the CABECA project, I installed nodes in Rabat, in Chad, and in Mali. Another CABECA goal is to train node operators who will themselves become trainers.

In the CABECA project, we are trying to implement a regional network that is badly needed in francophone West Africa. Among these countries the telephone exchange is relatively good and the costs are relatively low. The idea is to have a regional hub—ENDA-DAK—which will be the focal point for the region, through which all regional mail shall be routed. With this infrastructure, there is no need for mail addressed to the neighboring countries to be routed through European gateways. Putting our resources together will make regional networking more efficient and will reduce our costs for international traffic. We believe that once this

---

**BOX 3   Capacity Building for
Electronic Communication in Africa**

Funded by a grant from the Canadian International Development Research Centre (IDRC), the project on Capacity Building for Electronic Communication in Africa (CABECA) builds on the experience gained over the last four years from a number of IDRC-funded electronic networking projects in Africa. A public corporation created by the Parliament of Canada to support research designed to adapt science and technology to the needs of developing countries, IDRC has taken the lead in financing African electronic networking initiatives with the aim of demonstrating that the technology for deploying electronic connections throughout Africa is readily available and can be implemented at relatively low cost, taking into account the economic, social and political difficulties the region faces. The CABECA project design attempts to address the problems of the African region that have isolated it from the international networking phenomenon.

CABECA's overall objective is to provide technical assistance to bring about sustainable computer-based networking in Africa, at an affordable cost, accessible to a wide variety of users from both the private and public sectors. To build African capacity for computer networking, it will train a corps of systems operators who can train others in their area and offer continuing support to fledgling users to ensure the sustainability of national nodes with connections to international networks. The project's aim is to offer inexpensive and easy access to local and international information services on systems run by local operators and sustained by revenue from users. They will be able to exchange electronic mail worldwide at a fraction of the cost of fax or telex; they will also have access to conference mail, file transfer and databases. Efforts will be made to facilitate African connectivity to the expanding range of Internet information services.

---

infrastructure is set up, the region will be a zone for intensive information exchange. Organizations in the region have a great deal of information to share, the countries have the same language, the same currency, participate in the same economic organizations, and often are in the same ecological zone. Common interests and experiences should encourage the growth of networking in West Africa.

Some international organizations understand this very well and are discussing with us how to connect their projects or field offices to this low cost infrastructure. We are presently discussing with HealthNet the best way to for Senegal and other countries in the region to collaborate with this project.

Methodology for Sensitizing

In each country visited under the CABECA project, we organized a half-day workshop to sensitize NGOs and individuals to electronic networking. Some workshops, such as the one in Chad, brought together as many as 35 people. After a preliminary introduction to the technology, using a phone simulator I always carry with me, we split participants into three groups, each one sitting around a computer. That way, each group can prepare one or two messages addressed to the other two groups and then, through modems and the phone simulator, exchange mail. They can see how fast the message can go and also the other possibilities of the system.

After this hands-on training, all groups get together for a final discussion on how this technology can serve the national community, the advantages compared to technologies such as fax or even conventional mail. We always focus first on how this technology can serve information sharing and exchange within the country before opening up to regional and international networks.

Here we must not forget the context in which we work in many African countries: there are poor phone lines and electrical shortages and outages. In some of these countries, you can get a dial-tone only after working hours. In some others, it is even worse, as not only do you have to wait a long time for a dial tone but, once you get it, you are not sure your international call will succeed. In one of these countries you can dial directly only to France!

Difficulties in Sensitizing

There are people who are allergic to new technologies. In one of the countries I visited for sensitizing purposes, the Government computing department is now attached to a national service. During our meetings, the head of that service had been completely against the introduction of this new technology, despite the fact that minister and all his colleagues agreed that their country should be part of the process. They all wanted to join the growing networks and reap benefits from them. Yet, the head of the service was able to block progress. Every month, his office sends data concerning the country to their subscribers who pay for the information. The documents are sent by regular mail. After many demonstrations and taking into consideration the volume of information sent monthly to North America and Europe, that person still retains his original position—which makes his colleagues quite unhappy.

RESULTS, IMPACT, AND BENEFITS OF THE PROJECT

Some of our users told us that they were able to get rid of the international line they used to send faxes after they discovered our fax service. Now their fax machine is mainly receiving faxes from their correspondents who do not have email and this has dramatically reduced their communications costs.

NGOs have been changing their way of communicating—especially with their northern partners. They are not only sending faxes but they send and receive email

---

BOX 4   Using Email to Solve Problems

In Burkina-Faso, there is a daily newspaper that is issued at noon every day except Sunday. The editor told us that to send an issue to a town located 400 hundred kilometers from the capital city they have to transport it via "bush taxi." Due to lack of road infrastructure, the newspaper can be sold only the following morning. Using email technology, the newspaper can be transferred very easily and very quickly through the phone system, printed on the spot, and issued at the same time as the capital city.

---

messages and files. Some of them have been subscribing to listservs while the others, because of language problems, wait for the opportunity to have access to conferences in French.

NGOs have also benefited from the technology by being better able to participate in the preparations for such events as the United Nations environment conference. Through the NGO forum, even small and isolated organizations can be heard. ENDA itself, during the UN Environment Conference, issued a daily newspaper in French giving accounts and comments on what was happening. The newspaper was uploaded to Dakar and issued in both places on the same day. The newspaper was broadly diffused among NGOs in Africa via networking technology. (For another example of the benefits of email, see Box 4.)

ANALYSIS OF LESSONS LEARNED

- Sacrifices are necessary to begin a network. You must be prepared to work long hours, spend your own money, visit users who have problems that have nothing to do with the electronic communications system, and fix hardware and software problems.
- If you give people your home phone number, then you will be disturbed for anything.
- You also need to be patient with people. You may find people with laptops who will take minutes to write a single word.
- For strategic purposes, you will sometimes have to give free accounts.
- Fidonet is a simple technology to master for NGOs which do not have the resources and the time to invest in too sophisticated technologies. Presently this is an appropriate technology for some African countries taking into account the situation described above.

Fidonet has been criticized for its limitations, but for people who are interested in email only and fax services, this is no doubt often the best choice. In spite of all what is said, IT WORKS. . .

CONCLUSIONS AND RECOMMENDATIONS

Here is probably the best recollection I have from networking. Two years ago, I was surprised to find a message in my mail box saying:

"I have been searching the Internet for an electronic address in Africa and found yours for Senegal. My name is. . ., I am living in . . . . of the USA and I am 12 years old." For a while this young boy and myself have corresponded.

This would surprise any African—as we have not yet reached this level of computer use in Africa. Taxes continue to make computers unaffordable for individual use. And because of this we have a very low level of computer literacy.

One should note also that almost all NGOs use computers only for word processing, which really shows lack of computer skills.

When you try to convince NGOs or individuals who have access to computers to join the network, they are afraid of investing a lot of time learning something new. Those who do not have access to computers do not understand the necessity to invest money in a new technology of which they are afraid.

At this level, those who are connected are only interested in email and sending faxes. This is understandable as communication costs are very expensive in our countries.

NOTES

1. Doug Rigby came to Nairobi in 1989 to work at the Environment Liaison Center International (ELCI), which served as the node for several networking projects. While there, Mr. Rigby did much to extend networking technologies, principles, and training throughout Africa. Many local systems operators credit their current enthusiasm and success to Mr. Rigby.

2. The APC has contributed much to African networking. For more information about this organization see page 189 in this volume.

3. The following rates are applied: installation US$ 20.00; monthly fee US$ 5.00; charge per kilobyte sent US$ 0.10; charge per kilobyte received US$ 0.10.

ACKNOWLEDGEMENTS

I am deeply grateful to Jacques Bugnicourt, ENDA's Executive Secretary for his generosity and his open mind. He understood very quickly how crucial this technology was for his own organization and for the NGO community. And without his personal commitment and his encouragement, I would not have been able to work in this field.

To Abou Thiam, from ENDA, who first mentioned email to me.

Thanks to Doug Rigby for the role he played in electronic communications in Africa. He is the one who introduced the technology to me and to many African system operators.

Thanks also to wonderful friends and colleagues who played and continue playing a crucial role in African networking: Bob Barad, Karen Banks, Mike Jensen, Cesare Dieni, Youba Sokona and Ann Heidenreich.

Thank you also to the very good friends in the APC networks.

Background Summary

Satellife and Healthnet

SatelLife is an international not-for-profit organization whose mission is to improve communications and the exchange of information in the fields of public health, medicine, and the environment. It is an initiative of the International Physicians for the Prevention of Nuclear War, recipient of the 1985 Nobel Peace Prize. Not wanting to see space become a battleground, Dr. Bernard Lown, IPPNW co-founder and co-president, suggested the creation of a satellite-based global health communications system as a means of demonstrating that space can unite rather than further divide humankind.

SatelLife works in developing countries where libraries, hospitals and other organizations often lack adequate funds or foreign currency to subscribe to medical journals or to maintain ongoing subscriptions. Where communications facilities are intermittent, of poor quality, or expensive, the use of direct "real-time" voice or fax connections can be inefficient and frustrating. Health workers can become isolated from one another because of the high cost of telephone calls, fax services, and travel. Even with today's improved networks, communication in remote and rural areas is still difficult or impossible, and always extremely expensive. SatelLife has thus put much of its efforts into providing and improving access to "store-and-forward" message systems.

HealthNet, administered by SatelLife, is an information service that connects health care workers around the world. Using the most affordable and appropriate technology, HealthNet offers electronic mail and conferences as well as access to several electronic journals and publications. It also provides access to databases

continued

and experts. SatelLife initiated the *Library Partnership Program* to facilitate access to medical literature for libraries in the developing world. Finally, for its Internet users, HealthNet offers pointers to useful health mailing lists, Worldwide Web homepages, Gopher and FTP sites on the Internet. HealthNet is currently operational in the following African countries: Botswana, Burkina Faso, Cameroon, Eritrea, Ethiopia, Gambia, Ghana, Kenya, Malawi, Mali, Mozambique, South Africa, Sudan, Tanzania, Uganda, and Zimbabwe.

SatelLife began by linking medical education centers in Africa with medical libraries and other centers in the United States, Canada, and Europe via a low-earth orbiting (LEO) satellite. The satellite was expected to be an essential part of the solution to the communications problems in developing countries but, since its launch, modern telephone switch equipment has been installed in many cities in Africa, providing good international connections. Because of rapidly evolving technologies, dialed telephone circuits and error-correcting modems are often a more economical and efficient solution for international transfer of electronic data in developing countries than the LEO satellite.

Fidonet-based networks were in widespread use in Africa in the late 1980s and SatelLife joined the many NGOs supporting Fidonet use there. Fidonet provides an economical alternative to Internet email systems. The evolution of HealthNet has produced a large network of Fidonet nodes. The network is still growing rapidly, although much of its growth is in the "points" connected to network nodes rather than nodes themselves. SatelLife is committed to supporting this low-cost access system along with advanced Internet services so that services can be brought as close as possible to the end-user.

Since 1993 SatelLife has operated the Internet domain "healthnet.org" to support access by its member networks. While the cost barriers to providing international permanent leased lines are still prohibitive for most public health and medical education programs in the developing world, there are now several cases in which full Internet access is a realistic alternative to store-and-forward networks. SatelLife is helping its member networks take advantage of these circumstances as they arise.

The HealthNet satellite system offers Internet message services to any remote area where the local telecommunication infrastructure is poor or inefficient. The ground equipment needed to contact the satellite consists of an IBM-PC compatible computer, a Terminal Node Controller (TNC), a satellite radio, and antennas. At this stage, SatelLife is field testing a new radio design that merges the satellite radio and the TNC in one single box that can be portable.

Advances in satellite technology, opportunities in radio technology, and the growth of Internet connectivity to Africa, all mean that SatelLife will become increasingly diverse and complex. The only practical approach to handling this com-

continued

plexity is to base the system on a powerful software environment called UNIX. In the past two years, Linux, a public domain software for UNIX on personal computers, has become a stable and respected (and very low cost) alternative to commercial UNIX system software. SatelLife is working to bring together many different networking technologies (including full Internet, satellite packet radio, and Fidonet) into an automated system based on Linux. Its own engineering task will be to provide software to simplify the control and monitoring of this package so that the amount of training required is kept to a minimum.

This new network node technology will offer many new options in network services and will make HealthNet more useful and attractive to users of standard Internet mail systems. Using whatever technologies are available SatelLife and its HealthNet service network will continue to address the twin problems of an acute shortage of current health information and of the severe isolation of African health care workers from their colleagues.

MUKLA: Evolution of a Homegrown Network in Uganda
by Charles Musisi

Charles Musisi is Network Manager of MUKLA (Makerere University in Kampala) and pioneer of electronic networking in Uganda. He has an electrical engineering background. He has shared his networking expertise with colleagues in Kenya, Tanzania, Nigeria, and Ghana.

BACKGROUND AND CONTEXT OF THE PROJECT

This paper tells the story of the establishment of the MUKLA Electronic Network in Uganda. There is much in the establishment and growth of an electronic network that can be learned from our experiences. MUKLA is an example of a sustainable network bred from a homegrown desire to network. I say this because:

- Our primary emphasis is on self-sustainability;
- We are now in our fourth year of operation, with an increasing base of users, expanding facilities, and a financially viable operation;
- Starting from a university and grassroots NGO base, we now have established strong working relationships with various levels of government and other sections of the community;
- We are internationally connected to the Internet, the Association for Progressive Communications networks, United Nations organizations, major commercial networks, and facilities around the world; and
- All of this was accomplished with very little donor funding and no government grants whatsoever to commence operations. A small team of dedicated individuals in a unique government institution is running a sound business-based electronic mail service.

The need to communicate across distances on vital issues is far from new. An ever-increasing range of technologies has been applied to this need, from rudimentary tools before the age of transport to the constantly emerging suite of sophisticated services offered by the information age.

The ESANET Project

The MUKLA node began with the Eastern and Southern Africa Networking (ESANET) Project. Inspired by the communication needs mentioned above, the IDRC-funded ESANET research project was aimed at investigating various microcomputer-based methodologies for communications. The countries of the five participating institutions are all members of the Preferential Trade Agreement (PTA) region. The participating institutions themselves were the Institutes of Computer Science at the University of Nairobi and Makerere University, and the Computing Centres at the University of Dar es Salaam, the University of Zambia, and the University of Zimbabwe. The long-term goals of the ESANET project are given in Box 1 below; the specific objectives of ESANET were to:

- experiment with alternative techniques for data communications between the five nodes in five countries;
- evaluate the technical, economic, sociological, and management aspects of the communication network experiments;
- disseminate information to the research community within the region about the development and the results of the project with a view to increasing

---

BOX 1   Long-term Goals of ESANET

The long term goals of the ESANET project were to:

- achieve more cost-effective and relevant data collection and assessment by better identification of users, in both the public and private sectors, and of their information needs at the local, provincial, national and international levels;
- strengthen local, provincial, national and international capacity to collect and use multi-sectoral information in decision-making processes and to enhance capacities to collect and analyze data and information for decision-making;
- develop or strengthen local, provincial, national and international means of ensuring that planning for sustainable development in all sectors is based on timely, reliable and usable information; and
- make relevant information accessible in the form and at the time required to facilitate its use.

the awareness of possibilities, stimulating new and wider applications, and inviting feedback on related topics; and

• make recommendations to the research community (users and telecommunications authorities in the region) on cost-effective data communication modalities, and appropriate network models and policies for specific environments and applications.

The introduction of electronic networking to the wider community in Uganda began in May 1991 as a natural spin-off from the ESANET project. MUKLA was mandated to provide email services to non-governmental organizations (NGOs) within the NGOnet-Africa project, which is described more fully in Fall's case study on page 142. We also sought collaboration with the HealthNet project whose aim was to facilitate communication among health professionals within the African region and with their peers elsewhere. (See information on page 153.) While the mode of communication chosen by HealthNet was a store-and-forward, low-earth orbiting satellite (LEO) with tracking ground stations, the regional interconnection of the ESANET and NGOnet nodes was to be across regular, dial-up telephones lines using Fidonet technology.

Activities of ESANET

A start-up meeting for ESANET in November 1990 brought together representatives from all the participating institutions, as well as those from IDRC, SatelLife, and the Nirv Centre/Web of Canada. The start-up workshop focused on identifying suitable methods of communication and on drawing up preliminary lists of hardware and software requirements. We decided that the project would support a series of workshops in the different participating countries.

At a design workshop held in May 1991, in Harare, Zimbabwe we formally adopted Fidonet technology as the technology of implementation. Our review of the status of licensing of the HealthNet ground station revealed only Zambia at the time had obtained a license. Other highlights of that meeting included confirmation of lists of requirements by different nodes and the topology of regional mail traffic exchange. The nodes in Uganda and Tanzania were to route their regional traffic and international traffic via Nairobi, while Zambia would poll (or generate a computer call to) Harare, which would in turn poll Nairobi for regional mail.

The University of Zambia (UNZA) hosted an experimentation and review workshop in November 1992. Our aim then was to enhance internode telephone calls (polling) and review the progress of the project to date. At the time of the review workshop, we observed that some interesting trends had clearly emerged and we realized that the assumption upon which the topology had been drawn was evidently unattainable. For instance, the interregional polling in East Africa was not possible due to several factors: delayed arrival of equipment purchased from overseas suppliers; wrong power specification supplied; or poor telephone lines at the node on an old analog exchange. Hence, while activity was well under way in Uganda by February 1991 and a little later in Tanzania, the MUKLA node only became operational in August 1992.

MANGO, the NGO network in Zimbabwe, was an established Fidonet bulletin board by the time the ESANET project began and so only needed to integrate the ESANET activity early in 1991. UNZA was also fully operational early in 1991 but routed its regional and international traffic through Rhodes University in South Africa. Interregional polling between these two was never reliably successful owing to poor interconnecting telephone infrastructure between Zambia and Zimbabwe. All of the ESANET participating institutions and bodies met in September 1993 at an evaluation and closeup workshop held in Uganda.

PROJECT DESCRIPTION

As it happened, Doug Rigby, a networking consultant at the Environmental Liaison Center in Nairobi but also working for the NGOnet-Africa Project, visited Kampala in February 1991. I was then a final year student of Engineering at Makerere University but on forced vacation as a result of student riots that caused the closure of the campus.

My meeting with Rigby was helped by the student riots as much as by my volunteer work at an environmental NGO, called JEEP, a grassroots network organization. JEEP staff asked me to meet Rigby at the Entebbe airport. This was perhaps my longest wait at an airport for any visitor coming from abroad—as the scheduled flight, I later learned, had been a phantom one. All the same, I persevered until he arrived on a late evening plane and took the 35 kilometer journey back with him to Kampala. After hearing his stories enroute, I never regretted the long wait and I slept that night dreaming about this intriguing new concept of electronic mail! The following week was to usher in many more exciting ideas that have led, as it turns out, to a new and unforeseen career.

With Rigby, we went through the drills of Fidonet: installing a modem; communication software for end users; and even basic DOS commands. The team of trainees had now grown to five: the then three folks from the Institute of Computer Sciences; one representative from the Developmental Network of Voluntary Associations (DENIVA), an umbrella network body for local and indigenous NGOs in Uganda; and myself. A windup workshop of Rigby's mission brought together the first batch of potential users from different organizations. Among them were people from CARE (the relief agency), the Centre for Basic Research, the Makerere Medical School, a handful of DENIVA members, JEEP itself, the Makerere University's Vice Chancellor, and other independent participants.

While I may not have been the most conspicuous participant, I had apparently caught the eye of some people and I was chosen as the person to carry the mantle of making it work.

PROJECT EXPERIENCE AND IMPLEMENTATION

The Critical Years

I quickly realized that my new role would have to be accommodated within my academic life when campus reopened. That I did by working at the node after classes, not an easy thing to do for an engineering student. The next thing was that I had to do to this work as a volunteer. There would be no pay at first. I still remember those first meetings with prospective users—environment groups, missionaries, and other NGOs. This was new to all of us. Even as I crawled under desks to connect modems to telephones, and even as I made test polls to Nairobi, not one of us was sure that we were not going to get enormous telephone bills. I wasn't all that sure that I would be able to pay the actual telephone bills, even if they were not enormous! (See Box 2.)

The harder electronic networking seemed the more determined I was to prove that it worked. It was the best thing I could have done. The process taught me a great deal, refined my thoughts considerably, and led me into contact with many people whose expertise I would need if this was going to succeed.

Originally, I had planned to set up a non-profit network for NGOs to run parallel to MUKLA. That might have been ideal but, with my unfinished engineering degree in the way and a lack of clear institutional support from the NGO community, this seemed a formidable task. I labored to convince the director at the ICS that there was more to be gained in merging ESANET with NGOnet activities than there was in operating them separately.

> **BOX 2   Seeing Is Believing**
>
> I really thought everyone would be so excited that they would just put in some money and we would be up and going in no time. Not so, I learned. There was a lot more to do— and the hardest lesson of all was that, until I could prove that this thing saved money, there was no chance of it getting off the ground.

Shortly after the university reopened, however, we reached agreement and installed the ESANET equipment and procured a dedicated telephone line. The MUKLA node got under way and the real fun began! At the end of our first year of operation, we had nearly 50 users, quite a remarkable achievement and a good omen for an exciting future. We were beginning to fulfill many people's dreams for use of this media. At this point, I stood as the systems operator (sysop) and manager of an ever-growing network. I was confident that I had established a sound management structure to introduce cost recovery. The director's secretary would handle billing and accounting while I concentrated on software and hardware developments as well as other technical matters.

BOX 3   Help from Some Friends

There are many funny stories from those first few months. I grappled with the establishment of a node facility for which there were no textbooks - only a concept and some guiding hands from friends abroad. Invaluable help and support handily came in from Doug Rigby at ELCI, Mike Jensen at WorkNet in South Africa, Karen Banks at GreenNet, and later Bob Barad in Washington. I had considerably underestimated the technical complexity of what we were doing.

Project Synergy

The ESANET project, with its idea of electronic networking at the Institute of Computer Science, took second place to the higher profile and better funded UNESCO Intergovernmental Informatics Project (IIP). The IIP was aimed at sensitizing decision makers in government and other sectors of society on the use of informatics tools in decision making and management. The attention paid to the IIP reduced high-level interference in the day-to-day running of MUKLA. Electronic networking nevertheless benefited from the many IIP workshops organized where email was always on display.

As the rush to sign on to MUKLA grew, so too did the pressure on the hardware—then a 386 SX, 2 RAM 80 megabyte hard drive personal computer. So, by July 1992, with the user base standing at well over 150, the node personal computer was upgraded to a 486DX 33 MHz, 8 RAM and 170 megabyte hard disk from the IIP project consignment.

Challenges

At this level of expansion, MUKLA posed a real management challenge. With technical capacity to handle new installations and user support overstretched, we made a decision to get more members of the teaching staff involved. One person was put in charge of documentation and promotions, while a technical assistant was assigned to help me. (See Box 3.)

Billing and accounting were firmly put in the hands of an accounts clerk who also doubled as the director's secretary. I believe that the stability of our network caught the attention of other regional networking projects, based mainly in Nairobi, and that they borrowed ideas from our experience. We then had over 10 groups or users dialing-in on long distance trunk phone calls from Nairobi and other parts of Kenya.

Around this time I was drafted into a number of regional initiatives. I, for instance, participated in the design and implementation of the UNEP/Global Environment Facility (GEF) Greenhouse Gases project to link up researchers in six

African countries, namely: Uganda, Tanzania, Nigeria, Senegal, Morocco and the Gambia. I was also hired as an independent consultant for the CABECA project to setup and train systems operators in Uganda, Nigeria, and Ghana. (See CABECA box on page 147)

Between the UNEP/GEF and the CABECA project I have established a total of nine nodes in the above mentioned countries. I have also trained a score of in-country technical support people and have installed several end-user sites for access to email and the Internet. I have also set up email access for the UN's World Food Programme (WFP) offices in Dar es Salaam, Mombasa, and Kampala. Only recently I was on mission to war torn Burundi on an International Alert of London mission. There, I set up email so that the UN's special Representative to Burundi could access information and participate in discussions aimed at better informing the world and also the warring factions in conflict resolution.

Present Situation

From around mid-1993 to the present, we began routing MUKLA's international traffic through the GreenNet's GnFido node in London via four daily polls. This link works satisfactorily well, though disruptions in the past often occurred due to factors such as adverse weather conditions. Lately, the unreliability of the GnFido node can be attributed to over-stressed hardware facilities coupled with lack of support staff.

As of January 1995, MUKLA had an installed user base of over 300 sites. The majority of these are around Kampala but there are about 15 sites in Entebbe (35 Km from Kampala), five in Jinja (80 Km east), three in Mbale (150 Km east, close to the Kenya border), three in Mbarara (220 Km southwest), and three in Kabale (400 Km southwest, close to the Rwanda, Tanzania, and Zaire borders). The upcountry installations all have to make long distance calls to Kampala.

It therefore became imperative to set up local access points in these towns. In February 1995, a node was established in Entebbe at the Uganda Virus Research Institute with equipment supplied by the HealthNet project. Similar nodes are planned for Mbarara, Kabale, Mbale and Jinja during the first half of 1996.

Even now a few users call in from Nairobi, though the majority of regional traffic flows to MUKLA via Sasa Communications System. This company, based in Nairobi, is an initiative of the East Africa Internet Association. (See Box 4.)

Recent Developments

Throughout 1995, I consulted for a commercial enterprise (StarCom) to help establish a full Internet (IP) link for the Uganda market. In August 1995, another company (InfoMail) opened full IP access from Uganda—thus becoming the first site in East Africa and the Horn of Africa region to give full access to the Internet, including facilities such as World Wide Web. Starcom became operational in No-

---

BOX 4   The East African Internet Association

The East African Internet Association (EAIA) is a not-for-profit group formed in April 1995, seeking to promote and expand cooperative electronic communications and inter-networking in the East African region. Its members include the majority of electronic service providers, serving at least 3,000 users, in the following countries: Eritrea, Ethiopia, Kenya, Tanzania and Uganda. Partner networks abroad are also members, as are a number of interested individuals. Membership is open to all interested parties for a nominal fee. The Association is in the process of being officially registered in each country.

EAIA's aims of cooperative internetworking in Africa are also supported by: Capacity Building in Electronic Communication in Africa (CABECA, UN Economic Commission for Africa), GreenNet (London), UN Environment Programme (Kenya), UN World Food Programme (Kenya), RIO/ORSTOM (France), Web (Canada), Wolfnet Communications (London) and SangoNet (South Africa).

Discussions take place on a private Internet mailing list.

---

vember 1995. It is noteworthy that both these companies implemented international access using very small aperture terminal (VSAT) satellite technology in preference to the overpriced and unreliable digital leased lines from the Uganda Posts and Telecommunication Corporation (UP&TC).

As seen from the information in Appendix A, the electronic network market in Uganda is now fully liberalized with not less than five providers with services ranging from email access to full Internet. However, the usage charges remain high. The charges given are accurate as of January 1996.

RESULTS, IMPACTS, AND BENEFITS OF THE PROJECT

Beyond Email

While the bulk of our traffic on MUKLA remains electronic mail, there is a new trend towards user participation in electronic conferences. MUKLA at the moment carries over 50 different conferences mostly from the Internet and APC networks, with a few specifically regional or local ones. Perhaps the most notable among these is a discussion list on Uganda-related issues and news, appropriately called Ugandanet. Through this conference, over 600 Ugandans from all over the world link with each other on a daily basis to interact with lively discussions on various topics ranging from the constitutional process, to entertainment, to sports and news.

Perhaps responsible for the bulk of growth in the beginning was the email/fax service that MUKLA provided. Users are able to send, at the price of email, faxes to destinations all over the world. Its popularity was mainly due to the exorbitant international charges levied by Uganda Post & Telecommunication.

Sectoral Involvement

University

Electronic mail has had a particular attraction for research activities to many researchers. Students are also increasingly getting to use email. About 25 percent of MUKLA traffic is for university related activities.

Non-Governmental Organizations

These form the single largest group of MUKLA users accounting for over 40 percent.

Government

The involvement of government in any major way has not come yet, although from the early days government departments were interested in what we were doing and, in 1992, we were approached by many government bodies for connectivity. Presently, however, only isolated projects within government departments are connected, usually for very specific reasons, such as easy access to a donor office abroad. We have been approached by the Ministry of Foreign Affairs to explore possibilities for linking Ugandan embassies, especially in particularly hard-to-reach places like Zaire and Rwanda.

Business Sector

This perhaps remains a weak and under-represented section of the network. Nevertheless, from the early days, business users concerned with sustainable development issues began to join us.

Others

There are many other individuals and independent groups that MUKLA knows are interested in electronic networking. We have yet to tap this group.

Finance

Though MUKLA benefited from the ESANET research fund as seed capital, cost recovery was instituted at an early stage to supplement this. As of now, and at completion of the ESANET project, MUKLA is fully self-financing through fees levied on users. A check is put on users via shadow billing whereby an itemized bill for all users is prepared at the end of the billing quarter to check on excessive use and possible abuse of our lenient terms. There is no additional charge for the fax facility though strict monitoring is done for each of categories above. When excessive use is noticed, the user is upgraded to the higher billing group.

Results

The ESANET project introduced the idea of electronic mail communication to researchers and other users at Makerere University campus—though the focus of the project was then on experimenting with various computer-based communication technologies and working out the technical bugs involved with poor telephone lines, erratic management of the telephone long-distance dialing system, and hardware and software equipment.

As of September 1993, most of these problems had been ironed out. The electronic mail system using the GnFido system has reached a level of reliability that surpasses that of fax machines. A cost-effectiveness analysis was carried out at the end of the ESANET project and this provided the evidence needed to prove that this venture could be sustainable, given the proper setting and management.

The ESANET project established that microcomputer-based electronic communication was a viable, sustainable technology and appropriate to the context of the region in which it has operated. There is a proven demand for electronic communication, both regionally and internationally. Following are the recommendations from the ESANET project:

To the research community, we recommended that:

- Relevant institutions be encouraged to consolidate and expand their user base.
- We should undertake more research into improving and expanding technologies used.
- Manpower requirements for this activity be consolidated into the establishment of the institutions concerned.
- Appropriate mechanisms be established for operational cost recovery and institutional funding to cover system operation and expansion.
- Cognizance be taken of the ever-improving nature of electronic communication worldwide and relevant upgrading be considered.

To the telecommunication authorities, we requested:

- Further investment be made in improving regional telecommunication links to enhance electronic viability of using national telecommunication infrastructure for modem related activities

- Special tariffs be applied to the academic and research communities for packet switching and leased line facilities thus enabling greater access to computer based communications regionally and internationally.
- Liberalization of user terminal equipment connected to national telecommunication networks be encouraged.
- Pragmatic policies be established with regard to licensing of alternative communication methodologies such as packet radio and low earth orbit satellite.

To the donor community, we recommended that:

- In view of the fact that national communication networks are an indispensable component of national development, providing as they do for an efficient and effective information delivery system in diverse sectors, continued funding be made available for establishing infrastructure related to computer-based communications for capacity building in order to facilitate transfer of technology.

To regional governments, we recommended that:

- They recognize the importance of national and regional networks for all aspects of development and for human resource and manpower interactions. The final meeting of the ESANET project paid tribute to the invaluable contribution that IDRC had made through this project in furthering the case of electronic communication within academic, health, and other related communities. We accordingly asked IDRC to:
  - Ensure that ESANET nodes be covered in any forthcoming regional electronic network support programs.
  - Share the findings of this project with other donor and development agencies.
  - Be receptive to future requests from ESANET community to consolidate and expand what has been achieved so far.

ANALYSIS OF LESSONS LEARNED

The ESANET project provided the participating institutions the opportunity to experiment with regional and international microcomputer-based communication. The aim of the experimentation was to establish the viability of the regional computer networking for data communication from the technical and management perspectives. We acquired data and experience from the experimentation phase of the project using Fidonet and packet satellite technologies. Based on this experience and data, we made the following specific observation on hardware, software, connectivity, network management and research activities.

Hardware

For modems, we have observed that:

- 9600 baud or higher modems (e.g., Telebit Worldblazer) perform better for international connections, while 2400 baud modems (e.g., GVC 2400) are sufficient for local connections.
- External modems perform better and are easier to handle than internals.
- Modem power supply should be 240V AC.
- Modems should be Hayes compatible.

For the node computer, we recommend a machine with the following specifications:

- 386 or higher,
- a minimum of 4 megabytes RAM,
- 120 megabyte hard drive minimum (max 12 ms cached),
- dual floppy,
- fast serial ports,
- 220 V AC supply, and
- UPS with stabilizer.

There is always a need to have a backup computer.

Software

We used the following software packages in most of the our node operations:

- FrontDoor 2.1+ — mailer
- Gecho — conference mail processor
- Msgtrack — mail tracker,
- ReDir — mail redirection
- GUS, Echovol — for conference tracking,
- AC — for accounting and billing

Connectivity

We observed that GnFido, Rhodes University, or WorkNet polling into ESANET nodes was cheaper and easier than direct polling between ESANET nodes. This has been the case for regional as well as international traffic. We thus disproved the earlier assumption on which the interconnectivity topology had been based.

User Base

We also observed that:

- A massive effort was required to develop and support a user base. We needed advertising, workshops, and maintenance visits.
- There was a need to clarify to the users what installation and support imply and discourage frivolous requests.

Network Management

To sustain the network it is important to:

- train system operators and establish official positions for system operators at various universities and
- put into place efficient and cost effective cost recovery mechanisms.

Some Fidonet management tools are available in basic node software. Additional software was developed during the project period to supplement these basic tools. Examples are: AC (accounting) from the Zimbabwe node and MTMON and HISMON (monitoring) from the Zambia node. However there is still need to develop more tools. Whereas there was sufficient documentation for point operation (the lowest level of the Fidonet hierarchy), there was need to develop more documentation for node operation. Nodes are the individual systems that belong to Fidonet. They are responsible for passing mail between the points and the next hierarchical level of Fidonet—the hub.

Research and Development

We need to encourage technical innovations to improve the system and we can use student resources for such projects. Technical innovations are required in the following areas:

- Terminal Node Controller (TNC)
- The packet satellite upload program (PG)
- Modems and modem testing/evaluation
- Mailer interfaces

Beyond the ESANET Project: Future Developments at MUKLA

While the interest in using electronic mail among researchers is strong, the technical capacity to meet this demand remains severely constrained due to lack of adequate funding. Additional funding is needed both for the personnel involved in its spread and for the purchase of hardware upgrades for the present installation. Although a number of groups and individuals have expressed interest in using and learning more about electronic mail, there are no adequate pedagogical materials nor the funding to have technical experts available to advise on both hardware and software problems as well as to do the installation and training.

Given the lessons learned from the experimentation phase, with the outlined constraints, it is imperative that MUKLA seek to improve its institutional capacity to effectively spearhead a development plan. We will seek support for recruiting trainers whose job will be to build on the achievements to date and enhance the existing network amongst all these groups. We will also seek support to update the hardware at the existing nodes and to create a pool of modems to serve as seed investments in new areas where electronic communication is to be introduced.

Specific goals should be towards:

- upgrading the hardware and software at the MUKLA node to full Internet status via leased line;
- developing appropriate educational materials and formats for workshops and short-courses;
- providing technical assistance and training; and
- facilitating communication via email amongst users within the country and region.

There are two sets of activities to look at in the process. The first would involve the acquisition of the necessary funding and identification and purchase of the necessary hardware for a full IP connection. Simultaneously, we would prepare training materials for the use of electronic mail, instruction on both hardware specification and troubleshooting, and hands-on training with the software. The second set of activities will include the provision of regular and ongoing technical support to users. This will be necessary both to iron out technical problems encountered in the daily operations of the electronic mail, as well as to sensitize and train new users.

New Nodes

We expect that the user base will have grown to an estimated 2000 installed sites by the end of 1996. It is time now to consider new nodes to improve services in areas outside of Kampala. Some possible sites for expansion of MUKLA are given below.

Entebbe is a major seat of government ministries and headquarters to many international United Nations bodies and NGOs. It is ripe to have a node established that could serve as hub to all users in and around Entebbe. This node would periodically poll MUKLA to transfer national, regional and international traffic.

There is potential for up to 150 installed sites within one year; this would also relieve the pressure on MUKLA. Kabale located about 400 Km from Kampala has good potential to play a node role for Rwanda, Burundi, and some parts of Western Tanzania that fall within the Kagera Basin. Kabale is the gateway to these countries that have traditionally used the northern corridor trans-Africa highway to link them to the Kenyan seaport of Mombasa. There is an automatic exchange that is part of a large telecommunications project linking the countries that comprise the Kagera Basin Organization (KBO): Burundi, Rwanda, Tanzania and Uganda. With 3,000 lines, the exchange is the most modern to be installed in Uganda. The KBO regional telecommunications project consists of a microwave transmission system interconnecting the four countries. It is aimed at the promotion and development of agriculture, forestry resources, and telecommunications links between member states that share the river Kagera.

Goals of Expansion

The nodes in Entebbe and Kabale, together with a series of training workshops for users in Jinja and Mbale, would constitute the first phase of the expansion program.

Existing national and international mechanisms of information processing and exchange, and of related technical assistance, would be strengthened to ensure effective and equitable availability of information generated at the local, provincial, national, and international levels, subject to national sovereignty and relevant intellectual property rights.

National capacities would be strengthened, as would capacities within governments, non-governmental organizations and the private sector, in information handling and communication, particularly within the East African region.

Improved Services

MUKLA would offer its clientele the full benefit of a wide range of Internet services. Electronic mail and conferencing, public and private access to Internet mail and other worldwide networks might be provided via partnership with the Association for Progressive Communications. MUKLA can also provide consultancy services on network establishment for organizations and government departments.

Future Needs and Possibilities

One of the difficulties we face as we prepare for future developments is to clarify the role of what is essentially a well meaning private enterprise with the responsibilities in this area of various tiers of government and public in Uganda.

The question of appropriate ownership structures for networks like ours is quite complex. Our decision to operate as a private company was indicated at the time of our birth. The people are sufficiently interested to devote time and financial energy to the project and do not have any particular philosophical attachment to a mode of operation.

However the structure has served us well amidst the politics of governments and NGOs. We have always regarded ourselves as the carriers of information related to these issues, rather than as a policy body or an arbiter of truth and best practice. In the early days, this structure and philosophy allowed us to engender cooperation between NGOs who did not see eye-to-eye on all issues. In later days, the same stance has allowed us to assist cooperation between tiers of government and government departments, which have been known to jealously guard their own interests rather than cooperate. And, more importantly, we have managed to remain credible with both government and its more radical opponents. It is probably our strongest point, that we can operate independent of the political will of any tier of government or its funding priorities.

The future holds many specific problems to address—questions of cooperation, questions of standards, and questions of access to information will have to be addressed. Much work will have to be done towards these ends by both ourselves and government bodies.

Regional Interconnectivity

There will be immense savings by sharing costs and collaborating with other regional providers. The East African Internet Association (EAIA) effort could be one way to foster further regional interconnectivity. (See Box 4 on page 164 for more information about EAIA.)

CONCLUSIONS AND RECOMMENDATIONS

My experience suggests that there is far more to establishing a successful network than purchasing and learning the technology. Indeed, technology expenses have been a minor part of our budget. Outlined below are some basic principles I believe are essential in establishing viable networks.

User Friendliness

Experience indicates that the issue of user friendliness is one where there should be no compromise. Simplicity of interface is crucial; however, simpler interfaces, those that use graphics, for example, also require more computing power. It is important to have machines with adequate power, memory, and speed to perform the necessary tasks. This is where a full needs analysis is necessary. The simplest looking interface may not do the job; nor will old or obsolete equipment provide enough sophistication to run programs such as Windows.

Adherence to Standards

The only trade off in user friendliness that might occur would be in the area of adherence to standards. Here, important standards have to be considered if contact with global networks and global relevance of data collected are concerns.

Promotion and Education

The most common mistake we can make in large scale electronic messaging installations is believing that somehow the system will "introduce itself." Not so! You can only successfully train the converted. The network has to be actively promoted. Its benefits have to be known before people will use it. Its applications to work areas and advantages have to be received with enthusiasm. Without this, the basic aims will not be achieved.

Training

Equally, training is an absolute must for a successful implementation. Links should be made to existing training organizations. Training materials must be available for any software used. (See Box 5.)

Product Champions

The concept of a "product champion" is often mentioned in sales literature. It essentially refers to enthusiasts who promote concepts and products willingly because they believe in them. All networks need them. Product champions sometimes create problems for organizations with their over-enthusiasm and are rarely popular with administrators. But they are totally necessary and need to be identified and supported.

Adequate Funding

An under-funded initiative that fails can delay a concept such as sustainable development networks in a country by a decade or more, and a few failures can

---

Box 5   Training Needs

A typical mistake made in electronic messaging implementations is to spend all available funds on hardware, bandwidth, and software development and find that no funds are available for training. This has been noted in many universities where typically less than 13 percent of academics actually use systems. It's not surprising - they are presented with very basic interfaces, no help desk, no manuals, and only the very brave and technically-inclined actually make it.

ruin the concept altogether. It is far too easy to attempt to stretch available funds too far and to leave behind a string of underdeveloped projects with little chance of success. It is also far too easy to get carried away by enthusiasm and to start a project without sensible financial plans to ensure viability.

Appropriate Ownership Patterns

This is a difficult question for which there is no immediate formula. An appropriate ownership pattern has to be one which will not restrict the participation of any governmental or non-governmental body whose cooperation is needed.

Plans for Financial Sustainability

Unless the venture is to be a continual financial burden to funding organizations, a realistic business plan has to be adopted to ensure that the network is self sustaining within a given period (perhaps 2–4 years).

Managerial, Sales and Technical Expertise—in that order!

The need for managerial expertise must be obvious, as is the need for technical expertise. What is less obvious is the need for sales expertise. Even if a facility is not expected to raise revenue, it surely is expected to engender use and that's a sales job.

In conclusion, I would state that the world is not a series of isolated ecosystems bearing no relationship to one another and capable of resolving their own problems. National sovereignty does not rule the atmosphere, nor the oceans, nor indeed the rivers that meander happily across borders with no care to the politics of the government of the day. Global cooperation is vital, and access to the experiences and knowledge of others is essential if we are to solve the problems facing us.

Indeed, this paper is written in the belief that what we have achieved and learned in Uganda is valuable, and may be of assistance to people in other countries wishing to establish similar facilities. We would be happy to assist and advise based on our experiences here.

APPENDIX—INTERNET/EMAIL PROVIDERS IN UGANDA

1. MUKLA Institute of Computer School
Makerere University, P.O. Box 7062, Kampala
Info@mukla.gn.apc.org
Contact: Charles Musisi, Network Manager

Services offered: Electronic Mail, Listservs, APC conferences/Usenet, Faxing

Usage charges

Students	$ 10
A monthly individual/small NGO	$ 30
A monthly corporate rate	$ 50
Big corporate/International	$100

2. StarLight Communications (U) Ltd (STARCOM)
Sheraton Complex, 14th Floor, Ternan Ave., P.O. Box 10524, Kampala
Staff@starcom.co.ug
Contact: Kiggundu Mukasa, Internet Manager

Services offered: Email and email fax, World Wide Web, Telnet, FTP

Usage charges:

E-mail only (unlimited usage)	$ 30
Shell account	$ 50
SLIP/PPP account	$100
Full IP	Negotiable

3. Infomail (U) Ltd
Plot 2 Clement Hill Rd. P.O. Box 11465, Kampala
Info@imul.com
Contact: M.M. Otyek, Manager

Services offered: Email, World Wide Web, Telnet, FTP

Usage charges:

	Monthly	Duration	Setup	Overtime
Basic	$ 50	3 hours	$50	$20
Premium	$120	8 hours	$50	$20
Big corporate	$250	20 hours	$120	$15
Very big corporate	$500	50 hours	$120	$10

4. Transmail Ltd
Blacklines House, Suite 2B4, P.O. Box 7482, Kampala
mawanda@tmail.gn.apc.org
Contact: Patrick Mawanda, Manager

Services offered: Email, Electronic Fax, Mail Broadcasting, Conferencing

Usage charges:

Traffic not exceeding 420KB	$50/month
Traffic not exceeding 910KB	$100/month

5. InfomaNet
4th Floor Impala House, P.O. Box 8945, Kampala
xtina@infoma.com
Contact: Christine Nantongo

Services offered: Email, Fax

Usage charges:
    Quick start plan:

Setup	$30
Email sending	$1.20 per page
Email receiving	$0.70 per page
Fax sending	$2.95 per page

    Power user plan:

Installation	$50
Security deposit	$50
Subscription	$15
Email sending	$1.00
Email receiving	$0.40
Fax sending	$1.95

THE UNIMA Fidonet Network: Computer Networking for Communications in Malawi

by Paulos Nyirenda

Dr. Paulos Nyirenda is Head of the Department of Physics and Electronics at the University of Malawi. He has a PhD in electrical engineering from the University of New South Wales. He has been working on networking at the University of Malawi since 1992. He asks that this chapter be dedicated to his late wife, Gemma.

BACKGROUND AND CONTEXT OF THE PROJECT

Malawi is a landlocked country located on the southeast side of Africa. It shares boundaries with Mozambique, Tanzania, and Zambia. The country has a population of about 9 million, of which about 90 percent live off subsistence farming. Malawi's economy is agricultural-based, with few manufacturing or mining industries.

The University of Malawi is the only university in the country. It is made up of five colleges spread out over a wide geographical area in the central and southern sections of the country. There are many research institutions in the country, most of which are linked to the agricultural sector and, as such, are located in remote locations across the country. Most of these research centers have access to direct exchange telephones that work most of the time but are of relatively poor quality, just as in some other African countries. Also, as in other African countries, the telephone penetration into the population in Malawi is very low.

Communications in Malawi is difficult and expensive. Research and data communications have been achieved primarily by physical travel to a site—often over seasonal roads in poor condition—or by fax where available. This is also the case for most governmental and private sector communications. Most needed research and other data and information do not reach the people and decision makers who require this data to make important national and international decisions.

However, even as early as 1992, most research, governmental, and major commercial offices had computers. Most of these were IBM-compatible desktop computers or Apple Macintosh computers.

PROJECT DESCRIPTION

Realizing the difficulty of communicating among widely separated university colleges and research institutions, I proposed a project titled *Study of Computer and Telephone Network Based Communications in Malawi*. The proposal was submitted for funding to the University of Malawi (UNIMA) Research and Publications Committee (RPC) in February, 1992. The original budget was for Malawi Kwacha (MK) 5123[1] or roughly $1,000. The main objectives of the project were to:

- investigate the feasibility of establishing computer and telephone-based communications in Malawi; and
- demonstrate more efficient and effective communications among researchers and academics within Malawi as well as among those in Malawi and outside.

With these objectives and minimal base funding, the Malawi Fidonet network was started. The network, now called *UNIMA*, has grown to be a public, nationwide network serving all sectors —government, non-governmental, and commercial—of the Malawi economy. It thus serves a much wider population than the academic and research communities originally envisioned and for which I had budgeted. It is a public network in the sense that anyone and any organization in Malawi can be linked to the network—provided they have the basic resources required for such linkage. The project has since attracted funding from various national and international organizations.

PROJECT EXPERIENCE AND IMPLEMENTATION

The proposal I made to the University led to the establishment of the UNIMA Fidonet network. The specific objectives of the proposal were to:

- experiment with modems, microcomputers, and the telephone network for data communications within the University of Malawi;
- design and build electronic interface devices for connecting direct telephone lines and switchboard (PABX) extensions to one computer and modem node to handle both local college and direct line connections;
- evaluate the quality of the Malawi telephone network for data communications; and

- evaluate the cost of computer communications using modems and the telephone network and compare it to other electronic communications modalities.

At the time the UNIMA project was started, there was a regional project called the East and Southern Africa Network (ESANET) funded by the International Research Development Centre (IDRC) of Canada. (For a complete description of the ESANET project, see Charles Musisi's case study on page 158.) The UNIMA project had similar general objectives to ESANET, which linked university computer centers in Zimbabwe, Zambia, Tanzania, Uganda, and Kenya. Because I was involved in these activities, the UNIMA project benefited considerably from the ESANET project in the beginning, even though Malawi was not a participating country in ESANET. The startup modems and non-commercial Fidonet software that enabled UNIMA to take off were obtained under ESANET.

My proposal to study computer and telephone-based communications in Malawi was accepted by the RPC in January 1993. I next needed to request security clearance from the Malawi Government, as well as from the Malawi Posts and Telecommunications to start the project. The government issued the security clearance on 15 June 1993, one day after citizens passed the referendum that introduced multiparty politics into Malawi. The Malawi Posts and Telecommunications Department then cleared the project in July 1993. The direct telephone line required for the node or hub of the telephone-based computer communications network was installed at Chancellor College in Zomba on 24 September 1993.

We next installed the equipment for the node: an IBM-compatible 386 computer running at 20 MHz with a disk space of 40 megabytes (borrowed from the Physics Department at Chancellor College); a VIVA 2400 baud modem donated by IDRC under the ESANET project; and non-commercial Fidonet communications software (FrontDoor 2.02) obtained under ESANET and tested earlier. This startup setup was then used to negotiate the network address, initial mail routing, and initial polling procedures required for the network. In the startup phase, the network address was negotiated under ESANET to be a Fidonet point address off the University of Zambia electronic mail network. Malawi now has its own network number and the node established has the Fidonet address 5:7231/1.[2]

Connecting to the University of Zambia Fidonet node was very difficult and, when the connection was finally made, the line quality was poor. We decided in November 1993, to switch connections to the Africa Zone Gate directly at Rhodes University in South Africa. This improved the connection success rate as well as the quality of the connections. In May 1994, the UNIMA network started receiving funding from the Capacity Building for Electronic Communications in Africa (CABECA) project also funded by IDRC but managed under the Pan African Development Information System (PADIS) in Addis Ababa, Ethiopia. (For more information about the CABECA project, see Fall's case study on page 147.)

Under CABECA, the UNIMA network received more modems and assistance from the Southern Africa Non-Governmental Network (SANGONET) in Johannesburg. SANGONET polled the UNIMA system twice a day at first but this was upgraded to three times a day to cater to the increased volume. Also under CABECA, we upgraded the node with the installation of a Telebit WorldBlazer high speed modem. This modem was eventually replaced by a US Robotics modem.

Figure 1 shows the general Malawi Fidonet network and its linkage to other networks in the world. The number of points running off the node has increased

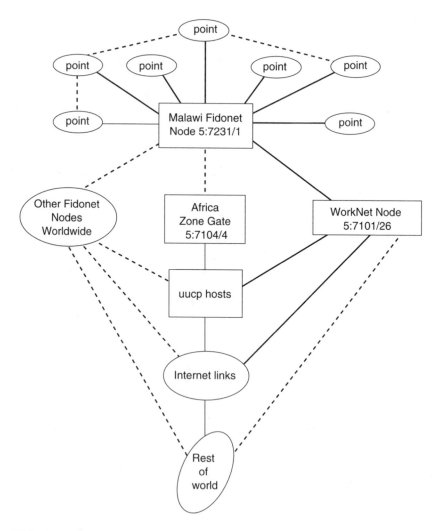

FIGURE 1   Fidonet structure in Malawi.

rapidly even though the single most important constraint to the growth in the user base has been the availability of modems at an affordable price within Malawi.

We replaced the computer borrowed from the Physics Department with a dedicated computer borrowed from UNIMA RPC. This was also an IBM compatible 386 computer with the same speed but with a 104 megabyte hard disk and more memory. This computer made it possible to perform multitasking using DesqView and QEMM. This allowed us to operate two telephone lines, using *intermail* as the communications program on the node. With this setup the node is now able to handle two data connections simultaneously, one on a direct exchange telephone line and another on a PABX telephone extension that caters to the local Chancellor College campus computers. Putting in the line from the local PABX helped to reduce congestion considerably on the direct line.

The use of a multiline mailer that enabled the node to handle more than one telephone connection at the same time made it unnecessary to develop hardware devices to achieve the same results. However, there were problems with rescanning the mail every time it was collected from the node. As the message base and user base grew, this mail rescanning took more and more time and eventually led to lengthy in-between call processing, leading to delays in answering calls at the node.

After observing the significant contribution that the Fidonet UNIMA network was making towards improving data communications in Malawi, the World University Service of Canada (WUSC) provided funds to the UNIMA network in February 1995 to purchase a Gateway 2000 IBM compatible 486 DX2 computer with 730 megabyte hard disk and running at 66 MHz. This has considerably improved the performance of the node, which can now process mail much faster and has removed the waiting that users experienced between calls while the node computer was processing received mail and extracting billing information. In addition the network has also received support from the Canada Fund of the Canadian High Commissioner to Malawi to purchase modems to assist the public sector in getting connected to the network so as to improve their communications.

UNIMA Network Operation

Under Fidonet, electronic messages and files are prepared offline to reduce telephone connection costs. The messages and computer files are then transferred onto the network in compressed files or packets to reduce the time of the telephone connections and to improve efficiency. When a point has a message to send, the message is normally sent to the node to be routed to its destination. If the message is destined for another point on the UNIMA network, the message waits at the node to be picked up by the destination point. Before April 1994, the node originated international calls to the Africa Zone Gate at Rhodes University for delivery and collection of international mail. All international mail is now routed via SANGONET, which polls the UNIMA node three times a day. International mail from Malawi is made to wait at the Malawi node in Zomba for international delivery during one of the polls from SANGONET.

When mail is received at the UNIMA node, it is processed by the non-commercial Fidonet mailer and other mail processors. Gecho.exe (version 1.01) is used as a mail and conference processor and also for mail compression and decompression. Netmanager, Netmgr.exe (version 0.99), is used as a general message processor for message-by-message identification, distribution, and redirection. Message tracking is done by msgtrack.exe, which produces a message-by-message log indicating such data as message origin, destination, dates, and volume.

I have written additional software to produce bills sent to users for cost recovery and network sustainability. Most of the billing information is obtained from the data produced by msgtrack.exe. Other data used to evaluate the performance of the network and the telephone system is collected from the various log files produced by the mailer and mail processors and analyzed using tools developed at the UNIMA node.

RESULTS, IMPACT, AND BENEFITS OF THE PROJECT

Network Performance

The network performance reported here was monitored at the UNIMA Fidonet node. As outlined above, the node software produces log-files (logs) for the day-to-day, telephone call-by-call, as well as the message-by-message activities that the node performs in sending and receiving electronic mail and files. The collection of the data presented here started in October 1993 and ended in March 1994. Much more data has been collected at the node but this has yet to be analyzed. By processing the log files, the monthly international mail volume can be determined. This is shown in Figure 2.

Cost of the Service

Shown in Figure 3 are the costs of sending or receiving one kilobyte volume of mail and the monthly telephone bill in Malawi kwacha, as charged by Malawi Posts and Telecommunications Department. This calculation was done on a month-to-month basis as well as on a cumulative basis where the total bill and the total volume, up to the dates shown, were used to calculate the cost per kilobyte of mail. As shown in Figure 3, the cost of operating the network per kilobyte of mail has dropped from MK4.68 (four Malawi kwacha and sixty-eight Malawi tambala) in October 1993 to MK0.88 in March 1994 on a month-to-month basis and from MK4.68 to MK1.10 on the cumulative basis. Using these data, the node has recommended that users be charged at the rate of MK1.00 per kilobyte of mail sent or received internationally. This charge rate was still in place at the writing of this chapter.

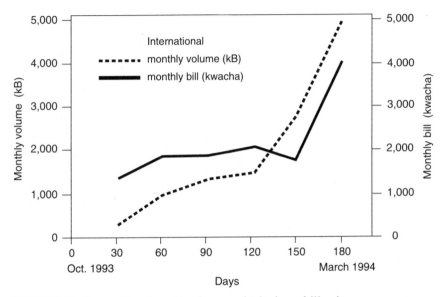

FIGURE 2 International email volume and telephone bill using a 2400 baud modem.

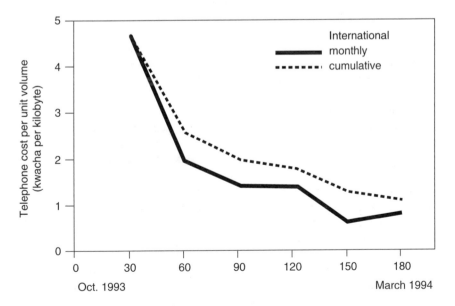

FIGURE 3 Cost per kilobyte of international telephone calls for email transfers using a 2400 baud modem.

Although the modem used for collecting the data changed from a 2400 baud modem to a 14400 baud one (with most good connections at 9600), the Malawi telephone charge per minute also changed upwards considerably from about $1.00 to $3.00 per minute in January 1995. We are currently collecting and analyzing data to check the effect of the modem speed change versus the telephone charge rate change.

A comparison between the cost of using the email system and using a fax to transfer text messages can be made based on the above data. One full page of text (as on this page) uses nearly 3 kilobytes and would therefore take MK3.00 to send by email. After examining several fax transmissions at Chancellor College, we found that such a page would take more than one minute to send but often less than two minutes. (The Malawi Posts and Telecommunications would therefore charge two minutes.) Most of the international mail transferred during the observation period has been for contacts outside Africa. The cost of sending such text messages internationally by email is therefore about 20 times cheaper than faxing similar messages at the current telephone rates and email charges at the UNIMA node.

Billing Users

Using the data collected from message tracking, a bill is sent from the Bursar of Chancellor College in the University of Malawi to each user once every three months. In addition to the volume fee outlined above, which now stands at roughly seven cents per kilobyte, each user account held outside the university is charged at 70 cents per month for account maintenance. Experience has shown that although these rates are very low, most Malawian users and organizations still have difficulties paying. I am currently proposing to conduct a study to find out whether this is due to genuine financial difficulties. I hope that user perception of "user pays" electronic communications will be better understood following the survey and analysis of the results.

I have shown in Figures 2 and 3 that even though the monthly bill and the monthly volume of mail sent and received internationally are increasing rapidly from month to month, the cost of sending mail per kilobyte has steadily approached a constant value. I expect that the speed of the modem used at the node will play a crucial role in determining the cost per kilobyte of international mail transferred at the node. At the moment this has been complicated by the international charge rate change made in January 1995. I hope that the further data analysis now being carried out will assist in clarifying the situation.

All the money raised from the bills is paid into a project account held at the Chancellor College Bursar office. Money in project accounts does not get absorbed into the University's pool account; although the money does not generate interest in such accounts, it is available when required to pay the bills incurred by the project. It also helps cover equipment maintenance and staff costs.

Failure Rates

Figure 4 shows the failure rate of telephone calls for data transfer as monitored at the node. All the calls at the node involve the Malawi Telephone system. Data transmitted during a call that fails in some cases have to be re-transmitted because the decompression of the data at the receiving side fails due to incomplete packets or files. Thus a failed call is a major concern to a user on the network. As can be seen from Figure 4, the proportion of calls that fail has come down considerably from nearly 100 percent in October 1993 to about 18 percent in March 1994. This improvement in performance can be attributed to various factors. The international mail route changed in November 1993 from via Zambia to via South Africa. We observed that fewer calls fail on the new route. We have also learned when to make the international calls in order to achieve higher success rates. This information was not available during the startup phase of the network.

The number of calls to the node from Fidonet points within Malawi has grown considerably as a proportion of the total number of calls recorded by fdstats.exe at the node. This means that while the performance reported in Figure 4 applied more to international calls in the startup phase of the network, it applies both to national and international calls in March 1994. We can estimate from Figure 4 that on the Malawi telephone system about 18 percent of the calls for data transfer

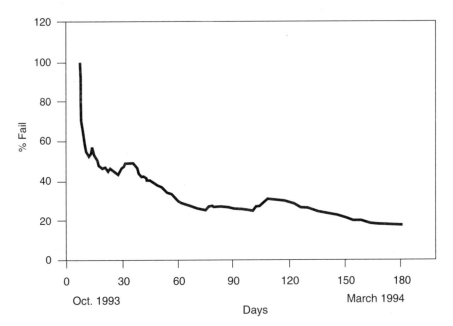

FIGURE 4   Failure rate of telephone connections using a 2400 baud modem.

using modems will fail. More data needs to be collected and analyzed to determine the separate failure rates of national and international calls on the Malawi
telephone system and to determine the rate which the graph in Figure 4 settles
down to.

•

ANALYSIS OF LESSONS LEARNED

Network Use

The main services on the Malawi Fidonet network are electronic mail and file
transfer. No remote login of any kind is currently supported. We need to conduct
a survey to determine and categorize the purposes of sending mail by users within
the University of Malawi and outside. During the experimental phase of the network, we have sought such information from users in the University and outside.
The message tracking software at the node collects information on the sources and
destinations of mail. We have observed that University of Malawi users use the
Fidonet network mostly for the following reasons:

- contacts with academic colleagues and supervisors;
- negotiating links with other universities at department level;
- submission of research papers, proposals and reports;
- applying for further studies abroad;
- coordinating research for staff on study leave abroad;
- library contacts;
- seeking funding for research and other projects;
- discussion of issues pertinent to Malawi;
- ordering equipment from suppliers outside Malawi;
- personal mail; and
- file transfer using *archie* and *ftp* by email.

In using the network, University staff and other users are finding it easier and
more efficient than before to request and access information from colleagues and
institutions outside Malawi. I hope that as the network grows inside Malawi it will
also become easier and more efficient to access colleagues and information sources
within the country.

A number of users on UNIMA were already on email in Malawi but they used
to make international calls to access email facilities abroad, such as CompuServe
or CGNET. Since the UNIMA Fidonet network was established, many of these
users have switched to using the UNIMA network and are finding it cheaper and
more convenient since it only involves a local telephone call. (See Box 1.)

Toward the end of 1994 and the beginning of 1995, users in non-governmental organizations and commercial companies began making up a fast-growing pro-

---

BOX 1   Reviewing the New Constitution

The UNIMA network made a significant contribution in the development of the new Malawi constitution. It made it possible for international lawyers in Malawi and outside to exchange information in a fast and more efficient way. It promoted discussion and editing as the constitution was sent worldwide for comments and review. This was reported in the local press in Malawi (*The Nation*). It was said that, without this mode of communication, the review of the constitution would have been lengthy and it would not have been possible to meet the deadlines for the review.

---

portion of the user base. These are high volume users who request and send large amounts of data over the network—mostly involving business related information. I expect that in the near future these users will be the main revenue generators for the running of the network.

Growing the Internet

With more than one hundred points on the UNIMA Fidonet network and over six hundred users, it is time for the establishment of a full Internet link in Malawi. The user base is there to support the network and our experience has shown that the users would also be able to pay the fees that such an installation would demand. At the point of writing, a leased line to South Africa seems too expensive and so we are suggesting that a VSAT connection be tried instead. VSATs or very small aperture terminals are satellites that provide two-way, high data rate services. VSATs appear to offer a low-cost telecommunication solution in developing countries.

Users on the UNIMA network indicate that they would not like flat billing. They would prefer message-by-message billing so that they pay for what they use. We will, therefore, have to carefully examine the current billing practices on UNIMA before full Internet connectivity is installed.

Equipment Shortages

The main constraint on the expansion of networks in Malawi will remain equipment based, with modems topping the list. I recommend to donors that, when projects are funded in a country like Malawi, each project should have an information technology section providing for the supply of computers and modems, when and where these are not available. Donors should also consider the expense of the installation and training of users of the information technology within the project. The minimum here should include electronic mail in any project proposal and implementation.

CONCLUSIONS AND RECOMMENDATIONS

A project to study computer and telephone network based communications in Malawi has been in progress in the University of Malawi since 1993. Under this project a nationwide electronic network using Fidonet technology has been installed and is being expanded. The network supports electronic mail and file transfer. This is a public network in the sense that anyone or organization with the required resources can link into the network. Most of the objectives of the project have been accomplished.

The project has shown that using the installed network for electronic communications is cheaper and more convenient than existing methods, such as fax and voice telephone. It has also shown that the Fidonet software can be used to generate data on a local telephone system that can be used to monitor the performance of the local telephone network. We expect that such data will be useful to the telecommunications operating corporation.

We have had many positive and congratulatory comments on the network performance and about how it has improved the communication efficiency of our users. So while the project began as a scholarly undertaking, mostly to determine the feasibility of establishing computer and telephone-based communications at the University of Malawi, it has resulted in the provision of improved communication services throughout the country. The small amount of seed money that we received from the University has been effectively multiplied and the impact of the project has been felt far beyond what we had originally intended.

NOTES

1. The value of the Malawi kwacha has changed considerably from roughly US$1=MK5 at the time when this data was collected to US$1=MK15 roughly at the time of writing of this report.

2. Fidonet uses a hierarchy to pass messages through the system. A Fidonet address identifies the zone, the hub, the node, and the point (if there is one) number of the user. This address, 5:7231/1, means Zone 5 (Africa), hub 7231, and node number 1. See Fall's case study for a more complete discussion of Fidonet.

Background Summary

A Global Computer Network for Change

The Association for Progressive Communications (APC) is an extensive global computer network, dedicated specifically to serving non-governmental organizations (NGOs) and activists working for social change. Composed of a consortium of international member networks, APC provides effective and efficient communications and information-sharing tools to NGOs and individuals. Member networks exchange email and participate in selected electronic conferences with over 50 partner networks worldwide. Many of these partner networks provide the only email access for NGOs in their countries. Through this global partnership, APC offers vital communication links to tens of thousands of NGOs, activists, educators, policy-makers, and community leaders in 133 countries.

APC member networks develop and maintain an informational system that allows for geographically dispersed groups to coordinate activities online at a much cheaper rate than can be done by fax, telephone, or for-profit computer networks. APC wants to assure that electronic communication tools are available to people from all regions in the world. By collaborating with over fifty partner systems in Southern countries, APC helps to increase the information flow between South and South. To further assure equitable access to computer technology, APC initiated a Women's Networking Support Program, which focuses on increasing access to networking technologies and information sources for women and women's NGOs.

The APC Networks are distinguished by the depth and quality of their information resources, by the global reach of their communication services, and by the diversity of their membership. APC developed from a dedicated grass-roots con-

continued

stituency and has become a true global community. The Network provides information in several languages, including Spanish, Portuguese, Estonian, Serbian, Macedonian, Bosnian, Croation, Slovenian, Russian, English, Swedish, German, Polish, French, and Esperanto. In addition, APC provides extensive user support and training to help people access the system easily and learn to use it efficiently.

The APC Networks are designed for use by NGOs, United Nations agencies, research organizations, government departments, educational institutions, multi-stakeholder groups, and individuals who communicate with NGOs. People use APC as an information and organizing tool for a wide range of issues, including peace, human rights, public health, environmental issues, population, social and economic justice, development, education, poverty, and demilitarization.

Dial Locally, Act Globally

All APC member networks provide users with an Internet email address. APC users can communicate with any of the over 40 million people who have an Internet email address; as well as with most commercial, academic and other networks. Many APC networks provide navigational tools to help their users access information that is otherwise difficult to locate on the Internet. For example, users can access any public computer on the Internet, including universities, libraries, research institutions, and public databases. Several APC networks make information publicly available on the Internet via the Worldwide Web (WWW) and via Gopher P—a user-friendly, text-based, menu-driven information search tool. Several APC networks offer SLIP and PPP access which allows the use of a graphic interface to Internet services.

APC provides the following networking tools:

- Electronic Mail (email)
- Electronic Conferences, both private and public
- Databases
- Fax and Telex
- Internet Navigation Tools: Gopher, Telnet, Worldwide Web, FTP, WAIS
- News and Information Services
- International User Directory

The APC is a community without borders. NGOs and activists worldwide use APC Networks for both their internal organizational communications as well as their public organizing efforts. In addition, many progressive news services distribute their publications electronically on the APC Networks.

Bringing the Internet to Zambia

by Neil Robinson

Neil Robinson is a Senior Communication Software Engineer with ZAMNET Communication Systems Ltd. He has been working in Zambia for six years. This case study describes the work that led to installing a full Internet link in Zambia and the attempts to make the provision of Internet services a sustainable enterprise, independent of external donor funding.

BACKGROUND AND CONTEXT OF THE PROJECT

On 22 November 1994, Zambia became the fifth country in Africa (and the very first sub-Saharan country outside of South Africa) to have full access to the Internet, the world's biggest computer network. This achievement was made despite Zambia's official status as one of Africa's poorest nations and followed three years of development by the University of Zambia of an electronic mail network serving non-commercial interests within the country. It was also achieved in a country that lacks a Computer Science degree course and where advanced computer skills are scarce. However, the technological achievement is perhaps less important than the ability to meet the considerable costs of Internet connectivity from within and thus to establish a sustainable service. ZAMNET Communication Systems Limited is the company that has been established to do this.

Computer Skills in Zambia

Despite a steady increase in the numbers of computers in use in both government institutions and private companies, the number of skilled computer specialists working in Zambia is still desperately small. Top quality staff command high salaries and other benefits (housing and transport) that are beyond the reach of government-funded institutions and the majority of Zambian companies. Most of

191

the top computer specialists work in the financial sector or for Zambia Consolidated Copper Mines in the (up until now) well-funded mining sector. There is a growing number of small computer sales and support companies in the capital, Lusaka, but the quality of service they provide is variable. Against such a background, the number of expatriate computer specialists working within Zambia is relatively high.

Zambia's highest national qualification in computing is a three-year computer studies diploma taught by Evelyn Hone College. The University of Zambia has no computer science department so people who wish to advance to degree level have to go outside of the country. The Mathematics Department in the School of Natural Sciences does provide a Mathematics and Computing degree but their department is desperately short of computers and is unable to provide the practical experience necessary in such a course. The locally produced graduates with the strongest computing background come from the Electronic Engineering Department of the School of Engineering. Many who succeed in acquiring the necessary skills and qualifications during training overseas fail to return to Zambia for very long, if at all.

The University of Zambia

The University of Zambia (UNZA) is the larger of Zambia's two universities (the other being the Copperbelt University in Kitwe). It has a student body of some 5,000 and approximately 500 academic staff. UNZA is wholly dependent on the Zambian government for its funding, although several schools within the University benefit from international donor support for their equipment requirements.

The University uses an old IBM 4361 mainframe computer for administrative computing requirements. The systems that run on this computer (personnel, payroll, admissions, examination systems, and so on) have all been written and are maintained by the University Computer Centre, a department of about 50 staff. Some 15 of these are technical programming and analysis staff. The rest are involved in the considerable data entry and computer operations requirements of such a mainframe-based system.

The Computer Centre is also responsible for providing technical support to computer users throughout the University. Up until about four years ago, this was largely confined to support for the mainframe computer to which students and staff were given access through a small terminal room at the Computer Centre. However, as elsewhere in Zambia, the number of microcomputers in use around campus has been growing steadily and the support requirement for the repair of hardware components and for the maintenance of microcomputer applications has also grown.

The vast majority of microcomputers within the University are donated and as such there is a diverse range of models and types of computers. However, in general, there are still far too few microcomputers to distribute access to the student level, and even in the mathematics department most student computer project work is carried out on the mainframe.

UNZA has recently embarked on a major project to downsize its administrative systems to a microcomputer-based network. A campus-wide fibre optic network is being installed to distribute the administrative tasks to the schools themselves. Once again donor supported (through the Dutch government), this should provide access to the first of the systems (student records) by the end of this year. It will also provide access for members of staff through departmental networks to the Internet, although the extent to which this happens will largely depend on the ability of each school to extend its own section of the campus network through its own buildings.

PROJECT DESCRIPTION

Since 1991, the Computer Centre at the University of Zambia has been the focal point for academic, non-governmental organization (NGO), and health-based email networks in Zambia. In that year, as a result of the International Development Research Centre (IDRC)-funded ESANET[1] project, Zambia was given a microcomputer and modem to provide the hub or "host" of the first University email system. The very first recorded message through this system was sent to the Baobab, an African interests network based in Washington, D.C., on 30 September 1991. This and other international messages were initially routed through the Association for Progressive Communication (APC) network in London. The first recorded user of the system was the School of Medicine's Medical Library.

The rapid growth and development of what was then known as UNZANET was assisted by an arrangement with Rhodes University of Grahamstown, South Africa which, in November 1991, began providing a link with Internet via thrice-daily, computer-to-computer telephone calls. These were paid for by UNINET, the South African Universities Network funded by the Foundation for Research and Development (FRD). This arrangement remained until December 1994, when full Internet access was achieved and by which time some 270 email points were linked to the network.

The Early Technology

From the beginning UNZANET was a Fidonet system using dial-up telephone lines to transmit messages via dedicated host computers. When UNZANET was first established in 1991, Fidonet had been successfully tried and tested in Zimbabwe and in Kenya for NGO networks.[2] Thus UNZANET was able to learn from the experiences of similar networks in the region and benefit from cooperation with them.

The UNZANET host system was configured to handle simultaneously three telephone lines attached to three separate modems. Two of these lines were direct external lines, while the third was an internal switchboard line for users on campus and with access to an internal telephone extension. The configuration of the Fidonet system remains in place today, primarily to serve rural users and those whose telephone lines are inadequate for interactive communication. It also serves users in advance of the completion of the campus network.

UNZANET'S Traditional Users

The original users of UNZANET were the schools and departments of the University. From the very beginning, a single site address or point number[3] was allocated to each school and administrative department. In the majority of cases, computers already existed in those departments and the email facility was installed using modems supplied as part of the ESANET project. Some of the computers used were old IBM personal computers, which were still perfectly adequate for email.

From very early on, it appeared to be inevitable and desirable that initiatives in academic networking would lead to collaborations with other sectors. Without expansion of the service into other, better-funded areas, the UNZANET system could never be sustainable. The development of a non-academic user base was encouraged especially for those users who had an immediate need for communication and for those who would have a growing need for communication in the future. These users would want to be part of a longer-term, more sustainable solution. However, with UNZANET's dependence upon donor support in mind, and particularly that of UNINET, the emphasis was always on non-commercial applications.

In Zambia, following the use at the University itself, there was widespread growth in the use of email among NGOs, health institutions, and aid or development agencies. Encouragement for the first two came about through external support, while the majority of aid and development agencies were able to fund the necessary infrastructure (modems, computers and telephone lines) themselves.

UNZANET'S Free Service

One of the reasons for the rapid growth of UNZANET was the fact that it was provided as a free service. Users only had to cover the cost of local calls into the UNZANET host or access the system through the University's internal switchboard. This allowed users to "taste" email and to experiment with it before they had to commit themselves to paying for the service. We feel that the growth of UNZANET would have been considerably slower had it been necessary to charge users from the beginning, although a culture of non-payment can have its disadvantages when a subscriber-funded service is introduced.

The Need for ZAMNET

Through the technical success of UNZANET, it was clear that email was a viable technology within Zambia. This was true not just for a rich urban elite, but also for smaller, less-wealthy organizations within Lusaka, the Copperbelt, and further afield. We had shown that email had the capacity to remove some of the communications barriers that otherwise engender a feeling of international isolation in professional communities. At the same time it was attractive to a large community of users outside of the academic sector. Email offered a fast, easy, and highly cost effective method of communicating compared to any other available technology. (See Box 1.)

However, a free service—provided through the generosity of others—could not be sustainable. The Computer Centre of the University, with its responsibilities to the University administration, was not in a position to sell and maintain a commercial service to customers from outside of the University, nor to pay the salaries of the high quality staff that such a service would require.

By the end of 1993, users were transmitting large volumes of international messages to and from the Internet, and there was a strong desire among users of UNZANET to expand the horizons of the system. The Internet was already expanding very rapidly: more and more data, journals, and information became available in electronic form; the nature of the information being offered broadened beyond the bounds of academic interest into business and recreation; and publicity about it was reaching the popular public media. The ability to transfer large files to and from other users; to directly access remote databases and electronic libraries; and to participate in electronic conferences and other peer group discussions had become of considerable interest both within and outside of the University.

To accommodate this growth and change in direction, the basic infrastructure of the UNZANET system and the way it was funded needed to be reviewed. The Computer Centre had already perceived the need for collaboration between the University and its fellow research institutions, as well as with the commercial and

---

BOX 1   Pooling Resources

At times it was suggested that the users in the NGO and health sectors should form their own networks (ZANGONET and HealthNet respectively)—independently of UNZANET. However, the need for a full-time system operator and the considerable advantages of pooling equipment and staff resources with UNZANET, dictated that both groups be maintained and administered from the University Computer Centre. The advantages of such an arrangement are even more apparent under the current self-financing service, which enables non-commercial NGO's and health institutions to be subsidized to some degree by ZAMNET's 'commercial' customers.

international organizations that had the resources to pay for the high quality, high volume access to information. Some of these other organizations were using UNZANET but, because they needed to transmit larger volumes of information more quickly, many had made their own direct links to their international head offices using a variety of electronic mail systems. Pooled access for these organizations to the Internet through a single service provider would clearly bring considerable cost savings, while improvements in speed and efficiency of communication, as well as the extra services available, would allow international organizations to better service their target communities.

The ZAMNET Proposal

By the middle of 1993, we made a decision to submit a proposal for donor funding to enable the University of Zambia to establish a direct link to the Internet. This was circulated among a number of major international donors but failed to attract any direct support. At the beginning of 1994, the University decided to establish a private campus company (ZAMNET Communication Systems Ltd.) to put in place the connection to the Internet and to sell access to the services that the Internet provides. Then the World Bank expressed interest in funding the ZAMNET project and agreed to fund 80 percent of the first year operating costs of the new company.

As a young campus company with no working capital aside from the grant from the World Bank, ZAMNET issued a nominal share holding, the major and controlling shareholder being the University itself. The board of directors is comprised of senior administrators from the University and the Deputy Minister of Health, with the Director of the Computer Centre as Managing Director.

The Budget

The project budget was estimated at $150,000 and covered the cost of:

*   the leased data circuit to the chosen (cheapest) point of Internet access;
*   subscription paid to the service provider at that point;
*   extra hardware required to provide the Internet link and to provide a service to ZAMNET's customers;
*   hardware required to provide a training facility for ZAMNET's customers;
*   consultancy fees for technical Internet experts to assist in the configuration of the service; and
*   salaries for one administrator and two technical staff (to be met from customer fees from the beginning).

The Proposed Service

We intended to distribute Internet services to users throughout Zambia using a variety of methods including:

- local leased lines providing full Internet access to regular high-volume users with their own local area networks (LANs);
- dial-up interactive access using SLIP or PPP for urban users on good quality telephone lines; and
- Fidonet and perhaps UUCP access for users in rural areas where poor telephone quality prohibited interactive access.

We anticipated that Fidonet would continue to play an important role within Zambia providing as it did a quick, easy-to-use entry to electronic mail. It had already proved to be relatively cheap on remote trunk lines and generally reliable in a rural setting.

The Project Objectives

ZAMNET Communication Systems Ltd. came into being officially in February 1994, although it was unable to employ staff or provide a service to its customers until the following year. ZAMNET has the following objectives:

1) Put in place the hardware and technical support necessary to provide a reliable full Internet service. To do this, we would need to:

- establish a reliable link between the UNIX network at the University Computer Centre and an Internet service provider;
- procure, install, and configure all necessary hardware to provide an Internet service;
- provide an access point for customers to dial into the Internet with sufficient capacity to avoid congestion;
- provide a software package for customers to use to access the Internet through ZAMNET;
- connect the existing Fidonet service to the new Internet service, thus removing the dependence on the Fidonet-Internet gateway at Rhodes University;
- develop locally based information services for local and international access;
- provide a training facility and develop training courses for customers; and
- produce or obtain user documentation for the system.

2) Put in place the administrative staff and procedures, and market the Internet service so that it would be fully self-sustaining after one year of operation, and after the World Bank funding had run out. To do this, we would need to:

- set up a computerized accounts system;
- determine a pricing system; and
- produce marketing materials (pamphlets, brochures, price lists, advertisements).

PROJECT EXPERIENCE AND IMPLEMENTATION

Although ZAMNET has been operating commercially for less than five months (at the time this report was written), the financial support from the World Bank is soon to come to an end. Thus, while in many ways the project is still ongoing, this is a good time to review progress on the ZAMNET objectives during the establishment of the Internet service to date.

Establishing the Link to the Internet

The establishment of the data communications link between Lusaka and Cape Town, critical to our service, proved very slow and time consuming. The Internet Company of South Africa or TICSA (now Internet Africa) of Cape Town had already generously agreed to carry our Internet traffic for free (for the time being) when, in April 1994, we submitted the application to the Zambian PTT for a leased, four-wire, 9600 baud, designated data circuit between our own offices in Lusaka and the TICSA offices. After the necessary surveying work, we were notified that it would be commissioned in July 1994. However technical problems over the satellite link between the Zambian earth station at Mwembeshi and Johannesburg meant that the line was not available to us to test until October of that year. Unfortunately our problems were not over.

Our original choice of modem to serve both ends of our Internet link was the Telebit Worldblazer. We had good experience with Worldblazers through our work with the Fidonet system. However when we installed the leased four-wire data circuit between Lusaka and Cape Town, we did not know that the Worldblazer is purely a two-wire modem and, therefore, unsuitable for the type of circuit that we were using. Unfortunately our email messages (our cheapest and what should have been the easiest route to assistance) to Telebit often failed to solicit a response and it required several long distance telephone and fax calls to establish the facts and to find out what options were available to overcome this problem.

Our first solution was to install hybrids to convert the four-wire circuit to two-wire over the local segment of the circuit in Cape Town and Lusaka. Both the Zambian and South African PTTs were extremely helpful in immediately inserting hybrids into their circuits. However, the resulting signal contained too much echo for the Worldblazers to cope with and, despite the further insertion of echo suppressors into the circuit by the PTTs, the resulting signal was inadequate for the Worldblazers at either end of the circuit to communicate with each other.

Eventually, after seeking advice from various sources, we decided to purchase two (quite expensive at $1,100 each) Telebit Fastblazer modems through their South African agents. Despite the availability of email, communication with them proved as frustrating as trying to communicate with Telebit in the United States. However, eventually, two modems were purchased and installed. Alas our problems did not end there.

The line between Cape Town and Lusaka uses microwave technology as far as Johannesburg, satellite to the Lusaka earth station, microwave once again as far as Lusaka's main exchange, but then uses copper wire for the last six or seven kilometers to the University. The signal loss over this section is high and the signal coming from South Africa was already quite low. Over such a long distance, the quality of the line allocated between central Lusaka and the ZAMNET office was highly variable and it required some intensive work from the Zambian PTT to identify the very best connections to provide for our circuit. However on 22 November 1994 the line was finally strong enough to carry a signal from our mail server to the Internet and vice versa.

The line has since been quite reliable (above 95 percent), the modems training up to 14,400 baud. Although capable of connecting at 19,200 baud, it appears that the signal loss over the circuit as a whole will prevent us from achieving such speeds. When the data circuit does fail, the technical staff at the two PTTs (ZAMTEL in Zambia and TELKOM in South Africa) have been quick to respond and restore our circuit.

Procuring, Installing, and Configuring the Internet Hardware

Most problems encountered during the installation and configuration of the hardware were due to our own inexperience with UNIX and our ignorance of much of the technology with which we were dealing. The staff involved were subjected to a very steep learning curve and inevitably much of that learning was through our own mistakes. (See Box 2.)

BOX 2   Danger from Lightning Strikes

A real problem during Zambia's rainy season is the threat of high intensity lightning strikes. All telephone lines and the leased data circuit to Cape Town are protected from lightning strikes using a surge protection box that diverts current surges down a thick copper wire into a copper stake driven into the ground outside of the equipment room. So far this system has thankfully not been tested by such a lightning strike.

The mail server

Through the RINAF (Regional Informatics Network for Africa) project, the University Computer Centre had received two identical Olidata (Olivetti) 486 computers. One of these was pressed into service as a new Fidonet host to cope with the rapidly growing number of users accessing that host. The other was set up on the Computer Centre network as a prospective mail server (puku.unza.zm).

A copy of SCO UNIX was installed on puku and this machine was configured to run SENDMAIL (for mail delivery), to run a POP (post office protocol) server (for mail collection by ZAMNET's customers), and to exchange mail with the Fidonet host using UUCP. We experienced some difficulty finding free Internet applications software to run under SCO UNIX (a commercial product) and, when we employed an expert to assist in the configuration of our mail server, we were advised to switch to FreeBSD-2.0. This was done in December 1994—after the Internet connection had been commissioned.

FreeBSD is a relatively easy operating system to configure and to manage, but finding precompiled binary versions of Internet applications has proved difficult. Compilation of ports and patches is cumbersome for those inexperienced in UNIX and keeping abreast of the constant updates is time consuming. The only alternative free UNIX system that runs on a 486 personal computer is Linux. Having already started with FreeBSD, there are few advantages in switching at this stage.

Puku is now running as the ZAMNET name server, as well as the server for mail/POP, Gopher, and WWW. All of these services appear to be running quite well. However from a hardware point of view we have discovered that a system with eight megabytes of RAM and a 400 megabyte hard disk is insufficient to tackle the range of tasks and to serve the number of users that we are asking of puku. A gigabyte hard drive and 32 megabytes of RAM is essential on such a pivotal system within an Internet service.

The router

The router required to connect ZAMNET to the rest of the Internet—a Cisco 3000—was provided as part of the funding of the Zambian regional node by the RINAF project. ZAMNET itself purchased a transceiver to connect this router to the ethernet network. The Cisco gave no problems in terms of configuration; however since its installation two problems have arisen.

First, one of the primary requirements of the router is to provide statistics that can be used to bill ZAMNET customers who link their networks with ZAMNET's using locally leased data circuits. Such customers are billed for all traffic carried. The data to enable this kind of billing needs to be analyzed on another computer on the network that is running UNIX. We have yet to find any software to analyze this data that will run under the FreeBSD operating system on puku, our mail server. The only such software that we have found is written for the SUN operating system (SUNOS) and we have since been advised that nobody would attempt to do Cisco accounting on a FreeBSD system!

The second problem is in trying to increase the speed of our link to the Internet. That link currently operates at 14,400 baud. It seems that by switching to an asynchronous connection using data compression it should be possible to increase the throughput of data on our link. To do this, however, the Cisco needs to have its auxiliary port configured to operate in asynchronous mode, which in turn requires a memory upgrade and a new version of the operating system to be loaded into the increased memory. With our whole system dependent on that one router we are somewhat reluctant to attempt this upgrade.

Providing Customer Access

To provide access to the Internet service to as many of ZAMNET's customers as possible simultaneously, 20 dial-up telephone lines configured as a hunting group were installed by the Zambian PTT, and a Livingston Portmaster 2e-30 with 30 configurable ports was purchased along with 20 Zyxel U-1496 modems to connect these lines to ZAMNET.

The telephone lines were installed when a new cable was being laid into the University and there were no problems in finding 20 new lines for ZAMNET. The hunting group is functioning well, although up until now (with 193 active, paying users as at the end of June 1995), we have rarely seen as many as seven of the lines in use at one time.

The modems that the ZAMNET customers dial into were purchased by mail order directly from Zyxel in California. Dealings with that company by email were very easy. The modems were purchased before the V34 (28,800 baud) standard had been ratified and they are all set to a maximum speed of 14,400 baud. However, given that this is also the maximum speed on our data circuit to the Internet, and that as yet there is no congestion on the dial-up lines, there is no disadvantage in restricting our customers to connections at this speed.

The Portmaster was chosen over a Telebit Netblazer on the grounds of its cheaper price and that its range of features was closer to our requirements. However we were unaware when purchasing the Portmaster that some of the software that is provided with it and that enables easy configuration and backup of the system would not run under the FreeBSD operating system that we are using on our mail server. The inability to back up the tables used to store user names and passwords has proved a serious weakness on two occasions when part of the user table was lost and had to be manually re-entered.

Provision of End User Software

For ZAMNET users continuing to use the existing Fidonet service or leasing local data circuits between their own LANs and ZAMNET, we did not need to provide any new software. The Fidonet installation had already been developed and proven over a number of years, while those linking through their own networks were responsible for their own software.

However, for our dial-up interactive customers we needed to find an easy-to-install, easy-to-use package for Windows, DOS, and Macs. When we found a set of books for each of these three categories, complete with software diskettes, we thought we had found the solution. However, we discovered that the DOS software contained a hard-coded login script that did not match the prompts provided by our Portmaster; the Mac software would not run on the systems on which we attempted to install it; and the Windows software contained frustrating bugs in its Mail program.

Software for DOS

The package distributed to DOS users is a slightly modified version of the SLIP/MINUET package developed by the University of Minnesota. While not as attractive as the Windows software, it does contain an easy-to-use mail program and a Gopher client. It lacks a WWW client and we are investigating how DOSLynx (a WWW client for DOS) might be integrated into the installation.

Software for Windows

After the frustrations encountered above, we borrowed the package distributed by GreenNet in London for their own PPP customers. Their package is based on shareware versions of the Trumpet Winsocket Manager, Eudora as a mail client, Netscape as a WWW client, plus FTP and Telnet clients. We modified this package for our own system and developed our own installation program. This package is stable, easy-to-install and has been found to be easy to use by our customers.

Software for Macs

The vast majority of computer users in Zambia use DOS-based computers. Consequently, providing support for the few Mac customers that ZAMNET has, has proved very difficult. The package distributed to Mac users is a combination of the diskette provided with the *Internet Tour Guide* and a second diskette obtained from GreenNet that they distribute to their own Mac users. The resulting package includes the Eudora mail client and Netscape and is very similar in its two main components to the Windows package. ZAMNET still does not possess its own Mac and so streamlining the installation is still some way off. Even copying the two distribution diskettes requires a visit to one of the two private individuals on campus who use Macs!

Integration of Fidonet and the Internet

When the Internet link was established in November 1994, we had just three weeks in which to commission the gateway between the Fidonet host and the mail server before UNINET started charging us for the use of their own gateway. On the recommendation of Bob Barad of the Baobab, we installed the new GIGO package and were pleased to find that it was very easy to install and configure, and what's more, it worked. Rhodes University had given us an experimental UUCP account and, for the three weeks prior to cutover, we polled (generated a computer call to) the Rhodes UUCP host on a regular basis. We encountered no problems with this link and the modification of the software to enable connections between the Fidonet host and our own mail server went equally well.

The only disadvantage of the link at this stage is that it requires a modem and telephone line to be dedicated to the mail server for the UUCP connections (none of our users use UUCP directly). Even using local phone calls at 14,400 baud the telephone bill for this exchange of mail between adjacent personal computers is quite high. It would be better to move this mail over the LAN if possible.

Development of Local Information Services

The ZAMNET Gopher

In December 1994, a Gopher server was set up (gopher.zamnet.zm) with a menu structure covering Agriculture, Engineering, Health, Communications and Networking, and ZAMNET News and Information. This proved to be a very useful way of publicizing our work and making contact and service information available to potential customers and other interested parties around the world. We also found the Gopher useful for advising our customers of the latest developments (or problems) on ZAMNET.

As customers became aware of the potential of the ZAMNET Gopher for the distribution of local information, they expressed an interest in storing their own information within its menus. To date a number of customers are paying for disk space on our Gopher server at the nominal rate of $1.00 per megabyte per month. For example:

- the National Farmers Union is providing weekly Agricultural Commodity Exchange prices;
- the Ministry of Agriculture posts regular food security and marketing bulletins; and
- the Engineering Institute of Zambia is publishing a range of information about the institute and its activities.

The Worldwide Web server

Our knowledge of the Internet has grown and we are aware of the rapid growth of the Worldwide Web (WWW) and the trend towards storing more information in hypertext form. Around April 1995, we installed our own WWW server. The ZAMNET homepage is accessible as www.zamnet.zm and contains pointers to information about Zambia, about ZAMNET, to the ZAMNET Gopher, and to a small but growing number of pages developed for ZAMNET's customers. For example:

- articles from the Post Newspaper are currently published twice weekly before the paper actually reaches the streets;
- the Zambia National Tourist Board has published information about travel and tourism; and
- the University of Zambia has published the text of a short leaflet giving background information about the University.

We plan to develop all of these areas. In particular several commercial customers are interested in posting information about their companies and services within our WWW pages.

Provision of Training Facilities and Courses

When ZAMNET was formed in 1994, it occupied one small office within the Computer Centre. In April 1995 we got our own offices that include a training room with capacity for nine networked personal computers. The room was equipped in May with seven multimedia Compaq personal computers and we have set aside three mornings per week to provide training to ZAMNET customers.

In addition, this facility has been used to provide sensitization seminars to the staff, deans, and administration from each of the schools at the University. When not in use for training, it is open for these members of University staff to book for an hour at a time, and is also open for members of the public to use at a rate of $7.00 per hour.

User Documentation

The Internet is a new concept to many people in Zambia and there are few books or magazines about it in the bookshops in the country. Since it is important for customers to have access to information that helps them make the best use of the service they are buying, we decided to provide a book, *The Internet Tour Guide,* with the ZAMNET subscription. In practice, as explained above, the software included with the books has not been very useful and the books are very American in style and language. However, there are few alternatives until we can produce our own software specific guides. We have spent some time producing detailed installation instructions for the software that we distribute and these certainly appear to have reduced the number of queries that we field during customer installation.

Computerized Accounting

The initial chart of accounts was put together by an accountant who has subsequently kept an eye on our progress. We are using *Mind Your Own Business (MYOB)*, a small business accounting package developed in the United States. While quite easy to use, it has been not been adaptable to the multicurrency system we operate (we accept payment in Zambian Kwacha and in U.S. Dollars). We are considering replacing it with a package better suited to our own particular requirements.

Determining a Pricing System

No two Internet service providers use the same method to charge for their services. Our own method of arriving at our fees was to draw up the budget over the next few years; decide how much emphasis we wanted to put on the basic subscription, the cost of international electronic mail, and the cost of connect time; estimate the number of customers and projected growth rate in each category; and to fiddle with the parameters until we could be sure of breaking even within one year.

Since we need to support our traditional users, we added a two-tier pricing structure for commercial and one for non-commercial customers. The resulting fee structure—which entails a signing-on fee, a basic monthly subscription, a per kilobyte charge for international email, and a per hour charge for connect time—has been well received within the country, although we have received some criticism from without. We are always reviewing these fees and plan to increase the free connect time to two hours per month. As yet ZAMNET is not sufficiently financially sound for any radical discounting of the prices.

Marketing of the Product

To promote ZAMNET to a largely unaware population, we employed a graphic artist to produce a leaflet and eight page brochure. This determined the "corporate image" of ZAMNET and its style has been copied on price lists, business cards, and advertisements. Over 1,000 brochures have been distributed so far. Advertisements have been placed in the *Times of Zambia, Productive Farming,* and *Profit Magazine.* However such has been the interest in the Internet that ZAMNET has benefited from free publicity in articles in all three of Zambia's leading newspapers, plus a lead article in *Profit Magazine.*

BOX 3   ZAMNET Salaries

Even at the relatively (for Zambia) high salaries being offered by ZAMNET, recruitment of the right quality staff was difficult. The package on offer of a two year contract with a salary but no fringe benefits was perhaps not so attractive in a country where housing and transport costs are so high and many employers still provide housing (or housing allowances) and transport to senior information technology professionals.

Staff Recruitment

The recruitment of the administrator/bookkeeper with a full Association of Accounting Technicians qualification and solid accounting experience proved a lot easier than the recruitment of the technical staff, although an initial plan to recruit a part time administrator was revised when it was fully appreciated just how much would be involved in administering the ZAMNET service. (See Box 3.)

Of only 30 applicants for the post of communications technician, six were suitable to interview. Few of these had UNIX experience, and none had any practical experience with internetworking technology. While one member of staff was recruited from the Computer Centre and had been involved in the development of the system from the beginning, the only external recruit is very much learning as he goes along.

RESULTS, IMPACT AND BENEFITS OF THE PROJECT

As part of the billing process it has been necessary to gather comprehensive statistics about the use of the ZAMNET system from the very beginning. A very simple analysis of the connection time and email statistics reveals very rapid growth of the service. ZAMNET is growing at roughly the rate of one new account each day and at the current rate this will lead to ZAMNET more than doubling in size over the next twelve months.

Table 1 shows the growth in the number of interactive accounts and the connect time that those accounts have generated. Growth has been constant—with accounts connecting to ZAMNET for an average of just over four hours per month, although the average number of connections per month has increased from 38 in March to 46 in June. This increase perhaps reflects the increased regular use of the system for electronic mail rather than Internet browsing.

Table 2 shows the steady growth in the volume of email, although it should be noted that the mail volumes include mail from the Fidonet system which, unlike the connect time data, would have been present before March. Nonetheless the

TABLE 1 Growth of ZAMNET by Month, January 1995 to June 1995

Month	Number of Accounts	Number of Connections	Total Connect Time (hours)
January	5	32	5.12
February	26	875	135.08
March	93	3,510	390.26
April	112	4,415	503.87
May	168	6,926	800.77

TABLE 2 Growth of ZAMNET by Month, March 1995 to May 1995

Month	International		Local		Total	
	Count	Size	Count	Size	Count	Size
March	3,505	7,629,575	2,057	7,316,013	5,572	14,945,588
April	4,103	8,535,996	2,522	8,300,020	6,625	16,836,016
May	5,633	13,571,732	2,422	7,498,555	8,055	21,070,287

volume of international mail being sent has nearly doubled in two months. This does not include incoming mail. Interestingly, while the volume of mail to international destinations has increased steadily the volume of mail to local users has remained nearly constant, perhaps reflecting the international requirements of the newer users, and the benefits of ZAMNET in economizing over traditional communication methods (fax, telephone and courier).

A Breakdown of the Users

The majority of urban users of the non-commercial Fidonet service prior to ZAMNET's formation have now subscribed to the Interactive service. Those remaining with Fidonet include:

- Users in rural areas (notably the health community) from where telephone calls to Lusaka are expensive, and telephone line quality is often too weak to support interactive communication.
- University users who will remain on the Fidonet system until the installation of the campus network has been completed.
- Long term users of the Fidonet system who are due to leave Zambia shortly and therefore do not wish to upgrade to the new interactive service.
- Some United Nations agencies that are currently planning to connect their own network directly to ZAMNET with a local leased data circuit but, in the interim, would prefer to continue to use the technology with which their users are familiar.

Looking at the geographical and categorical breakdown of the Fidonet and interactive subscribers, it is clear that the vast majority of users of both systems are Lusaka based. (See Table 3.) While this is not surprising, the significantly smaller concentration of users on the Copperbelt, Zambia's other major urban area, is more unusual and perhaps can be explained by the greater difficulty in fully supporting a service to users who are based outside of Lusaka. It will be necessary to consider a point of presence on the Copperbelt to rectify this and also to consider ways in which greater support can be provided to rural users.

TABLE 3   Users by Province

Province	Fidonet	Interactive	Total
Lusaka Province	38	165	203
Copperbelt	6	12	18
Southern Province	7	4	11
Western Province	7	3	10
Eastern Province	5	1	6
Northern Province	3	2	5
Northwestern Province	0	3	3
Luapula Province	1	1	2
Central Province	0	2	2
TOTAL	67	193	260

Analysis of the new interactive subscribers by category is particularly difficult. (See Table 4.) Beyond learning that companies are commercial, no attempt has been made to determine the line of work in which a subscribing company is involved. Many of the private individuals joining ZAMNET as non-commercial subscribers are attached to development organizations or international NGOs and use their points professionally. Again we have made no attempt to survey the uses made of email and so further analysis is impossible.

BOX 4   Email to Fax Service

ZAMNET has recently reached an agreement with GreenNet in London that allows ZAMNET customers to send email messages to fax machines. These messages are delivered to London via the Internet and are then delivered from there at the cost of the delivering phone call. For faxes to Europe and to North America, this results in a total fax cost of less than 50 cents per page. An informative acknowledgment email message confirms to the sender whether or not the fax has been delivered. Delivery times are usually less than 20 minutes after the email has been sent, which is perfectly satisfactory for ZAMNET's customers.

TABLE 4   Users by Category

Category	Fidonet	Interactive	Total
Private	2	53	55
Health	30	18	48
University/Research	18	11	28
Development	6	18	24
Agriculture	8	9	17
Religion	1	15	16
Government	0	6	6
Education/Schools	0	5	5
Environment	0	5	5
Tech Training	0	2	2
Journalism	0	1	1
Other	2	4	6
Commercial	0	46	46
TOTAL	67	193	259

Apart from the 55 private individual accounts and 46 commercial accounts, the largest category among the rest of the accounts is in health. As indicated by the number of accounts still using Fidonet, many health and agriculture accounts were users of the previous non-commercial service. Since the new ZAMNET service was put in place there has been a growing interest from a number of religious organizations active in Zambia (most of whom have head offices in the United States or Europe), and encouragingly recent interest from the Ministries of Finance and of Foreign Affairs.

Feedback

ZAMNET has received very positive feedback from its customers within and outside of Zambia. Zambian expatriates write to us saying how proud they feel that Zambia is only the fifth African country to establish a full Internet service. Starved of information about their home country, they are eager to see expanded news and information services through ZAMNET.

ZAMNET customers within Zambia are particularly pleased with the cost savings that communicating by email has brought. With international telephone calls to North America and Europe billed at $7.00 per minute, the ability to make a cheap local telephone call and send an email message for about 20 cents per page is very attractive. To find that this message is delivered reliably and within minutes is an added bonus. (See Box 4.)

Media Coverage

As the Internet has received more and more coverage in the international media, ZAMNET has correspondingly come under the spotlight within Zambia.

The *Zambia Daily Mail*, the *Times of Zambia,* and the *Weekly Post* have all published articles about the Internet and its arrival in Zambia (the Post subsequently subscribing to the ZAMNET service). *Profit Magazine,* Zambia's leading business magazine published a full leading article about ZAMNET complete with a front page image of some example WWW pages captured from the Internet.

The Zambia National Broadcasting Corporation has regular computing and business programs that make reference to information technology and the Internet. We hope that a full interview with the Managing Director of ZAMNET will be broadcast soon, while plans exist to connect ZNBC to ZAMNET in the near future.

Further afield, the efforts that Zambia has made to provide an email service and to establish a full Internet connection have been mentioned several times on the African service of the BBC World Service. In fact when the BBC began using email and started accepting questions to their Pop Science program, the very first email question that they received came from an email user in Ndola, Zambia.

ANALYSIS OF LESSONS LEARNED

Just four months after the ZAMNET product was made available to the public, its existing infrastructure is already creaking. Its communications link to the rest of the Internet is becoming congested at certain times of the day. Its mail server is overloaded and does not have the memory or disk capacity to cope with a significant increase in either the number of ZAMNET customers, or in the number of Internet users from outside of Zambia accessing its information services. Without a doubt the main area where ZAMNET might have been launched differently was in its technical capacity.

Capital Funding

ZAMNET's initial budgets should have been significantly higher and included items vital to the provision of a high quality, high volume, large customer base service. Namely, in hindsight, we should have begun with a SUN workstation, VSAT communications, a router capable of handling asynchronous communication, and a full set of equipment to provide backup in the event of system failures. While these items would have increased the initial cost of ZAMNET significantly, repayment of that cost could have been spread over a number of years.

Staff Training

Providing technical support from a position of considerable inexperience has been difficult. While the staff currently in place are learning fast, sustainability of the ZAMNET service is not only dependent upon them but also on the availability of suitable staff to supplement and replace the existing staff in the future. With this in mind there needs to be greater opportunities for Zambians to learn about Internet technology without having to travel outside of the region.

CONCLUSIONS AND RECOMMENDATIONS

ZAMNET is providing an important and much needed service to all sectors of Zambian society:

- businesses and industries need a fast, reliable and economical communications system in order to compete within the newly liberalized Zambian economy;
- international development organizations need to keep in regular touch with their projects in the field and their head offices overseas;
- the academic sector and researchers need access to the latest research and need to keep abreast of international developments in their field;
- government ministries need an efficient means of communication with district and provincial offices in the fields of agriculture, health and education; and
- private individuals wish to keep in touch with their friends abroad or simply wish to use the Internet as a vast encyclopedia.

Both commercial and non-commercial customers have shown a willingness to pay the fees that ZAMNET has set in order to cover the considerable costs of its service.

Because its customers now rely upon its service, ZAMNET needs to ensure its future both technically and economically. At the current, very fast growth rate, the system will be overstretched within twelve months, by which time the customer base should have more than doubled to over 600 accounts. The resulting reduced performance could seriously damage the positive image of ZAMNET. Meanwhile the lack of technical backup within the system leaves the whole service vulnerable in the event of an equipment failure. The downside of this is the capital expenditure involved in safeguarding against possible disasters. ZAMNET urgently needs to look at ways it can improve and upgrade its services.

Increasing the Bandwidth

The capacity of the Internet link between Lusaka and Cape Town will not be able to support 20 simultaneously connected users without a significant and noticeable deterioration in performance. The most promising option for increasing the capacity of this link appears to be a direct VSAT link from the ZAMNET offices in Lusaka to our Internet service provider in Cape Town, or failing that, an alternative link direct to the United States or United Kingdom. Although continued cooperation with counterparts in the region would be desirable, progress in negotiations with Telkom (the South African PTT) have not been productive so far. Based on the cost estimates provided so far, we know that the hardware costs of a VSAT link, plus annual rental and license fees should prove cheaper than the line we are leasing from ZAMNET and TELKOM at a cost of over $60,000 per year. The disadvantages of this strategy will be the expertise expected of the technical support staff and the cost of paying for both the existing and the VSAT link during the transition. Indeed it may be desirable to maintain the existing link to provide redundancy in the event of failure of the VSAT connection.

Increasing Dial-up Access

With the current customer base, we have rarely observed more than eight ports on the Portmaster modem server active simultaneously. Further expansion to serve 600 customers, while also accommodating increased activity among the existing users, is likely to put severe pressure on our dial-up. This expansion can only be accommodated through the purchase of a second modem server and a further batch of dial-up telephone lines. Over the next year a number of leased line customers will also subscribe to ZAMNET thus putting further pressure on the number of free ports available on the existing system.

Covering for Equipment Failures

The current system is highly vulnerable in the event of any kind of equipment failure. ZAMNET service would be lost in the event of:

- the loss of the leased line modem at either end of the data circuit that links ZAMNET to the Internet;
- the loss of the router linking the ZAMNET LAN to the Internet; or
- the loss of the Portmaster providing local access to the Internet to ZAMNET customers.

None of this equipment is readily available within Zambia and, even if finances were available, the resulting loss of service while replacements were being shipped from abroad could last for several days and have a serious impact on the image of ZAMNET among its customers. Spare items to replace those listed above would cost about $8,000.

Increase Capacity on Mail and Information Servers

The current mail server is running on a 40 MHz 486 PC with just 8 megabytes of RAM and a 400 megabyte hard disk and is already overloaded. As the number of customers and the volume of local information being provided to users outside of Zambia increases, the burden on this machine will also increase. A second machine is currently being configured as a News Server to accommodate the growing number of useful log files that the system generates. However this machine is itself only a 25 MHz personal computer, albeit with a one gigabyte hard drive.

ZAMNET needs to invest in a much more powerful personal computer with at least 32 megabytes of RAM and another high capacity hard drive. Ideally ZAMNET would seek to obtain a SUN workstation or equivalent, which is capable of running some of the software needed for maintaining the Portmaster and for monitoring traffic passing through the Cisco router. However the cost of such a SUN machine would be $10,000 or more!

Expanding the Range of Provided Services

There is an immediate need to provide a News Server to enable ZAMNET's customers to participate in the many discussion groups available over the Internet. Work to configure such a Server is currently under way, although the impact of a full news feed on the limited bandwidth of the Internet connection has yet to be determined. It is likely that such a feed would be dependent on the implementation of the VSAT link.

As the Internet develops further, other applications will be developed and ZAMNET needs to be in a position to make these applications available to its customers (within the limitations of the bandwidth of its Internet connection). Current examples include "Real Audio" and the ability to communicate by voice over the Internet.

Increasing Technical and Administrative Support

ZAMNET currently employs just three staff, one administrator and two technical support staff. This team is severely stretched in its efforts to provide support and to develop the ZAMNET staff. We have decided to employ an assistant administrator to ease the workload.

With the anticipated growth, it will be important for ZAMNET to employ at least one additional skilled and experienced technical member of staff within the next twelve months. With both the contracts of the ZAMNET technical staff due for renewal at the same time, the possible impact of these employees departing at the end of their contracts also needs to be anticipated.

Looking Forward

This chapter was written in June 1995 and I want to provide a quick update. By January 1996, ZAMNET had grown to accommodate 417 interactive accounts. These accounts generated 9,558 connections totalling 1,600 hours of connect time and 12,862 international messages. This is a growth rate of 100 percent in just eight months. We have taken several steps to ease the growing congestion on both the Internet link and the server computers and to provide protection in the event of system failures:

We ordered the VSAT terminal equipment and it has been shipped from the United States. We need to complete some administrative procedures before it can be used but we hope that a 64 kilobaud VSAT connection direct from ZAMNET's offices to Johannesburg will be operational before the end of March 1996.

We maintain the Portmaster users table on the WWW server machine using Livingston's Radius software.

We moved the WWW server from the mail server to a second computer, which has been configured as a News Server, although we still do not receive a full news feed from the Internet. We just ordered a new mail server (a Pentium 120 with 32 megabytes of RAM and a 2 gigabyte hard drive).

We have recruited a new assistant administrator.

Within the next year ZAMNET plans to increase the number of access telephone lines to 40 and purchase an extra 20 V34 modems and a second Portmaster to serve these lines; employ two additional technical staff, a marketing manager, and another junior administrator; and provide local telephone access to customers based in the Copperbelt.

We have proven that the provision of an Internet service is viable and can pay for itself. The costs of expansion require capital expenditure and, ultimately, an injection of capital from investors either in the form of loans or in the broadening of shareholding is required. Most importantly, however, several months before the end of the World Bank funding, ZAMNET is self-sufficient and is able to buy new equipment from its own funds and to guarantee repayment on any loans it requires. This healthy position should enable ZAMNET to significantly reduce its fees within the next three months and to continue to expand services to meet it customers' demands.

NOTES

1. The East and Southern African Academic Network (ESANET) is described more fully in Musisi's case study in this volume. See page 158.

2. Moussa Fall gives a more detailed description of Fidonet in his case study in this volume. See page 143.

3. Each member of the Fidonet system has a unique address. This address identifies the zone, the host, and the node. The point number will ensure that a message gets to a specific user in the node's subsystem.

CASE STUDIES ON THE COLLECTION, MANAGEMENT, AND DISSEMINATION OF LOCAL INFORMATION RESOURCES

Many STI projects focus less on the technology and more on the management of information and the content of databases. Databases from abroad do not generally give adequate coverage of research efforts in developing countries and African scientists have learned that they cannot depend on such outside sources for the services needed to keep them abreast of local developments in their subject fields. The following group of case studies focuses on efforts made to collect local information, to organize it into usable forms, and then to disseminate it to those who can put it to good use.

Thus one case study in this section is about a group of natural products researchers who banded together to form a professional network that unites them through newsletters, conferences, publications, and now, electronic means.

The next case study describes how a research institute in Botswana collected local data to produce an indigenous database on socioeconomic information. The project manager learned that she required expertise in subject analysis and indexing, system design, database management, and access to computer hardware.

The Kenya Medical Research Institute decided to focus on their institutional needs for information and designed an information system that included all aspects of their data needs. Their case study demonstrates that many management tasks can be aided by automated data processing and that the introduction of computers can aid the decision-making process, provide information about financial and human resources, improve turnaround time for data analysis and report writing; and improve the quality of data organization and analysis. By adding equipment for desktop publishing and CD-ROM searches they realized the same benefits of other case study authors.

The CSIR in Ghana took a serious look at its mandate and designed a system to improve national access to scientific and technological information. National systems are difficult to manage and finance but the rewards can be great, as demonstrated in this final case study.

NAPRECA and Its Role in the Dissemination of Information on Natural Products Research in Africa

by Ermias Dagne

Ermias Dagne is one of the founders and the immediate past Executive Secretary of NAPRECA. He is an associate professor in the Chemistry Department of Addis Ababa University. He gratefully acknowledges the editorial assistance of Wendimagegn Mammo in writing this paper. Dr. Mammo is also an assistant professor in the same department.

BACKGROUND AND CONTEXT OF THE PROJECT

This paper describes the background history, objectives, and main activities of the Natural Products Research Network for Eastern and Central Africa, known in short as NAPRECA. We give particular emphasis to the role of the network in improving the scientific and technological information (STI) scene in Africa.

Origin and History

The Fourteenth IUPAC (International Union of Pure and Applied Chemistry) International Symposium on the Chemistry of Natural Products was held in July 1984, in Poznan, Poland. Over one thousand participants from all over the world attended that symposium, including six Africans.[1] As we Africans met during the breaks and the social occasions, we realized that there were no such fora in Africa, even though there were many natural products there who could benefit from the exchange of experiences and ideas. Our meetings took on a more formal character as we discussed ways to circumvent the isolation and alienation that African researchers faced. We unanimously resolved to found a network to bring scientists engaged in natural products research in Africa closer together and to link those researchers with colleagues around the world who were involved in tackling research problems of relevance to Africa.

We felt that the task of a network should not be to build infrastructure, new centers, or new laboratories but instead to work towards strengthening national capabilities through regional and international cooperation. We called for the sharing of existing facilities and resources in the sub-region. As a first step in this direction, we agreed to concentrate on information dissemination and exchange of ideas through publications, including a biannual newsletter and other means. These discussions led to the crystallization of the network's constitution.

Before the end of the Poznan meeting, we resolved to name the network the *Natural Products Research Network for Eastern and Central Africa*, or NAPRENCA. Later an "N" in the acronym was dropped and the Network came to be known in short as NAPRECA. We felt that Africa was too big an area to encompass initially and, for the sake of expediency and modesty, we realistically started with a sub-regional approach. Had there been participants from other parts of Africa in that meeting, the arguments might have been different. In any case, the geographic definition for the network satisfied all those present and the consensus reached heralded the birth of NAPRECA.

I was elected Chairman and Editor of the Network's newsletter and we asked Berhanu M. Abegaz of the same department as myself at Addis Ababa University to serve as Secretary and Treasurer. The rationale for this decision was to avoid having the two officers in different countries, a situation that would have paralyzed the Network right from its inception.

PROJECT DESCRIPTION

Upon returning to our homes, our initial enthusiasm did not wane; on the contrary, all concerned received the idea of founding a regional network for natural products scientists with joy. In Ethiopia, B.M. Abegaz prepared the final version of the constitution and came up with invaluable suggestions and ideas on how to launch NAPRECA and initiate the newsletter. (See Box 1.)

The maiden issue of the NAPRECA Newsletter came out in September 1984, immediately after the founding meeting of a NAPRECA branch in Ethiopia. The editorial of that issue stated that:

BOX 1   The Chairman as Editor

The idea of entrusting the task of editor to the chairman of NAPRECA was judicious. As one of the main tasks of a network is information dissemination, anyone exercising the leadership of a network should take this duty to heart and ensure the continuous flow of information through publication of a newsletter and other circulars. The *raison d'etre* of a network depends on how well this task is handled. Consequently this was a task that could not be delegated but executed right from NAPRECA's top position.

"in order for the African scientist to be worthy of the noble name . . . the current state of isolation has to be combatted and scientific fora created which will contribute to the amelioration of the present dismal state of research and academic activity."

This issue also echoed the importance of contacts and exchange of information. The editorial made a strong appeal to all natural products researchers in the region to interact with each other and to initiate programs of mutual interest. It stated, "the birth of an organization *per se* is not a historic event. What is more significant is whether such an organization will live up to its name." The publication and worldwide distribution of this issue was made possible by contributions from the members in Ethiopia.

In Kenya, J. Ogur, senior lecturer of chemistry at the University of Nairobi, brought together a large team of researchers and educators and founded NAPRECA-Kenya, where he emerged as chairman. This branch was formally registered by the Kenya Registrar of Societies in January 1986. Although no Tanzanian took part in the deliberations in Poznan, colleagues at the University of Dar es Salaam were swift in taking up the idea and founded a branch that was registered in October 1985. At the same time a branch was also founded in the Sudan.

Colleagues in Zimbabwe decided to merge the NAPRECA concept with an existing association with similar objectives, namely NAPRAZ (Natural Products Association of Zimbabwe). This was fraught with problems from the start. Although an understanding was reached from the outset that NAPRAZ would be like a NAPRECA branch, in reality this never worked. In December 1988, a separate NAPRECA-Z was founded. This turn of events contributed to a weakening of the branch in Zimbabwe, a problem that has not been circumvented to date.

In Ethiopia, NAPRECA became affiliated with Addis Ababa University (AAU) and the Chemistry Department served as the seat of the Coordinating Office. This meant that NAPRECA benefited from the administrative framework of the University. Funds for the NAPRECA Coordinating Office were administered by the university as a project account. Since overhead charges are waived on most grant accounts in AAU, this arrangement was greatly appreciated right from the start. The network was also able to use such university facilities as guest houses, halls, and laboratories.

In March 1987, John Kingston, a senior officer in the Division of Basic Sciences in UNESCO, came to Addis Ababa leading a mission to the Ethiopian Science and Technology Commission. That occasion provided an opportune moment to discuss cooperation between UNESCO and NAPRECA. Jack Canon, an Australian scientist, senior UNESCO advisor, and chairman of the Australian Network for the Chemistry of Biologically Active Natural Products (NCBNP), strongly supported the idea of affiliating NAPRECA to UNESCO. The NAPRECA branches in Ethiopia, Kenya, Sudan, Tanzania, and Zimbabwe urged their respective UNESCO national commissions to support the motion of affiliation at the UNESCO

General Assembly in November 1987. NAPRECA was formally declared a UNESCO affiliated organization, entitling it to receive direct financial support from UNESCO's regular budget.

This recognition boosted the morale of the membership and gave the young network a wider international recognition. Its meager financial resources were also increased. It was then possible to call a meeting of the NAPRECA Coordinating Board, with representatives from each of the then five member countries, namely J.A. Ogur and R.M. Munavu (Kenya); A. Taha (Sudan); H. Weenen (Tanzania); N.Z. Nyazema (Zimbabwe), and, of course, ourselves from Ethiopia. The meeting took place in Addis Ababa in March 1988.

NAPRECA was pleased with UNESCO's decision to send the Director of the Division of Scientific Research and Higher Education in Paris and the Director of UNESCO-ROSTA in Nairobi to the March meeting. The International Foundation for Science (IFS) sent its scientific advisor as an observer. J. Ayafor (Cameroon) and J. Mungarulire (Rwanda) came as observers. The latter country joined NAPRECA a year later.[2]

At the First Meeting of the NAPRECA Coordinating Board, we adopted the constitution of the network, elected its officers, and decided that Ethiopia would be the seat of the Coordinating Office. I was elected Executive Secretary and B.M. Abegaz was elected Assistant Secretary-Treasurer. H. Guadey[3] joined as Program Officer and ex-officio member of the Coordinating Board. Although NAPRECA had existed since 1984, this board meeting heralded the active chapter in the history of the network. Since that time, we have held eight annual meetings and the number of member countries has increased. With the joining of Rwanda, Uganda, and Madagascar in 1988, 1989, and 1990, respectively, our membership rose to eight countries.

A day after the first NAPRECA Board Meeting, a scientific session was held. As all of the Board Members and most of the observers were active researchers in the field of natural products, each made a presentation followed by discussions. This hurriedly organized scientific conference was christened the *First NAPRECA Symposium on Natural Products.* The high quality of the presentations and the enthusiasm with which the one-day symposium was received gave a clear signal that such events in Africa were long overdue.

In the same year, the International Program in the Chemical Sciences (IPICS), based in Upsalla, Sweden, started to offer NAPRECA annual grants, particularly in support of the Exchange of Researchers Scheme, the Summer School Programs, and the symposia and specialized workshops. The IPICS grant was kept mainly in Sweden and used for settling expenses directly from there, relying on the efficient secretariat in Uppsalla. We have on many occasions also benefited from the advice and guidance of Rune Liminga, Director of IPICS, who has vast experience in networking in Africa, Asia, and Latin America.

The main aim of the network as articulated in the constitution is to "initiate, develop and promote research in the area of natural products in the Eastern and

Central African sub-region." Dissemination of information pertaining to natural products research is one of the major objectives of NAPRECA. The importance of establishing links with counterparts in other parts of the world was emphasized right from the outset, as one of the objectives of the network is to "foster and maintain links with such scientists who are actively working in specific areas of natural products that are pertinent to Africa." The sections that follow will attempt to show to what extent NAPRECA has been successful in putting these aims to practice.

PROJECT EXPERIENCE AND IMPLEMENTATION

Seven categories of activities will be described in this section. In short, these are:

- Dissemination of information through publication of a biannual newsletter, monograph series and symposium abstracts;
- Administration of a post-graduate scholarship program;
- Implementation of an Exchange of Researchers Scheme;
- Organization of the Natural Products Summer School;
- Convening of the Natural Products Symposium once every two years;
- Conducting training workshops; and
- Coordination of the UNESCO's Botany 2000 program.

Publications

The NAPRECA Newsletter is published twice a year. About one thousand copies of each issue are distributed free of charge to readers in various parts of the world. Sometimes the founding of organizations by novices will lead to the launching of some form of publication—invariably designated as Volume 1, Number 1. Too often, Volume 1, Number 2 never sees the light of day and the new organization or association withers to oblivion! When the first issue of the NAPRECA Newsletter came out, we were warned of such a pitfall. But, so far, we have succeeded in maintaining our publishing schedule and we have now distributed 24 issues of the newsletter.

Reactions to the maiden issue of the NAPRECA Newsletter were mostly congratulatory, although some people pointed out mistakes and offered advice. Thus Dr. M. William, Executive Secretary of IUPAC wrote:

"... I was most interested to receive the Maiden Issue of the NAPRECA Newsletter and to learn that the Network arose from the IUPAC symposium held in Poland in July 1984. . ."

J.I. Okogun of the Chemistry Department of Ibadan University, Nigeria wrote:

". . . the Newsletter serves its purpose to inform us all on developments in the area of natural products."

We also welcomed criticisms—such as the one by the botanist Tewolde B.G. Egziabher, then President of Asmara University, who wrote:

"There were some spelling errors in the maiden issue. . . similar errors should be avoided in the future. . . I suggest that you check the spelling of every scientific name before you print. Even if you feel you know the scientific name very well, it is worth checking each name routinely every time."

The suggestions and criticisms of our readership greatly contributed to sustaining the Newsletter for 12 years. Four years ago NAPRECA began publishing a series of monographs, the first of which was a NAPRECA Year-Book, entitled *Eight Years of Existence and Four Years of Intensive Activities,* Z. Asfaw (Ed.), 1992.

Administration of Postgraduate Scholarship Program

A postgraduate scholarship program was born during a visit by the German Academic Exchange Service (Deutscher Akademischer Austauschdienst, DAAD) delegation to Addis Ababa in October 1987. A conference for former DAAD fellows was taking place and on one evening during that conference, I happened to sit beside Mr. Richard Jacob, who then headed the Africa desk of DAAD in Bonn. I commented that international organizations like DAAD rarely support initiatives at local levels and that such organizations more often follow the top-down approach. I continued to narrate the story of NAPRECA and how much we would have appreciated it if some DAAD scholarships could have been administered by the network for the purpose of training the young in the natural products field. He suggested that, if we submitted a convincing proposal, his organization would offer the network five scholarships per year.

In March of 1988, the German ambassador to Ethiopia, His Excellency Dr. Kurt Stoeckle, personally brought to the Faculty of Science a letter signed by Dr. Berchem, President of DAAD, declaring the award of five scholarships to NAPRECA. Since then, NAPRECA has received a similar letter from the President of DAAD every year.

In this DAAD-NAPRECA scholarship program NAPRECA is responsible for selecting the candidates, who must enroll in a post-graduate program in a university outside of their own country. DAAD scholarships cover tuition, research costs, and subsistence allowances of the fellows in universities in the sub-region. The cost of the scholarship per student per annum varies from country to country but is within the range of six to seven thousand U.S. dollars. The first beneficiaries were two Ethiopians who, in September 1988, joined the MSc program of the University of Nairobi and three Kenyans who came to Addis Ababa to join postgraduate programs in biology and chemistry. A total of 39 scholarships have so far been awarded to selected individuals. Of these, 15 have completed their MSc studies; eight, including two PhD candidates, discontinued or were dismissed on academic grounds; and 16 are still pursuing their studies.

A follow-up conference was organized in cooperation with DAAD in November 1993. Former fellows were invited to interact with their peers and former instructors. Despite the problems, briefly dealt with in Section 5, we faced in implementing this program, we are of the opinion that the DAAD-NAPRECA fellowship program was one of the most rewarding offshoots of the network.

Implementing the Exchange of Researchers Scheme

In an early issue of the NAPRECA Newsletter, we described the problems faced by African scientists as:

"Isolation, lack of contact with each other as well as with peers elsewhere, absence of conducive atmosphere of research, coupled with meager resources. . ."

We thought that an Exchange Scheme might be one of the best remedies of these ills. NAPRECA, therefore, invested considerable energy and resources in implementing this scheme, thanks in particular to the financial support of two organizations, UNESCO and IPICS. Many junior as well as senior scientists have benefited from this scheme.

Under the Exchange Scheme, a selected fellow is granted the opportunity to spend a month or two in a laboratory within the sub-region. Preference is given to candidates who are able to find funds for travel and then the research and subsistence expenses are covered by NAPRECA. So far 32 individuals have benefited from the exchange, with an average stay of one and half months in a regional laboratory. (See Box 2.)

Organizing the Natural Products Summer School

One of the regular activities of NAPRECA is the organization and implementation of Natural Products Summer Schools. Six Summer Schools were organized between 1988 and 1994. The main aim of the Summer School is to enhance the research capabilities of participants, in particular in chromatographic, spectroscopic, and bioassay techniques. Research scientists and technical assistants working for various institutions in the region have used the opportunity to improve upon their laboratory skills. Usually about a dozen participants take part in the Summer School; half of these come from outside the country where the program takes place.

BOX 2   Benefits of the Exchange Scheme

One of the recent participants in the Exchange of Researchers program was Ildephonse Murengezi, Chairman of NAPRECA-Rwanda. Our efforts to locate him after the tragic events in that country led us to the refugee camp in Goma on the border to Zaire. At the beginning of 1995, as soon as the Ethiopian Airlines resumed flights to Kigali, we sent him a ticket and invited him to come to Addis Ababa as an Exchange Fellow, where he stayed for six months working in a natural products laboratory [See NAPRECA Newsletter, Vol. 12, No. 1]

Each Summer School was rated highly by the participants. Particularly those researchers who had little or no exposure to modern research settings have found this program highly beneficial.

Natural Products Symposia

As the NAPRECA concept got off the ground in an IUPAC Symposium on Natural Products, it is only natural for the network to pay special attention to organizing similar conferences in Africa. So far six natural products symposia have been organized in the five member countries.

The first symposium was indeed a modest one, convened immediately after the first meeting of the Coordinating Board in March 1988. No book of abstracts came out of that event. As our Kenyan colleagues were very keen about organizing a conference, the second was held quickly thereafter in Nairobi in September 1988. Sixteen participants came from outside of Kenya to the second symposium. We published a booklet with nearly 20 brief abstracts in advance of the symposium. We included pictures of the speakers at the end of the book, a feature that has been kept in subsequent symposia booklets.

The third symposium was held in Arusha, Tanzania, in May 1989. It drew over 40 participants from outside of the host country and the local organizers were able to publish an impressive book of proceedings, with 22 full papers and nearly as many abstracts. The Arusha symposium set a high standard not only in terms of the quality of the scientific presentations but also in the excellent way in which it was organized.

In the Third Coordinating Board meeting that took place in Arusha, we agreed to organize subsequent symposia every two years. That led to the fourth symposium in Addis Ababa, in December 1991. The increased number of papers required, for the first time, the holding of parallel sessions. The Symposium Book, published prior to the conference, was of high quality with 28 papers appearing as extended abstracts. In retrospect that was indeed a good decision. The preparation of conference proceedings is a thankless job, because it is done after the event is over. Extended abstracts published in advance of the conference, make it easier to put pressure on participants to submit papers of reasonable standard. This has made the NAPRECA Symposium Extended Abstracts frequently cited sources of information.

The fifth symposium held in Antananarivo, Madagascar, in September 1993, enabled a large contingent of researchers from South Africa to participate for the first time in a NAPRECA activity. Prior to this meeting, it was not possible for scientists from South Africa to mingle with their counterparts from other African countries. Nearly a dozen well known South African scientists came to the symposium and this had an impact on the quality of the oral as well as poster presentations. It was humorous to hear a South African professor say at the beginning of his lecture that he was extremely pleased because he was "for the first time in Africa." As Madagascar was a Francophone country there were several participants who came from Francophone Africa and France, and one parallel session was dominated by papers presented in French.

The sixth symposium that took place in Kampala, Uganda, in September 1995. This symposium attracted about 80 participants who came from various countries in Africa, Europe and North America. The scientific meeting covered 12 general and 28 parallel session lectures, as well as 32 poster presentations. A book of extended abstracts was published and distributed at the opening session of the symposium. Three pre-symposium short courses on Nuclear Magnetic Resonance (NMR), Mass Spectrometry, and Organic Synthesis were held at the same venue. The courses were designed to upgrade the skills of young researchers in applying or interpreting the results of these modern techniques in their own research. A total of 27 participants coming from seven African countries participated in the three short courses.

Participants' assessments of the symposium were very positive and some were unreserved with their kind words of praise.

"...The very successfully organized NAPRECA's sixth symposium was an event that one would wish to witness again. . ." wrote Gizachew Alemayehu, Ethiopia.

A leading natural products chemist, Joe Connolly, Glasgow, UK, commented:

"...Congratulations for the excellently organized NAPRECA's sixth symposium and the pre-symposium short courses . . . It was great to be in Kampala with your team."

I realize how far-reaching the impact of these symposia are when a Kenyan colleague who was sitting next to me during a session in the sixth symposium pointed to a group of scientists from Europe, and said:

"These people did not take us seriously when we started holding such conferences in Africa some years back, but now they listen to us attentively when we make scientific presentations."

Conducting Training Workshops

NAPRECA has organized four major training programs so far. The first was the IFS-NAPRECA Workshop on NMR Techniques, which took place in Addis Ababa in December 1991. NMR is one of the most useful methods in structure elucidation of substances isolated from plants. It is also one of those techniques that develops by leaps and bounds and it is therefore of paramount importance for a chemist to keep abreast of these changes.

IFS and NAPRECA held a symposium on bioassay methods in Antananarivo, Madagascar in September, 1993, as a pre-symposium program. The focus of the program was on ways to screen substances for anti-malarial activity. IFS support ensured that several participants could come from several countries in the region.

Another two month program, held from April to June 1993, was a training workshop on herbarium techniques, which was organized in cooperation with the National Herbarium in Addis Ababa. As plants are the major sources of natural products, their identification and documentation is of great importance for natural products research. This program was designed for technicians who work in herbaria of the region. It included lectures and practicals on botany and related disciplines.

The fourth in this series was a training program on glass blowing techniques which was held in Uganda in January 1995. The instructor was Mr. Wodajie Imru, senior glass blower of the Chemistry Department, Addis Ababa University. All the 12 trainees were glass blowers serving in various research and academic institutions in Uganda. This program speaks for the need to improve skills of research support staff. (See Box 3.)

Coordination of the UNESCO's Botany 2000 program

The Director General of UNESCO launched an initiative called Botany 2000, which is basically an interdisciplinary program that attempts to link three disciplines, namely botany, chemistry, and pharmacology. NAPRECA was designated to take the lead in coordinating the Africa Botany 2000 program. As part of that activity, NAPRECA organized a training program for Herbarium Technicians, sup-

---

BOX 3   Co-funding Opportunities

Funding from one agency often opens the door for funding from another. For example, in the first training workshop, a grant from DAAD enabled us to bring a topnotch NMR specialist, Dr. S. Berger, to lead the one week intensive workshop. IFS made it possible to bring some of the leading natural products researchers of Africa, selected on the basis of their scientific output.

ported activities in documenting rare and endangered plant species of Africa, and supported exchange programs that fall within the scope of Botany 2000.

RESULTS, IMPACTS, AND BENEFITS OF THE PROJECT

Many research groups in Africa and indeed in many other parts of the world are engaged in the isolation, characterization, and evaluation of the biological activities of natural products occurring in plants and animals of African origin. Currently, most of the studies on natural products from African plants and animals are conducted by research groups based in Europe and North America, cooperating in some cases with groups in African universities and research institutions. Consequently, most of the scientific papers describing the output of such work appear in scholarly journals published outside of Africa. In too many cases researchers in the country where the plant material of the research originated are not fully aware of the research results.

It is important to follow the literature in the field to know more about our own resources and take measures for their sustainable use. Following progress in the field, is also of paramount importance to ensure that the county of origin shares in the benefits resulting from the use of natural products discovered from African plants and animals.

There are many international natural products chemistry journals that deal with plant constituents and their biological activities. Of these, the three with wide international coverage are: *Journal of Natural Products, Planta Medica,* and *Phytochemistry.* These journals frequently publish research results on the study of the constituents of African plants. We therefore dedicate one regular column in the NAPRECA Newsletter to list all those papers on African plants that appear in these journals. The column attracts the attention of many researchers whose libraries do not subscribe to these journals.

A compilation of the information in this column in the period 1984–1994 now forms the basis of a database. In the three journals, we found nearly 1,000 articles dealing with either the chemistry, biology, or pharmacology of plants collected from different parts of Africa. The full details of this database are now published in Monograph Series No. 8.

In the 1,000 articles various types of compound classes are reported from the African plants such as alkaloids, anthraquinones, flavonoids, and steroids. In terms of utility of the products, anti-cancer, anti-fungal, anti-bacterial, anti-malarial, anti-feedant and molluscicidal activities are by far the most prominent. Over 56 papers give chemotaxonomy as a significant outcome of the studies and 29 deal with the culturally and commercially important essential oil bearing plants of Africa.

The limitation of the above mentioned database is obvious, as it is based on articles in only three international journals covering just an 11 year period. Nevertheless, it gives an indication on the wealth of information that is coming out in the field of natural products from Africa. The database could also serve as a starting point in literature surveys on topics of interest to phytochemists and other natural products researchers interested in investigating African plants for the benefit of the peoples of Africa and elsewhere.

The publications of NAPRECA amply demonstrate that the network has achieved some of its objectives to a satisfactory degree. These publications have turned out to be frequently cited sources of information and ideas. NAPRECA has helped many researchers break their isolation. The symposia, training workshops, and summer schools organized by NAPRECA have served as excellent fora for the exchange of ideas and information. The benefits of all of these to promote research and development in the field of natural products research in Africa is obvious.

ANALYSIS OF LESSONS LEARNED

The most serious problems facing African networks are a consequence of poor communication and lack of appreciation for promoting inter-African contacts. Travel within Africa is indeed very difficult. Slow and undependable mail systems and poor fax, telephone, and telex connections exacerbate the problem. Going from one country to another requires the use of expensive air transport and, in most instances, one also has to take into consideration stringent visa requirements. There is very little opportunity for African scholars to visit other countries in the region, and many get unpleasant surprises when the first travel to another African country. We were taken by surprise when the first DAAD-NAPRECA fellows from Kenya came to Addis Ababa and spoke of culture shock and difficulties in adjusting to their new environment.

There is also a great deal of dependence on foreign currency. Fees to universities and other institutions, hotel bills, and airport taxes have to be paid in U.S. dollars. Many African scholars are accustomed to the generous travel arrangements offered by international agencies who organize conferences in or outside of Africa. NAPRECA could afford no luxuries. For example, a Ugandan lecturer was sent to Madagascar on a two-month exchange scheme. He returned home after 10 days because he felt the allowance he was given by NAPRECA was not sufficient. On another occasion, we secured a round trip air ticket from the Commonwealth Science Council in the United Kingdom for a senior lecturer to come to the sixth NAPRECA Symposium in Uganda. He failed to show up at the conference presumably because the donor did not provide him with per diem as well. By the time we learned of his decision, it was too late to use the travel grant.

On the other hand, there were several exemplary instances where exchange fellows did everything possible to sustain themselves with the very little we could give them in the form of allowance. Mesfin Bogale, an Ethiopian exchange fellow, wrote the following after his two months research visit to the Institut Malagache de Recherches Appliquées (IMRA) in Antananarivo, Madagascar:

". . .The subsistence and housing allowance given to me was $200 per month. On this allowance I could not afford to stay even in the cheapest inns in Antananarivo. Since the guest houses at IMRA were still under construction, the only option I had was to sleep in a room near the laboratory. . . The laboratory where I stayed had no facility for bathing. I could wash my hair in the laboratory sink. But I had to wash my body on the floor using buckets of water and mop the floor at the end."

During his stay in Antananarivo, Bogale tested forty-five samples for their antimalarial activity. The samples he found active were further tested for other kinds of activities. He wrote:

"The laboratory facilities and the working conditions are very good. This research visit to IMRA enabled me to complete my thesis project. In addition it provided me with a good opportunity to learn more laboratory techniques. . ."

Our experience has shown that organizing programs in Addis Ababa was much easier. This is because NAPRECA was entitled to use the guest house, student quarters, laboratory, lecture halls, and other facilities of the Addis Ababa University. Consequently many of the Summer School and Exchange of Researchers programs took place in Addis Ababa.

Network programs thrive on a give and take basis. One is a host at one time and a guest at another. He who gives in one round receives in another, and he who responds to a request at one moment also gets a response to his call in time of need. If we set aside the problems, network activities bring to all those participating many moments of joy and satisfaction. For me the most rewarding experience is the feeling of being at home whenever I am in any one of the NAPRECA member countries.

Looking back to the formative years of the network, just as there were moments of success, there were equally many instances of frustration and setbacks. The unprecedented tragic events in Rwanda, where many of our colleagues lost their lives or were forced to flee their country, is by far the worst of these setbacks.

Despite the above problems, it is gratifying for NAPRECA, in the words of Prof. P.J.M. Ssebuwufu, Vice Chancellor of Makerere University, to have "developed into an organization which has achieved a deservedly notable prestige within and outside of Africa." Equally uplifting are the kind words of the Nobel Laureate and President of the International Organization of Chemistry for Development (IOCD), Jean-Marie Lehn, who made the following remark while announcing a travel grant for participants of the sixth Symposium, "We believe support given to NAPRECA and its programs can multiply the impact of our modest contribution considerably since NAPRECA is a truly indigenous action among natural products chemists in Africa."

CONCLUSIONS AND RECOMMENDATIONS

The present office bearers of NAPRECA, E. Dagne, B.M. Abegaz, and H. Guadey of Addis Ababa University have served the network for the constitutionally allowable two terms since 1988. The 8th NAPRECA Coordinating Board meeting held in September 1995 in Kampala, Uganda, elected for a four-year term Drs. M.H.H. Nkunya and M.A. Kishimba of the Chemistry Department, University of Dar es Salaam, Tanzania, as Executive Secretary and Assistant Secretary/Treasurer, respectively. We believe, that the most important task of the new officers is to ensure the continuity of the network by not only maintaining the current tempo but also meeting new challenges and adding more dimensions to its activities while leading it into the 21st century.

Jack Canon, the Australian scientist closely associated with NAPRECA since its inception, reflected as follows on the challenges ahead:

". . .You are certainly handing on a very smoothly running organization to Tanzania and, as NAPRECA has now achieved a 'critical mass' of first class research workers I am sure that it will continue to flourish. I think that it is a reflection of the strength of NAPRECA and the goodwill existing between its members that it has been able to cope with the tragic madness which took place in Rwanda. I am sure NAPRECA will be able to help re-establish research in that country when full peace finally returns. . ."

There are also many other issues facing NAPRECA. In light of the improved email facilities in the region and possible Internet connectivity of several of the member countries in the near future, the new challenge for NAPRECA will be to tap these opportunities to advance networking among its membership and to provide them with vital information services.

For some of us, what we have achieved in the last decade is like a dream come true. I have witnessed that a handful of dedicated individuals can make an impact if they are committed to a cause. The concept of NAPRECA thrives because there are individuals who devote their time and energy for the accomplishment of the Network's ideals. We in NAPRECA have also learned the important lesson that we can make meaningful contributions to our respective nations, and to the sub-region at large, only if we pool together our meager resources for solving our common problems.

NOTES

1. The Africans in attendance were: J.A. Ogur, Chemistry Department, University of Nairobi; M. Gundidza of the University of Zimbabwe; A. Taha and M. Younis from Sudan; N. Matos from Mozambique; and myself. Matos was, at the time, a PhD student in Humboldt University, East Berlin. He is now the Director of the Association of African Universities which has its headquarters in Accra, Ghana.

2. It is interesting to note that colleagues in Cameroon and Ghana tried to establish a parallel West African network. Despite support from UNESCO and a founding meeting held in Ghana during the IFS and Kumasi University-sponsored scientific meeting in September 1990, the NAPRECA parallel network failed to take off.

3. Hailu Guadey was the first Ethiopian to get a University degree in chemistry, BSc (McGill University, Canada, 1950) and MSc (Howard University, U.S.A., 1959). He was assistant minister of health in the Haile Selassie regime and was retired in 1974 when that government was overthrown. He was then employed by NAPRECA as a program officer.

ACKNOWLEDGEMENTS

Finally, it is only fair to conclude this brief account by paying tribute to all colleagues and friends in the region and elsewhere in the world who have supported our efforts to make NAPRECA a successful venture. Special gratitude is also due to the donor agencies—in particular to SAREC (Swedish Agency for Research Co-operation with Developing Countries), UNESCO, DAAD, IPICS, IFS, TWAS, and IOCD who provided generous support for implementing NAPRECA's activities and programs.

A Socioeconomic Development Information System for Botswana
by Stella Monageng

Stella Monageng is the Senior Documentalist at the National Institute of Development Research and Documentation at the University of Botswana. She has wide experience in the development and management of computerized databases and has been working in this area of expertise since 1983.

BACKGROUND AND CONTEXT OF THE PROJECT

This case study describes my experiences in developing databases at the National Institute of Development Research and Documentation (NIR) of the University of Botswana. I will discuss a project entitled Development Sciences Information System for Botswana (DEVSIS-Botswana), which is the system we created to facilitate the collection, organization, and dissemination of Botswana's socioeconomic development information.

DEVSIS is a project that dates back to the mid-1970s, when a number of international agencies, including the International Development Research Centre (IDRC) of Canada, established a system that would help meet the information needs of planners and decision-makers responsible for economic and social development planning. The concept was never implemented as the global scheme that had been envisaged. Instead, a number of national and regional development information systems evolved out of the program. DEVSIS-Botswana is one example of such a national information system. In collaboration with the Pan African Development Information System (PADIS), the NIR launched our project in May 1984 with the financial assistance of IDRC.

The National Institute of Development
Research and Documentation (NIR)

The NIR was established in 1975 as a documentation center. In 1978, it added a research component. Its objectives are to:

a) Coordinate and conduct research on issues of socio-economic and environmental development affecting Botswana;

b) Develop the national research capacity within Botswana; and

c) Publish and disseminate the results of the research conducted.

The research activities focus on agriculture and rural development; education; environment; health and nutrition; Basarwa[1]; and women and gender issues.

The Documentation Unit of the NIR implemented the project. The Unit was established in 1975 and later developed into the present research institute. Its main objective is to collect, process, and disseminate unpublished or grey literature on or about Botswana. The Documentation Unit has a library through which the information that is collected and processed is disseminated.

The Documentation Unit and its library deliver the following products, technologies, and services:

- *Reference Service* through which we assist users in accessing the library's computerized databases.

- *Selective Dissemination of Information* through which we offer a current awareness service to the Institute's researchers through their research interest profiles.

- *Newspaper Clipping Service* through which we clip and file key articles falling within the research areas of the Institute.

- *Referral Service* that links NIR with other major information centers such as the National Library National Reference Collection, the University of Botswana Library Botswana Collection, and several Government department libraries.

- *Photocopying Service*, which is provided for a fee. This service is not only used locally but is also used by a lot of researchers from outside Botswana.

- *Computerized Databases* maintained by the library, the first of which was set up in 1986. Until quite recently, when the University of Botswana Library computerized its operations, the NIR Library was the only one with a computerized information system. This attracted a lot of researchers because it made retrieval time shorter and helped to inform the users whether or not certain information was available.

- *Devindex-Botswana*, which is an output of the computerized databases. Documents are collected, cataloged, abstracted, and indexed and then input into the computer. When a reasonable number of these have been processed, an index is produced.

- *Technologies* used include: electronic mail, through HealthNet and Internet; Facsimile; and CD-ROM. The Documentation Unit has been selected as a POPLINE site for Botswana and will therefore have the POPLINE CD-ROM database.

PROJECT DESCRIPTION

History of the Project

In 1981/1982 many information professionals were trying to establish an information system called the Southern African Documentation and Information System (SADIS). The envisaged aim of the system was to assist countries in the region to build up their information infrastructures as a basis for a coordinated regional information system. Unfortunately, the system never got off the ground.

Botswana, however, through the initiative of the NIR, decided to set up its own socioeconomic development information system. We approached PADIS for assistance in computerizing our documentation system and also in acquiring funding for the exercise. The NIR circulated a proposal among various government ministries for comments and suggestions. The responses received were so positive that the Ministry of Finance and Development Planning approved the proposal and agreed to submit it to IDRC for funding.

NIR decided to maintain the momentum started by the SADIS efforts for several reasons. First, we realized that the situation regarding the documentation of Botswana's socioeconomic development was far from satisfactory; much development information was generated but it was ending up in very inaccessible places. We also found it necessary to establish such a system so that Botswana could benefit from development information available in other countries. (See Box 1.)

Objectives of the Project

The principal objectives of the project were to organize the national economic and social development information in support of the planning process in Botswana and to strengthen Botswana's capacity to participate in the regional PADIS network and in the proposed SADIS program. The specific objectives of the project were to:

a) Collect, organize and disseminate Botswana's national information and documentation related to its economic and social development;
b) Participate in the regional PADIS network;

BOX 1   DEVSIS Solves Information Problems

When we were making efforts to establish SADIS, the Government of Botswana also decided to focus its development efforts on the communal areas; that is, those areas where land tenure and resource management still follow the traditional communal pattern. There was a feeling that the problems of effecting meaningful, self-sustaining improvements in the standard of living in the communal areas were among the most intractable Botswana faced. The Government's wanted to tackle these problems by driving for development in these areas but they recognized that their efforts would be hampered if they were unable to take advantage of the wealth of information that already existed. DEVIS—Botswana was the perfect way to confront their concern.

---

c) Train staff in the organization and operation of a specialized documentation center; and

d) Determine the computer equipment, staff and training that would be needed in order for NIR to carry out its mandate as the primary national focal point for all information and documentation in the country and to prepare for it to participate in regional networks such as SADIS and PADIS.

Another objective of the project, although unstated, was to gauge the volume of socioeconomic information being generated on or about Botswana each year.

PROJECT EXPERIENCE AND IMPLEMENTATION

DEVINDEX - Botswana

Soon after the project began, the Project Coordinator, who had actually been involved in the conception and design of the project, had to leave NIR. I had to take over the day-to-day management of the project because identifying another project coordinator would have delayed implementation. My initial role was technical coordinator and I was responsible for abstracting and indexing documents and checking on the quality of cataloging.

DEVSIS-Botswana was conceived as a national project to collect, organize, and disseminate information related to Botswana's economic and social development. Unfortunately, we lost track of this objective somewhat as we implemented the project. For example, throughout the project implementation period, there was no contact with the Government ministries nor with other institutions that had been consulted when the project proposal was prepared. The project, therefore, was generally regarded as an NIR one and not as the collaborative effort that it had been intended to be. We lost the potential national support that had been promised at the initial stage.

I should, however, point out that there was no deliberate decision on the part of NIR to exclude other important partners. We were very much conscious of this fact but the implementation schedule of the project was such that we had to give priority to the production of a printed version of *DEVINDEX-Botswana*. Because of this production schedule, there was also little time to focus on identifying new information sources for the proposed database. We therefore had to reprocess the documents already available in the library.

When the project started in 1984 nobody knew anything about operating a computer. No software had been identified for the proposed database. The reason for this, however, was that it had been decided that the computer processing of data would be done in PADIS and this had seemed feasible until the implementation of the project. The library was already using its own manual information processing and retrieval system, which was tedious but very appropriate for the collection. The form we used for information processing was simple but adequate for our purposes. However, processing documents for the PADIS database required that we use different and more complicated information processing methodologies designed by PADIS. This caused long delays in the processing of documents. We did not realize until much later that the delays were not being caused by the methodologies we were using but because we were using two methodologies simultaneously. The situation changed when we decided to adapt the PADIS methodologies to suit our internal operations.

PADIS sent one of its indexers/abstractors for three weeks to assist in the manual processing of the documents. His stay was very valuable since we did not have any experience with processing information for a computer-based system. The input sheets were then sent to PADIS for entry into the computer and eventually to IDRC for the production of the first *DEVINDEX-Botswana*. The ensuing issues of the index were to be a collaborative effort between NIR and PADIS. This arrangement had some practical problems and it was eventually decided that NIR should do the best that it could. After a lot of trial and error, two more indexes were produced. To date, six issues of this index have been produced. In a way, however, this trial and error provided good training.

The information in the six indexes was not selective. Everything on Botswana that had been processed over a particular period was included. Initially, there was no problem with this since the collection was small but, during the production of the sixth issue, it became clear that some criteria were necessary for selecting what should be included in the index. The problem was not only the size of the index but the cost of its eventual distribution. It turned out that the problem was that the index was rather general in terms of subject coverage and this made it difficult for us to target specific audiences.

In retrospect the manual processing of documents should have been followed by the creation of a computerized database at NIR and the actual production of printed indexes. This would have provided a practical training program that would have included everybody in the Documentation Unit and would have helped us avoid the number of problems that we experienced. It was not, however, until 1987 that the first library database was created at NIR.

Specialized Databases

Research institutions and information centers tend to be subject-specific. There are of course, big libraries in America, England, and Europe that are interested in all the information about a country, but these are very few compared to the subject-specific ones. I decided that the main library's bibliographic database should be structured to enable us to produce specialized indexes and bibliographies according to the focus areas of NIR: agriculture; education; environment; health and nutrition; rural development; and women and gender issues.

This does not, however, mean that there are six different databases: instead, there is one comprehensive database, subdivided by codes. I find this system good because searching can be done on one database or across different subject areas. The actual production of specialized indexes or bibliographies can be subject-specific. This not only makes networking more effective but makes marketing of the products a lot easier. *DEVINDEX-Botswana* will, however, continue to be produced containing information about Botswana that does not fall within the specified areas. My experience with the specialized databases shows that there will still be some overlap.

The Meetings Database

The main purpose of this database was to collect information on forthcoming meetings, conferences, seminars, and workshops and to disseminate this information to users. The database focuses on meetings taking place outside Botswana because the information about these is available through journals, magazines, and newsletters that NIR receives. One problem we face is that the information often reaches NIR very late and users do not have enough time to register their interest or, more importantly, arrange for funding. The information collected, however, still serves a useful purpose. Because we knew what meetings are taking place, we are able to ask for reports of those meetings. Electronic mail should make it possible for information to be obtained as soon as it becomes available.

Newspaper Clippings Database

The Documentation Unit provides a newspaper clippings service. When the service started, about ten years ago, articles found relevant were clipped and then

---

BOX 2 Secondary Information Sources

It is worth noting that a lot of libraries and documentation centers do not seem to appreciate the very important role that newspaper cuttings play as a supplementary source of information, particularly in developing countries where research has a very recent history.

---

stored in folders, where they were seldom used. I decided that each newspaper article should be entered into the computer to facilitate immediate and easy access and to make it possible for one article to be used for different purposes.

A good example is that of AIDS, where an analysis of the issue can be made from a variety of angles: AIDS and Women; AIDS and Youth; or AIDS in Botswana. Computerizing the newspaper article collection has put more emphasis on easier and quicker retrieval of information. This is actually an easy income-generating activity since a lot of articles are requested through the photocopying service. (See Box 2.)

Mailing List Database

For a long time the library maintained a mailing list of all the institutions with which it had any links. The main purpose of the mailing list, however, was for exchanging information and, particularly, distributing the Institutes' publications. The system used was a manual one, which was effective but very tedious and time-consuming. The only way that this information could be retrieved was by name of institution.

A proper mailing list is a very important management tool that many organizations tend to take for granted. I came to appreciate this only after I had computerized the library database using Micro CDS/ISIS. In its computerized form, it is now possible to retrieve only those institutions or individuals that should receive the NIR's publications list, for instance. It is also possible to retrieve names of institutions and/or individuals that should receive certain publications free of charge or only information about the availability of those publications, so that they can decide to order.

One of our researchers had travelled overseas and desperately needed a list of institutions with which we had exchanged agreements within the area of health. It was possible to provide this information in the shortest time possible because the database is structured in such a way that the computer can pull out first those institutions with whom we have an exchange agreement with and then narrow down the selection to the relevant subject area.

THE RESULTS, IMPACT, AND BENEFITS OF THE PROJECT

Impact of the DEVSIS-Botswana on the Documentation Unit

The Documentation Unit felt the most immediate effect of DEVIS. Before the project, we used a card catalog that was very tedious—from the production of the cards to their management after they had been filed. No longer do we type the cataloging information onto a stencil that then has to be reproduced elsewhere. Of course, the list of possible tasks that always took priority over the production of the cards was endless and all too often the machine was out of order. No longer do we go through the most tedious exercise of filing the cards. Since we were using a controlled vocabulary, we had to update the cards everytime the thesaurus was changed or updated. The automated database relieves us from all of these clerical chores. The information can be easily updated and we can concentrate on providing quality services to our users.

Impact of the DEVSIS-Botswana Project Outside the Institute

The impact of the project outside the NIR Documentation Unit can be judged by the number of requests for assistance with database development that we have been receiving and continue to receive. The following are excerpts from some of these requests:

"In terms of computerization, our center has acquired the necessary hardware and chosen Micro CDS/ISIS software. I believe your documentation center uses this software and therefore offers the best prospects for attachment training. . . The training program that we have in mind is one that can provide: a) an understanding of the database concepts, and expose participants to the skills required for the design and implementation of a database management system; and b) skills in analyzing, designing and implementing computer based information systems." (National Council for Scientific Research, Lusaka, Zambia, 1988)

"Mr. M has recently attended a short course on Improving the Effectiveness of Small Libraries and Information Centres held at the University of Botswana, where among other things he was introduced to CDS/ISIS software and PADIS methodologies. From his report on the course, we are made to understand that the National Institute of Development Research and Documentation of the University of Botswana is one of the best and most successful national information centres within the PADIS. It is in this regard that we would appreciate it if you can arrange for a study visit to enable Mr. M to gain practical experience on the application of various techniques of information handling, storage, retrieval, and dissemination." (The Institute of Finance Management, Dar es Salaam, Tanzania, 1990)

"I would like to take advantage of my contact leave to come and visit your Documentation Centre, and have a first-hand practical experience with your newspaper indexing project." (Mr. E.R.T. Chiware, Periodicals Librarian, University of Zimbabwe Library, 1991)

"The University of Bophuthatswana is in the process of setting up a documentation center. I, therefore, wish to send two professional librarians, to study your setup, especially the organization/processing of materials." (University Librarian, University of Bophuthatswana Library, 1993)[2]

"Through Professor Heywood I heard about your computerization project and DEVSIS-Botswana, and I am greatly interested in paying you a visit to study your work in this regard." (Director of the National Archives of Namibia, 1991)

The above are only samples of the many requests that we have received. As can be seen from excerpts, however, the requests come from a variety of countries and institutions. This, in my opinion, is a clear indication of the impact that the project has had outside NIR. I would like to point out that, unfortunately, it has not been possible for us to satisfy these requests due to staff constraints. Attachment programs require a lot of time for participants to get the maximum benefit out of them. We have, however, had some people spend one to three months with us learning the processing and management of unpublished literature through the use of micro CDS/ISIS.

ANALYSIS OF LESSONS LEARNED

Project activities should be integrated into the normal activities of the organization. This has implications on the type of organization selected to undertake a project such as DEVSIS-Botswana. I believe that whatever amount of success that NIR may boast about is due to the fact that we did not have to deviate a lot from our normal tasks in order to accommodate the project activities.

If, as was the case with the DEVSIS-Botswana project, immediate results are expected, professional and experienced staff should be employed. In the case of the DEVSIS-Botswana, the aim was not only to obtain immediate results, but also to strengthen the staffing situation.

The schedule that we actually followed when implementing DEVIS-Botswana was neither efficient nor effective. It was dictated more by circumstance than by design. If I was able to start over again, I would definitely follow a schedule that looked more like the following:

1. Employment and orientation of a professional librarian who will be responsible for database management.

2. Training of the professional Librarian for about three months in computers and database management. The latter should include thorough training in abstracting and indexing since these are very important skills for a database manager.

3. Familiarization visit to PADIS by the Project and Technical Coordinators. The Project Coordinator should always be someone who was involved in the initial designing of the project. The Technical Coordinator is responsible for abstracting and indexing of documents.

4. Putting a network in place for purposes of identifying information sources. The sources should not only be for printed documents, but also for information about research activities taking place. This way, we would have ended up with two types of databases—a bibliographic one and a research inventory database. I found that simply tracking hard documents misses out on getting to know who the real information generators are.

5. Collecting documents that will be processed for the project.

6. Employment of support staff, including a Data Entry Clerk. It is very important that the latter be employed at the beginning of the project so that data entry is given full-time attention. The mistake that NIR made was to depend on the secretarial staff of the Institute who always had other tasks to take care of and also never really got to learn the library software since they did not use it all the time.

7. Training of the project staff in basic computer skills and PADIS methodologies by PADIS.

8. Processing of documents and entering data in the computer.

9. Publicizing the project, including organizing seminars for potential partners and policy makers and working with the press.

10. At this stage the database manager should be back from training and can start checking on the data entered.

11. Production of printed outputs, which would include not only one index but also some specialized bibliographies. A conscientious document collection exercise should result in a big enough collection to facilitate this. Two research directories would also be produced: one on ongoing and completed research and another on research institutions. The advantage of leaving the production of printed outputs until the very end is that there will be very little editing to be done.

Another lesson to learn is not to allow or encourage the development of bibliographical databases independently of the ones that have been created by the

> ## BOX 3 Lost Information
>
> This mistake was made at NIR: a few databases were created as special projects. Information was entered in computers outside the library and no arrangements made to transfer this information back to the library. The result was that, for a number of reasons, these databases disappeared and a lot of valuable information was therefore lost. This was unfortunate because the program that is used for the development of databases in the Institute has facilities for merging different databases.

library or documentation center. Work can be subcontracted to individuals to set up these databases but the information should always be transferred to the main database. (See Box 3.)

The NIR also embarked on a research program to build a database on whatever documentation was available on the Basarwa (bushmen). I succeeded in making this part of the existing library database. The good thing that came out of this negotiation is that this information is not only used for the Basarwa research program but is also used for research on the remote area development program that is intended for disadvantaged communities, including the Basarwa/San.

This helps prove that, once information has been collected and processed, it cannot and should not be compartmentalized. It cannot be argued that because a database is developed on environmental issues, it will only be of interest to environmental researchers. For example, I set up a database on energy up for the *African Energy Policy Research Network*. As I processed documents for this database, I noted the close relationship between energy and environment. Fortunately, I had already negotiated that the database be done as part of the existing library database. I have tried as much as possible to check how often the information from this database is used by other researchers outside the energy field and there is a strong indication that merging the two databases was the best decision.

CONCLUSIONS AND RECOMMENDATIONS

In conclusion, I would like to recommend the adoption of the Basarwa Database/Bibliography as a model database development project for two reasons. First, the Documentation Unit was fully involved in the project from the beginning—even though it had been conceived elsewhere. Second, this project includes the following "main ingredients" of a database development project.

Pre-Project Consultations Among Potential Project Participants

The idea of the project came from Professor Sidsel Saugestad, Research Facilitator for the Remote Area Development Program (RADP). The NIR Director, various officers at the Ministry of Local Government, Lands and Housing, other individuals interested in the Basarwa issues, and I all consulted on the project. I was involved to ensure that all the technical aspects were taken care of at the beginning. It was very important that the Ministry was involved so that the necessary link between NIR and Government could be established at the very beginning.

Collection of Documents for the Database

A research assistant was employed to go through the NIR library databases and identify Basarwa-related documents so that they could be re-indexed with the potential users of the database in mind. The research assistant also visited other local libraries. Through visits by the research assistant and enquiries from individuals involved in Basarwa research by Professor Saugestad, we came to know of the existence of many documents that we would not otherwise have known about.

We are using a very interesting method for collecting documents. We try and make contacts with researchers who have published widely in the area of the Basarwa studies and ask them to send us lists of their published and unpublished works and the actual publications. We have received a number of these lists and are using them to follow up more documents. The advantage of having these lists is that we are able to check against what has already been collected and what is available.

Provision of Funding for Production of Abstracts

Very often, organizations realize the need for information on specific subjects but never seem to realize the need for providing funding to make this possible. The result is that, through donor funding, databases are developed as special projects that end as soon as funding is exhausted and printed copies of those databases have been produced.

For the Basarwa Database, funding for the production of abstracts was provided. This left me only with the responsibility of checking the technical aspects of the database and editing the abstracts. Some people may wonder why I am emphasizing the inclusion of abstracts in a bibliographic database when they are so demanding to produce. I can only say that it is not until you provide these that you realize just how important they are to your users.

The availability of funding made it possible for us to be selective in our choice of abstracters. Mrs. Janet Hermans, an anthropologist with very keen interest in the Basarwa issues abstracted about 200 documents. Then we hired Shelagh Willet, an anthropologist and retired librarian. She also collects Botswana documents for the Library of Congress and therefore has a lot of experience in collecting grey literature. I therefore recommend that where the situation allows, a specialist in the field should be employed.

Immediate Availability of Documents

One problem we encountered when developing other databases is that documents located in other organizations but processed by us for the database were not retrievable by users at a later date. We could produce a fantastic database but the service falls apart when readers are unable to locate the source documents. All the documents that are being processed for the Basarwa database are already available in the NIR Library. These are being consulted by the researchers in the Basarwa Research Network, university students, government officials, and the general public.

Formalization and Regularization of the Attachment Program

I gave examples above of the requests we receive for assistance with the development of databases using micro CDS/ISIS. I would recommend that an attachment program be formalized and properly and widely publicized so that other people can benefit from our experience. Judging from the number of requests from Botswana and outside, there would definitely be enough participants for the program to run every year.

The program could be structured to provide practical training in information management and micro CDS/ISIS. This would be a lot cheaper for institutions in Africa. At the moment, we only take participants from one organization at a time. This, I feel, is not at all cost-effective. I would recommend that the training be done for groups of participants so that they can share experiences and learn from each another.

Our program does not teach participants the basic concepts of computers and information science; we require that they already have experience in running their libraries or documentation centers. Instead, we expose them to the various information services that we provide. We then work with them so that they get to know the various processes involved in providing those services. Finally, we let them work on their own like the other staff in the Documentation Unit, but with very close supervision. That way they get to experience a lot of practical problems and through the assistance of the staff, find solutions to those problems.

So, in conclusion, I would say that we faced and overcame many problems in implementing the DEVINDEX-Botswana database project. We have also managed to produce databases that are very important to our users. The lessons we learned in this process have been put to good use as we design and implement additional databases. Although there were a lot of problems during the implementation stages, in retrospect, they were a very good eye-opener for me. Dealing with the problems gave me an understanding of indigenous information management that I would never have had otherwise.

NOTES

1. Basarwa is a term used in Botswana for a group of peoples known variously as the Bushmen, Khoisan or San of Southern Africa, and for the purpose of this case study, this is the term that I shall use.

2. Bophuthatswana is one of the "states" that was created during the apartheid era in South Africa.

KEMRI's Management Information System

by James N. Muttunga

James Muttunga is a Senior Research Officer at the Kenyan Medical Research Institute (KEMRI) and head of their information systems. He carries out consultancies for research projects in information management that have been funded by the Commonwealth Regional Health Community Secretariat. He is a biostatistician by profession.

BACKGROUND AND CONTEXT OF THE PROJECT

The Kenya Medical Research Institute (KEMRI) was established in 1979 by the Science and Technology Act of Parliament. Its Board of Management is accountable to the Minister for Research, Science and Technology and it is primarily funded by the Kenya Government. KEMRI is mandated to conduct research in the biomedical sciences and its main objectives are to:

- cooperate with the other research organizations and institutions of higher learning in training programs and in matters of relevant research;
- work with other research bodies within and outside Kenya carrying out similar research; and
- cooperate with the Ministry of Health, the National Council of Science and Technology, and the Medical Science Advisory Research Committee in matters pertaining to research policies and priorities.

The Member Research Centers

KEMRI has about 1,200 staff members, of which about 450 are either scientists or technical staff. They operate through eight research centers. One is in Busia (near the Kenya/Uganda border); another is in Kisumu (in the lake Victoria region). The rest are in Nairobi: four at KEMRI headquarters and two centers near the Kenyatta National Hospital. The research centers are:

- Alupe Leprosy and Skin Diseases Research Centre (ALSDRC)
- Biomedical Sciences Research Centre (BSRC)
- Clinical Research Centre (CRC)
- Vector Biology and Control Research Centre (VBCRC)
- Virus Research Centre (VRC)
- Centre for Microbiology Research (CMR)
- Medical Research Centre (MRC)
- Traditional Medicines and Drugs Research Centre (TMDRC)

PROJECT DESCRIPTION

In 1987, KEMRI appointed a team to write a proposal to develop our management information system (MIS). The team suggested that KEMRI first embark on a pilot project that would:

- Study and identify KEMRI's data processing needs and requirements;
- Provide some additional hardware to facilitate immediate processing requirements; and
- Facilitate exchange of knowledge through training visits to institutions with an operational information management system.

Professor Dean Haynes, then the Deputy Director of the International Center for Insect Physiology and Ecology, an international research center located in Nairobi, helped us by identifying consultants who had the relevant experience and had carried out similar activities. The chosen consultant first reviewed KEMRI's current inventory of microcomputer hardware and software. The proposal team then reviewed the training needs for the data processing support staff, the scientists, and administrative support staff. We interviewed scientific, technical, and administrative support staff and asked about their present operational systems, the available resources for information technology, and current needs for research production.

We also arranged to train two KEMRI scientists at the Tropical Diseases Research Center at the World Health Organization (TDR/WHO) in Geneva. There, they were able to familiarize themselves with an operational management information system. The training program included working visits to each program and familiarization with the existing techniques for data capture, automation, and analysis.

We completed the study after about six months and presented the report to the KEMRI Board of Management for approval. Based on the initial study and the experience from the training visits, the management board adopted the study report and used its recommendations and identified needs as the basis for a comprehensive proposal for the development of KEMRI's MIS. The primary objectives of this project were to improve KEMRI's capability in:

- Data processing and information management, through the acquisition of relevant hardware and software;
- Literature search services, through online and CD-ROM searches;
- Desktop publishing, through provision of necessary hardware and software; and
- Human resource development, by providing training aimed specifically at scientific, technical, secretarial, library, clerical, or data entry staff.

The main project proposal underwent a number of revisions and reviews and was not approved for financial support until the second half of 1991. This project benefited from the technical input and support of several reviewers and consultants who shared their opinions, concepts, and understanding with us. The process was in itself tedious and, at times, was affected by standard bureaucratic processes resulting in substantial delays in implementation and funding. The main bottlenecks were mainly due to two factors:

- Lack of adequate information and understanding on the size, magnitude, and extent of operations at KEMRI on the part of the review teams named by the potential donors; and
- Inadequate knowledge of microcomputers systems and the costs of these processes on the part of KEMRI staff.

The hurdles were, however, overcome and the project was finally accepted and funded by the Carnegie Corporation of New York. The original budgets and planned activities were, in the end, drastically reduced to facilitate a well-phased development and implementation schedule. This allowed us to follow the strategy of implementing the system according to the primary needs of KEMRI and then building the secondary systems as needed and as resources permitted.

PROJECT EXPERIENCE AND IMPLEMENTATION

The final project provided five main initial services, which are described in some detail below.

Research Strengthening Support

The study of existing hardware revealed that computer systems of differing capacities and types had been acquired through assorted project grants. Neither the various systems nor the software were initially compatible with each other.

The Board of Management recommended that the equipment acquisition process be better coordinated in order to identify the necessary systems, select software that could be supported by the technical staff, and facilitate the exchange, sharing, and compatibility of all new systems and software. We therefore adopted a policy of standardizing all microcomputer systems to a common configuration to facilitate compatibility between machines and the exchange of data sets and software applications.

The project provided two microcomputer systems in each of the eight centers and in the secretariat for data management, analysis, and report preparation by scientific, technical and support staff. We also acquired a dot matrix printer and an uninterruptible power supply (UPS) for each center. We strengthened the central computer facilities by acquiring powerful systems that could support KEMRI's large data management and analysis projects. The project also installed appropriate software for data management, analysis, graphics, word processing, utilities, communications, and desktop publishing.

We also stated that all new projects that were expected to have massive data analysis requirements would have to include funds for the necessary equipment in their budgets. Thus a number of projects acquired the necessary support systems. Some of the research programs that benefited from this new policy are listed in Table 1.

TABLE 1   Research Programs that Included Acquisition of Computer Equipment

Donor	Centers Funded	Research Programs
JICA	CMR, VRC, CRC, BSRC, MRC	Filariasis, Schistosomiasis, Hepatitis B, Acute respiratory infections
Wellcome Trust	CRC, VBCRC	Malaria
WHO/TDR	CRC, VBCRC, ALSDRC	Clinical trials, Filariasis, Malaria, Leprosy, and skin diseases
Rockefeller Foundation	CRC, MRC	Reproductive health
KEMRI	Secretariat	Personnel, Administration
IDRC	MRC	Pesticide use and health
CDC/Walter Reed Army Hospital	CDC, VBCRC	Malaria

BOX 1   Sudden Depreciation

The project suffered a nearly 40 percent loss from the sudden depreciation of the Kenya shilling against the U.S. dollar during its second year. This problem has affected all KEMRI projects and has led us to seek authority to run two external accounts, with one running as a straight U.S. dollar account and the other as local external account for all projects.

We initially planned to acquire the hardware and software through local firms that could provide the necessary support and maintenance. We learned, however, that the prices of these systems—even when ordered duty-free—were excessively higher than what we had budgeted. We decided on this strategy: provide, first, the new technologies that were not available directly from the local dealers. These included the CD-ROM systems for the library and the communication hardware and all the software applications that we had identified for use throughout KEMRI.

We acquired the other systems after attending the first meeting of the network of Carnegie grantees in May 1992. This meeting was organized by the U.S. National Research Council and held at the African Regional Centre for Technology (ARCT) in Dakar, Senegal. During the meeting, I learned about computer manufacturing firms who were selling high quality systems at competitive prices in the United States—through a direct-mail order system—and who had already supplied some to ARCT. I used this new contact to order the new systems at prices comparable to what we had budgeted! (See Box 1.)

The equipment acquisition process has improved gradually and we have now identified other dealers who can provide equipment. The sourcing of new products is presently carried out after soliciting different quotations from a few international firms.

Documentation and Library Support

The project acquired two microcomputer systems and the hardware accessories (UPS and dot matrix printer) for use in the library and at the central computer facility for online literature searches and internal database development. Two external CD-ROM drives were installed together with Small Computer System Interface (SCSI) cards and we subscribed to MEDLINE and POPLINE databases on CD-ROM. These databases formed the core sources for literature searches performed by scientists at KEMRI. We did learn that the CD-ROM drives should be dual or multiple drives to improve on easy access and to minimize "disc swapping." Many large databases are carried on several discs and it is quite convenient to be able to search all the discs at one time. This is not possible in a single drive system.

The availability of MEDLINE on CD-ROM provided us with a unique and unexpected opportunity. For nearly three years we had been trying, without much success, to provide the Board of Management with a current list of publications and of research developments from KEMRI's scientists. The scientists had responded very poorly to our requests for copies of their published papers because they were unable to provide us with hard copies. We decided, therefore, to search MEDLINE and POPLINE—as well as our own annual medical proceedings—for information written by our own scientists. We then compiled a book of abstracts that covers the scientific output of KEMRI staff.

In early 1993, we compiled and published the first summary, covering material published between 1985–1991. In 1994, we compiled, printed, and circulated among scientists and institutions a second summary, covering 1980–1984. These abstracts now cover the period between 1980–1993, and part of 1994. They have been entered into a central database and are being edited and formatted for eventual publication on disk and in hard copy. We hope that this publication will be the first step toward the development of local databases.

Human Resource Development

The project has trained many staff groups. The type of training provided is summarized in Table 2.

Desktop Publishing

The project supports the dissemination of research results by providing desktop publishing (DTP) services. We have acquired software and a laser printer, scanner, and other accessories. DTP was initially used for the production of the proceedings of the annual scientific conference that has been convened for the last

TABLE 2 Training Program

Type of staff	Type of training offered
Scientific and administrative staff	Introduction of microcomputers and to software applications for data management, graphics, word processing, and spreadsheets. CD-ROM and use of email sytems.
Secretarial staff	Introduction to microcomputers and to the software applications for operating systems, database management, word processing and spreadsheets.
Technical and support computer operations staff	Specialized training in specific applications, programming, and LAN and Novell administration courses.

15 years by both KEMRI and the Kenya Trypanosomiasis Research Institute (KETRI). This conference has improved in quality and has been expanded to a regional "African Health Science Congress," which is now held in different countries on a rotating basis within the African region.

The production of the conference proceedings has also improved and a new journal, *The African Journal of Health Sciences,* has evolved. KEMRI selects quality papers from the congress and from scientists in the region for peer review and publication in the new journal. In addition to typesetting and producing camera-ready copy for the journal and the proceedings, KEMRI DTP staff also publishes the annual report and the quarterly *KEMRI News.*

Email and Communications

The project has also acquired some 2400 baud modems and has installed two telephone lines for use in electronic communication among scientists in the centers, as well as among local and international organizations and associations. This has facilitated the exchange of information among local scientists and with the international scientific community.

RESULTS, IMPACTS, AND BENEFITS OF THE PROJECT

Hardware and Software

KEMRI has experienced a dramatic growth in provision and use of microcomputer systems for various research activities. With the funding provided by the Carnegie Corporation, we have acquired 22 new computers. In addition, a

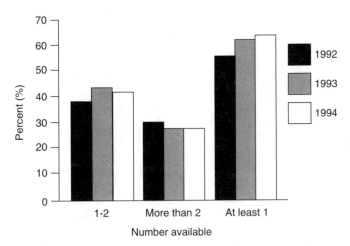

FIGURE 1 Percentage of Scientists at KEMRI with Access to Computers

TABLE 3   Hardware and Software Donations

Donor/Organization	No. of systems	Software packages
Carnegie Corp of NY	22	14
JICA	3	2
WHO/TDR	3	2
Rockefeller Foundation	3	1
Wellcome Trust	3	3
Walter Reed Army Hospital	3	3
IDRC	2	2
KEMRI	2	3

number of systems have been acquired through the research activities supported by other donors and collaborating institutions. These systems all have similar specifications since all computer acquisitions are arranged through the technical support group.

Standardized software has now been acquired and installed in all the existing systems—irrespective of the funding source. A summary of these acquisitions and the donor that supported their purchase is provided in Table 3.

Usage

Figures 1 and 2 show that access by staff to computers has risen from 46 percent in 1992 to about 60 percent in 1994. Word processing is the most used application. Use of spreadsheets (Lotus 1-2-3) and presentation software (Harvard Graphics) has remained below 20 percent but the ability to use MEDLINE on CD-ROM rose from 30 percent in 1992 to 46 percent in 1994. Email services have been poorly used overall with user rate ranging between 4 percent and 12 percent. Eighty percent of the scientists are aware of the existence of MEDLINE on CD-ROM and 64 percent have conducted a search at either the Library or the central computer facility.

The KEMRI Library has, over the past few years, experienced a reduction in the number of journal subscriptions it was able to carry. With the total number of journals reduced to about 20, a shrinking budget for books and other literature services, and inter-library loan transactions taking anywhere from weeks to months, the scientific process had been rendered a myth. The introduction of the MEDLINE database on CD-ROM has transformed this process. The CD-ROM service is complemented by the traditional process of providing reprints as requests are received by the librarian. In terms of volume, the number of requests forwarded to the main library for reprints has declined from about 415 in 1990, to 208 in 1991, to 135 in 1992, to 83 in 1993, and to 45 in 1994.

Comparatively, the total requests for MEDLINE literature searches on CD-ROM have shown a positive increase during the past two years with about 180 requests in 1993 and rising to 240 in 1994. This in itself is an underestimate as it includes only those scientists who were assisted during the search sessions or who had their searches printed. It excludes those scientists who conducted their own searches or who downloaded the search results to floppy disks.

Other Benefits

There are many other benefits of this project. These include the following:

- The tendency to use the literature available in the MEDLINE database is contributing substantially to the production of quality papers and reports in KEMRI.
- All the reference, documentation, and library automation services, including on-line searches using CD-ROM and the development of localized databases, are wholly provided by the project.
- The training of the scientific, technical, and administrative support in use of microcomputers for various operations has been provided through the project activities.
- The project provides full support to all email, communications, and desktop publishing services that exist within KEMRI.

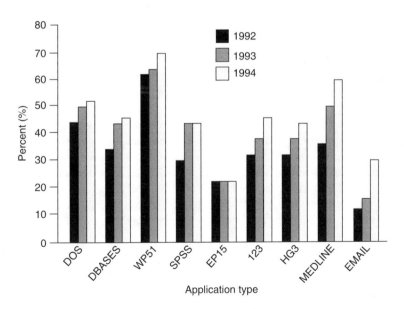

FIGURE 2 Percentage of Scientists at KEMRI Able to Use Specific Software Applications

---

Box 2   Timing the Training Sessions

Before the project got fully under way, IDRC, which was funding one of KEMRI's large, field-based diarrhoea projects, agreed to support a training workshop for about 30 scientists in the region—of whom about 50 percent were senior scientists in KEMRI. The training course content included an introduction to microcomputers, operating systems and standard software, and online literature searching and library information systems. The data processing staff in KEMRI coordinated and facilitated these training workshops. However, since KEMRI had not yet installed computer systems, the demand for computer access that the training workshop generated could not be met. As a result, more than half of this first group needed to be retrained four years later when the equipment was more widely available.

- Nearly 90 percent of the software available and in use in all the centers and computer laboratories has been provided by the project, inclusive of those systems that were acquired and donated by the other operational projects in the institute.

ANALYSIS OF LESSONS LEARNED

In the course of the project implementation, we discovered several things that we should have done differently. First, the training of staff should ideally be planned to take place immediately after the acquisition of the microcomputer systems. If training is conducted prior to the availability of computers, then many of those trained will not be able to use their new skills and will need to be retrained. (See Box 2.)

Second, we learned that hardware installation should be targeted to those services that are generating data and reports. These services require "power users" who have a genuine need for the technology. Some of the applications aimed at institutional strengthening were not used as much as we expected, simply because there was not a strongly felt need for them. We also discovered that computer services located at a central facility help to promote usage and access. Gradually, the access can be decentralized while the support, training, and maintenance are centralized.

In this same vein, we learned that email services should be provided initially to those scientists and researchers who are the most motivated to communicate with colleagues in other countries or regions. Those who share a common interest in a research area or in problem-solving will readily adapt to a new technology that makes communication relatively quick and inexpensive. Their enthusiasm encourages others to try the technology.

We were pleased with our early decision to establish standards for the acquisition of both hardware and software. By setting up such procedures for coordinated procurement, we were able to avoid incompatibility problems and by selecting a standard suite of software, we were able to facilitate sharing and exchange of information and data sets.

Another part of our project that worked well was the identification of a "computer coordinator" in each department. This person acted as the link between the users, the technical support team, and the procurement officers. The coordinators were members of the oversight committee that managed the implementation and development of the MIS project.

Finally, the project should have built in mechanisms oriented toward self-sustenance. Evaluation systems need to be in place from the beginning. This involves the identification of tangible process indicators that can be used in measuring the impact the project.

CONCLUSIONS AND RECOMMENDATIONS

We are enthusiastically planning the next phase of this project. In that phase, we will do the following:

- Install a local area network to facilitate easier access to hardware and software by more staff.
- Replace the single drive CD-ROM readers with multiple-drive machines in order to improve search services. We will continue subscribing to MEDLINE and other databases.
- Promote the development of more local databases.
- Strengthen the desktop publishing operation in order to efficiently produce the new journal; put these services on a self-sustaining basis.
- Install a communication system in order to promote the use of email and to take advantage of Kenya's newly-achieved access to the Internet.
- Implement new training strategies aimed at strengthening the technical staff with sufficient skills to support and maintain the LAN and at sensitizing more of the staff to the available services.

The idea for this project dates back to 1987 and it seemed to take an incredible amount of time to actually launch it. Looking back, however, we can see that we have accomplished much since we actually began implementing the project in 1991. The project is responsible for about 80 percent of all data management, analysis, and report productions systems and services currently available at KEMRI. Furthermore, the project has helped to develop an information culture at KEMRI and this has had a positive impact on every aspect of our activities.

The Ghana National Scientific and Technological Information Network (GHASTINET) Project

by John A. Villars

John Villars is Director of the National Science and Technology Library and Information Center, which he helped to found in 1964. His current interests include the popularization of science, science education, and the application of information technologies in support of science.

BACKGROUND AND CONTEXT OF THE PROJECT

The Republic of Ghana is located on the West African coast along the Gulf of Guinea. In 1995, it had a population of 17.1 million, with about 1.4 million in the capital, Accra. Since attaining independence from Britain in 1957, Ghana has experienced frequent political changes. Over the years, Ghana has had nine governments, five of which have been military and four civilian. In November and December 1992, parliamentary and presidential elections were held respectively for a Fourth Republic, and a new constitution is currently being implemented.

Ghana is predominantly an agricultural country which, for a long time, has depended rather heavily on a single export crop, cocoa. Ghana's economic development is constrained by several factors, including the overall low level in investment, which is estimated at about 16 percent of GDP. Of particular concern is the relatively low investment in social infrastructure, especially in basic education and training. The paucity of basic education and literacy is more acute in the rural areas, which account for nearly 85 percent of Ghana's population and which are responsible for almost all of Ghana's agricultural production.

The Host Institution

The host institution of the project is the Council for Scientific and Industrial Research (CSIR), which was established as the National Research Council in 1958. It is a government subsidized organization that has the status of a public organization outside the civil service. It enjoys a status similar to that of a university institution.

The mandate of the CSIR is to implement government policies on scientific research and development and to advise the government on scientific and technological advances likely to be of importance to national development. Another goal of the CSIR is to collate, publish, and disseminate the results of research and other useful technical information. Past attempts to promote the popularization of science and technology in the society and to market research results have not made a very significant impact and CSIR is taking steps to improve the situation.

The commitment of the CSIR to information activities stems from its recognition that information constitutes an integral part of the research enterprise. CSIR has thus established the National Science and Technology Library and Information Centre (NASTLIC), as well as library and documentation units in several of its institutes. There are in some institutes various categories of officers engaged in providing, processing, repackaging, or disseminating information.

The role of the CSIR in information activities is essentially a dual one of a parent organization and a user. As a parent, it acts as promoter, supporter, and facilitator of such activities. It plays this role by setting out broad policies; recruiting and paying salaries of personnel; providing buildings, books and equipment, and other physical facilities; and obtaining funding from government and other agencies for the development of information services.

As a user, the CSIR needs information to support its research and managerial functions. Its current mandate aims at regulating research and the application of science and technology in development, enabling private sector research and development activities in the Council, and encouraging commercialization of research results. For a long time, the CSIR was perceived as an "ivory tower" institution whose research activities have not been of direct benefit to society. This view has changed, following the general realization that it is ineffective mechanisms for marketing research results that create the impression of CSIR as an ivory tower. The CSIR must show even greater commitment to information and its repackaging and transfer.

PROJECT DESCRIPTION

The Ghana National Scientific and Technological Information Network (GHASTINET) project is located within NASTLIC. NASTLIC is the national focal point of the project, which includes nine sectoral nodes and several special resource centers. NASTLIC provides leadership through meetings, discussions, and guidelines and also promotes and fosters collaboration and cooperation among network participants.

The main objective of the project is to make scientific and technological information (STI) available in appropriately packaged forms for the benefit of users. The beneficiaries include government officials, private enterprises, scientific researchers, including university staff and students, and also small-scale and cottage industries.

To achieve the above objective, a number of functions and activities have been identified for which resources are being provided. Such resources include personnel, buildings, equipment and funding, as well as clear guidelines on operating procedures and linkages with external agencies. These resources and other relevant issues are discussed below.

Human Resources

The present core personnel of NASTLIC consist of eleven professionals, three technical level staff, four administrative staff, and fifteen clerical and junior personnel. We have plans to recruit four more staff, including two technical support level, and two junior staff.

All the professional staff have basic academic and professional qualifications. They have acquired other skills but could use more practical training through attachment to similar organizations. Additional training is required in technical areas such as database development and management, abstracting and indexing, handling user inquiries, and information searching. All library staff need more and better skills in using new information technologies. Many have little confidence in the use of computers because they do not have ready access to them.

Most senior professional staff need training in management and leadership skills. This is particularly essential because most of them are expected to provide liaison between the national focal point and the sectoral nodes and special resource centers of the project. They are therefore required not only to be highly trained professionals but also good managers with leadership skills. The technical support staff also require more training, especially in the use of computers and in the new information technologies. Such training, for which the present resources are inadequate, should ideally be provided in house.

Local training facilities are generally either not available or are inadequate. The only school for training in library and information science has a poor resource base in terms of teaching staff and equipment. This is particularly acute in the area of modern information science and technology. The school has only in the last year acquired six personal computers. Training provided tends to be rather theoretical with relatively little opportunity for practical skill acquisition in spite of a three week attachment program for students in working environments.

The attrition of librarians to other professions or to neighboring countries, as experienced about a decade earlier, has ceased, mainly because of an improved

---

BOX 1   Staff Mobility

Staff mobility and turnover has largely been a one-way—from the public library to the special or university library. In recent times however, as a result of a certain degree of saturation, especially at NASTLIC, there has been some exodus to financial institutions and to a large oil exploration company.

---

economy and the competitive salaries of librarians as compared to salaries of university lecturers and researchers. (See Box 1.)

Information and Communication Technologies

The project has received various items of equipment, most of which were gifts. One personal computer, donated by a local computer company, developed a problem with the motherboard after only six months and it took several months to have it replaced. During the last three years, the project has acquired a total of eight personal computers. The computers are mainly IBM personal computers, or clones running MS-DOS, that have capacities ranging from 50 to 120 megabyte hard disks. There are two laser printers and two dot matrix printers. All the computers operate on DOS with Windows and they have VGA color monitors. Other equipment includes a CD-ROM drive, a Telebit 1000 modem, and two mouses.

We have four CD-ROM databases namely, the CAB International Abstracts, AGRIS, TropAg and Rural, the Maize Germplasm Databank, and a couple of demonstration disks. We currently use standard software, including WordPerfect Version 5.2, Lotus 123, Borland Reflex for DOS version 2.0, Dbase 4, Aldus Pagemaker, and CDS-ISIS Version 3.1. There is also a Fidonet-based communication software, Frontdoor, used for electronic mail exchange with the Association for Progressive Communications in London.

The equipment and software are used for database management, word processing, desktop publishing, accounting, and electronic mail. All the software is user-friendly, although some observers complain that CDS-ISIS often poses problems and that its operation is sometimes cumbersome.[1] Technical support for the equipment has posed rather serious problems in the past, partly because of the lack of information about local suppliers, their products, and their competence in the repair and maintenance of electronic equipment. (See Box 2.)

Although technical support is now available, it is rather expensive. Lately, however, with the establishment of a repair unit in a local research institution, there appear to be prospects for much cheaper rates and more reliable arrangements for maintenance. Another bit of good news is that October 1995 the import duty on personal computers was lifted.

BOX 2   Repairing Modems

We had an interesting experience with our modems. We could not find a local company that could repair them so we took two modems across Africa to far-away Nairobi and Addis Ababa, where we were attending conferences. We could not repair the modems in either place, however, because they were not accompanied by their corresponding cables. So they went back across Africa and remained broken until, by sheer coincidence, a staff member complained casually to a relative. This person was able to fix one of the modems merely by inserting a pointed object into one of its pin-holes.

Attempts at developing a national policy on informatics are currently in progress. Over the years, certain major issues have been identified as being pertinent to a national policy on information technology. Some of the issues include:

- recognition of the importance for ministerial responsibility for informatics;
- the establishment of professional training centers for software and hardware applications;
- better methods for disseminating public information and raising awareness about information issues;
- the need to review trade restrictions and other legislation, regarding standardization and improvement in telecommunications infrastructure;
- the need for greater reliability of electricity supply;
- support for local manufacture and assembly of computer equipment;
- ways to promote investment in the information sector; and
- the establishment of a system for effective monitoring of trends in the industry.

Systems and Processes

The systems and procedures of the project arise from its objectives, functions, and activities. The activities have been assigned to six sections: Administration and Finance; Collection Development; Technical Services; Information Technology; Marketing, Publicity and User Service; and Reprography and Conservation. These activities ensure logical work flow and smooth communication among the various sections.

Financial Aspects

The project is funded predominantly from central government sources but it has benefited from funds provided by the International Development Research

Centre (IDRC) of Canada and the World Bank. The World Bank supports the National Agricultural Research Project (NARP), which is developing the library and information system for agriculture—the Ghana National Agricultural Information Network (GAINS). GAINS is a sub-network of GHASTINET.

Another source of funding is from the photocopying service, but this is rather meager and covers only the cost of paper. We also hope to cover the costs of providing email service. In this regard, our revenue has been limited by an increasing number of email service providers in the country, some of whom are offering service free-of-charge—at least in the short term. With the installation of desktop publishing software and a microfilm facility, we plan to generate some additional income. There are also plans to introduce charges for literature searches provided to industrial or commercial firms. We increasingly feel the need for a vigorous marketing and publicity campaign to attract customers for these services. Our effort to generate income falls squarely in line with the CSIR's new policy directives that require all its institutes to commercialize as much as possible.

PROJECT EXPERIENCE AND IMPLEMENTATION

The first phase of the project developed, equipped, and strengthened the national focal point to a level that enabled it to lead the gradual establishment and growth of the entire national network. To do this, we:

- developed an efficient system for the bibliographic control of indigenous STI;
- created computerized databases for indigenous STI, ongoing research projects, high-level scientific and technical manpower, and a union list of S&T periodicals;
- from these databases, generated and produced publications and other promotional material;
- established a facility for microfilming indigenous STI;
- arranged training programs and workshops for network participants; and
- promoted the implementation of the network and its services.

By its various activities, the project is expected to arouse the awareness of information personnel to the importance of science and technology information. With the ultimate objective of providing STI to assist in the socioeconomic development of the country, the project envisages carrying out a national survey to find out the information needs of various user categories including the research and academic; the government and public policy makers and planners; the private or public commercial and industrial houses; and the small-scale and cottage entrepreneurs and peasant farmers.

Ghanaians are innovative as reflected by the ingenuity shown among the small-scale or cottage industrialists. Attitude to information and knowledge is very positive, especially if the information has direct relevance to needs and if it is cheap

---

BOX 3   Acceptance of Technology

Generally, Ghanaians as a whole value education and learning. This attitude and the desire for high economic attainment has however seemed to wane. In the last decade, there has been a slight drop in the respect accorded to education and schooling. Attitude towards the new technology is positive but not many are willing to take risks, especially among the very highly educated. A case in point is my own attitude: for fear of it catching fire, I would not risk leaving a computer on overnight for electronic mail purposes.

---

and easily accessible. There is a tendency to give up the chase if information is hard to get or if it is not cheap. This attitude stems partly because information may not be easily accessible—either because it is not known to exist, because its location or source is not known, or because it has not been packaged or organized in a readily useable form. There is also a general attitude of wanting things free-of-charge. This is even more acute in the case of information, probably because it has always been provided free or because it tends to be taken for granted, unless it is a matter of "life and death." (See Box 3.)

Information Transfer

In many areas of science and technology activity, especially in agriculture, environment, and health, there are instances where information has played a vital role in the alleviation of problems. For several years, Ghana had experienced the problem of low-yield of local maize varieties and their high susceptibility to serious insect attack, both on- and off-farm. The role of information in alleviating these problems is not so much in the form of publications, but rather in the form of effective knowledge transfer and communication between the Crops Research Institute, the Extension Division of the Ministry of Agriculture, and farmers and maize consumers.

The solutions most commonly proposed for the above problem include knowledge transfer through effective extension and communication with farmers whose confidence is thereby won. By this means, information and feedback are easily obtained from experiences of the farmers who are generally illiterate and whose attitude to research may be one of suspicion or mistrust. Other means of solving the researchers' problems include faster and easier access to foreign journals or publications and inexpensive communication with their peers in other countries, as well as with other agencies like the International Maize and Wheat Improvement Center (CIMMYT) and International Institute of Tropical Agriculture (IITA).

Both the researcher and the farmer have interchanging roles as providers and users of information and they therefore exhibit certain patterns in the information life cycles in which they are involved. They both generate information either through research or from experience. The farmer produces and distributes information mainly orally and by demonstration. Researchers publish papers in journals or other media. They may distribute information at conferences or seminars, through invisible colleges among peers, or in electronic form on diskettes, tapes, and CD-ROM. They can also communicate by means of electronic mail or bulletin boards.

These media also provide the means of storage and easy retrieval and facilitate wider dissemination in a relatively short time. Modern electronic media can be used to capture, store, and communicate the farmer's orally delivered or demonstrable experiences. The mode of acquisition for both user types ranges from word of mouth and demonstration for the farmer, to document procurement by the individual researcher or a library and information center through gift, exchange, or purchase.

User Reaction

Users who have reacted positively to the project are predominantly the research scientists of institutes and academic staff and students of universities. Their reaction is initially one of approbation of the objectives of the project, especially with regard to the databases and the publicizing of the collection of indigenous STI. The policy makers and planners in government and public organizations who know about the project also approve of the objective of the databases, especially those that cover ongoing research and high-level manpower.

Researchers and academic staff however express disappointment with the poor availability of current journals and with difficulties in obtaining full-text articles when searches are conducted from CD-ROM databases. They also complain about the high cost of photocopies and lack of translations of materials in foreign languages, especially French. Industrialists hardly use the services of the project because they are not aware of it, and the small-scale and cottage industries do not have any direct contact with the project as yet. This is partly because they do not know about it and also because, even if they did, the information would not be easily assimilable since it has to be repackaged. It is also partly because of the general perception that libraries only have storybooks and not information or technical information for that matter. This state of affairs calls for sound information repackaging and marketing.

Information Marketing

Marketing of the services and products of the project has been minimal and this is being remedied with the recent appointment of an Information Marketing and Publicity Officer. So far, the only marketing methods adopted are announcements in the project's *GHASTINET Newsletter.* Other publication outlets include a

---

BOX 4   Popularizing Science

As part of the CSIR program to popularize science, a new radio program is in the pipeline. This program, "From the Research Files," is expected to start in August or September 1995. As part of the World Science Renaissance Day of Africa, which is celebrated on 30th June every year, NASTLIC participated in this year's program. It compiled a directory from a computerized database of small-scale industries in a suburb of Accra and distributed it to various agencies engaged in supporting or promoting small-scale enterprises.

GHASTINET Brochure, a flier advertising the project, and another advertising the electronic mail service. There is also a *Ghana Science Abstracts Bulletin* issued bimonthly, in which summaries of indigenous STI are provided and distributed to research and academic institutions. We are in the process of planning effective marketing of the project and its services.

Popularizing Science

Following the creation of a Ministry for Environment, Science and Technology and the concern of government for the need to market research results and to popularize science and technology, the CSIR has embarked on developing programs for this purpose. Accordingly, I am chairing a special committee on science popularization and we have held preliminary meetings with the Ghana Broadcasting Corporation (GBC) and all public relations personnel in the CSIR. During the last six months, we have prepared a set of proposals in a project document. The proposals have been discussed with the CSIR Director-General and officials of the local secretariat of UNESCO. A short request for basic equipment, including a video camera, has been submitted to UNESCO for consideration in 1996. (See Box 4.)

With regard to user education and training in information searching, not much has been done. Formally, only a couple of demonstrations of CD-ROM have been organized for selected user audiences. The major one was conducted among all agricultural research institutions, stations, and university faculties. It was combined with an interactive survey on user preferences and on their perceptions and opinions on services being provided. Following a full-day seminar and demonstration of CD-ROM to about forty researchers and academic staff, our expectation that we would be inundated with demands for searches proved to be a pipe dream—requests for searches remained as before. We have also taken advantage of national fairs and exhibitions to give demonstrations on the use of CD-ROM and of electronic messaging.

BOX 5   Importance of Science and Technology

The project has made an indirect contribution to the increased recognition of research as a necessary tool for development. Science and technology research has received considerable recognition and as a result, a Ministry of Environment, Science and Technology has been established. Hitherto science and technology did not have such prominence.

RESULTS, IMPACT, AND BENEFITS OF THE PROJECT

On the whole, we can say that the project has been of limited benefit to users in the various categories targeted. More could have been achieved if we had developed a vigorous and sustained information marketing program. The responses we obtained during the survey of users in agricultural research institutions indicated the benefits derived and the impact of the project, even though the demonstration did not result in an increase in requests for CD-ROM searches. These benefits included skills in using thesauri, abstracting and indexing journals, and in CD-ROM searches. For many, the project provided a first opportunity to use a computer database and for some, a first opportunity to use printed abstracts.

We are placing a great deal of emphasis on how to get science and technology to contribute to national development objectives and on ways and means of providing adequate funding for research. (See Box 5.) The former Minister of Science and Technology consulted with his peers and senior personnel in other ministries to determine areas in their programs to which science and technology could contribute. Ghana has also taken steps to establish a National Science and Technology Fund (NASTEF). Expected contributions from industrialists may raise the funding for research in science and technology to close to the target of one percent of GDP by the year 2000, as suggested in the Lagos Plan of Action. (The level of S&T funding since 1992 is only about 0.3 percent of GDP.)

As part of the effort to maximize the impact of science and technology and the contribution it can make to society, the legislation establishing the CSIR is being amended to give it a wider scope in commercializing research results. The CSIR Council is also being restructured to make it less cumbersome and more effective.

A recent development was the invitation to the Director-General of CSIR and some institute directors (including myself) to a special session with the Parliamentary sub-Committee on Science and Technology. We discussed issues relating to how well S&T had been covered in a Presidential Report to Parliament. The report, which is entitled *Ghana-Vision 2020: The First Step,* seeks, in the President's words, "to provide a framework within which we can realize the long-term vision of raising Ghana into the ranks of the middle-income countries of the world."

One notable impact of the project at the national focal point has been the increased awareness and the newly acquired skills of staff in the application of new technologies, especially computers, CD-ROM, and electronic mail. They accomplish assignments faster and their information products are more impressive, especially the publications produced by desktop publishing. Staff have become computer literate and their understanding of modern information work has been heightened considerably. The information literacy of users has also increased considerably, especially as a result of their exposure to CD-ROM and electronic mail facilities.

It is, however, too early to determine if users' information query formulation has also improved since rather few users are physically present during searches. However, as a result of their exposure to these new information technologies, both staff and users are better able to cope and feel more confident in handling the technologies, and they have become much more aware, not only of a wider scope and volume of information sources, but also of the potentials offered by the new technologies.

Benefits

The users who have been exposed to services offered by the project have benefited in a variety of ways. For example, those who have used the email facility have been able to contact their colleagues overseas for information or for some solution to a problem.

The project staff have benefited because they have learned new skills in computer use, database creation and maintenance, word processing, desktop publishing, spreadsheets, CD-ROM searching, and electronic mailing.

The CSIR as a whole has benefited from the introduction of computers into the organization. As a result, some secretarial staff at the headquarters had their first exposure to computers and this encouraged them to seek training in applications of word processing and spreadsheets. CSIR now appreciates the potential of the technology and is taking steps to have the project provide assistance for the development of a management information systems (MIS) and in automating accounts in the CSIR.

Nationally, the project attracted the attention of the Ghana National Commission for UNESCO, which designated NASTLIC as the national organization responsible for matters relating to the General Information Programme (PGI) and the Intergovernmental Informatics Programme (IIP). Accordingly, the CSIR Council has approved proposals by NASTLIC to set up a Special Committee to handle issues on informatics. The Committee is expected to be inaugurated early in 1996. NASTLIC also attracted the attention of the government's National Development Planning Commission and as a result it is represented on a special committee known as the Information Technology Planning Group.

ANALYSIS OF LESSONS LEARNED

Major Success Factors

Human, financial, and external support factors contributed to the success of this project. Essential human factors include the perceptiveness of authorities in the parent organization; their understanding and appreciation of the role and value of information in their work; and the commitment and dedication of staff on the project. Added to this is the vision for the project, with its clear and well-articulated plan, objectives, and expected benefits. The most significant human factor in this connection is the mutual understanding between authorities of the parent organization and the project leader. Another factor derived from this is good management practice, involving planning and constant review and evaluation.

Funding, especially from the Ghana government, has not been easily forthcoming; however, the limited funding that was available and the support of IDRC in the form of equipment and training, have contributed immensely to the success of the project. In fact, the external support has always served as bait for obtaining government funding and very often it has been used as a threat to withhold external assistance if government funding was not forthcoming. In spite of the generally weak economic situation of the country, even the rather meager government funding can be considered as a success factor simply because it serves as evidence of government interest in the project.

In this connection, another success factor has been the sometimes unorthodox public relations approach of project staff, especially at the individual level, to government officials in the funding ministry. This personal and informal approach helped drive home more effectively the not easily recognizable principle that STI is a vital ingredient to national development. My persistent reference to the importance of information at virtually any meeting of CSIR directors often led to remarks like "Oh yes, there goes the information man."

The issue of funding is directly related to external support factors that have contributed to the success of the project. The quality of any organization's library and information services is a reflection of the importance and commitment attached to such services. So, while the general economic and political situation had an adverse impact on the project, as evidenced by the delay in its take-off and in the occasional hiccups, it can still be said that the project has benefited from the generally enabling environment in the CSIR and the government. This was partly due to the timing of the project, which may be described as propitious, and also partly due to my persistence and the many years of sustained effort from me and my colleagues.

Problems

The problems that have prevented the project from reaching its full potential can be traced to the general lack of a sufficiently strong conviction and realization of the importance of STI in all spheres of national development. This is also partly due to the inability of the project, like many a library or information project, to adopt a more aggressive marketing, user education, and publicity approach. The weak marketing itself derives from an apprehension that the resulting demand for information may not be adequately met and will, therefore, lead to loss of confidence in the system. There have been a few examples of this, especially with regard to the email service, which broke down because of faulty equipment that could not be repaired quickly.

Lack of personnel has been a problem to the project. Special services, such as literature searches on CD-ROM, and the personal touch in carrying out such services, could not be sustained simply because the skilled staff were not available. There has also been a tendency for some staff to be apathetic due to insufficient motivation because of low wages.

Funding, as already mentioned, has been a perennial problem. Not only is it insufficient, but it is not always guaranteed. A case in point was when there was a one-year ban on construction works in public organizations. The most recent example was the freezing of allocations made for equipment in the 1995 approved budget estimates. It is also partly due to the relative low priority accorded to library and information projects. The limited funding may be partly due to our inability to articulate more forcefully and effectively the importance of the project. We need convincing and concrete evidence to justify our very existence and continued support.

Equipment repair and maintenance has also been a serious problem. The story of the faulty modems is a typical example. We have also lost large volumes of data due to faulty equipment, interruptions in the power supply, and dust collecting in computers.

CONCLUSIONS AND RECOMMENDATIONS

One solution to these problems is the intensification of user education, especially among the senior personnel in CSIR. They need to better understand the real value of information in their work as researchers and as decision makers. Training at all levels of information workers needs to be strengthened and we believe that the project should set up a special unit to conduct all training programs.

We should explore avenues of collaborating with the media and with other professional societies and organizations. We need to develop guidelines and standard procedures and begin services for systems reporting and evaluation. Good management practice is paramount.

Generally, the GHASTINET Project may be described as a success story because it has provided the stimulus and acted as a catalyst in creating awareness and arousing interest in STI generally. It has taken about thirty years to get this far and the little that has been achieved needs to be sustained and improved further. There is the urgent need to re-examine the project in the light of new circumstances and to intensify collaboration with agencies that generate or disseminate information in one form or the other.

There is further need to create the awareness that information management is not the exclusive prerogative of the librarian or other information professionals. Information is a resource that practically everyone needs and that practically everyone handles and uses in one form or another. There is a need for an STI culture in Ghana as part of a science and technology culture.

Finally, I recommend that external agencies, be they international or bilateral, be aware of the need to relate aid programs to STI where relevant and to emphasize information technologies and services as integral components of assistance programs.

NOTE

1. We are consoled by the fact that many information centers in Africa and the developing country members of UNESCO use it and it has become a *de facto* standard. Its use might promote uniformity and compatibility and therefore facilitate information transfer and data exchange.

CONCLUSION

COMMON PROBLEMS—INNOVATIVE SOLUTIONS

These sixteen case studies tell very compelling and specific stories about the introduction of selected information and communication technologies into African institutions. They also demonstrate that considerable progress has been made since the 1989 Nairobi conference, organized by the National Research Council, at which the participants identified problems and gave recommendations for their resolution. The case study authors demonstrate that, while many of these problems still remain, they have taken positive steps to resolve others.

Those information technologies and services that had been identified in Nairobi as most appropriate—CD-ROM, desktop publishing, electronic networking, and the collection, management, and dissemination of local information resources— are beginning to be adopted across the continent and their benefits can be seen throughout the research community. As the services and technologies become more readily available and easier to use, others are encouraged to experiment with them. Information and communication professionals in Africa are discovering many opportunities to develop innovative and effective information systems. As they do so, the link between information and communications and economic development becomes more clearly established. The importance of ICT, networks, and linkages among institutions becomes even more evident to project managers and to the directors and ministers to whom they report.

The sixteen case study authors recount that they still face common problems and barriers. Some problems, such as incompatible equipment, poor access to consumables (such as paper and toner) or peripheral equipment, a shortage of repair options and spare parts, and poor institutional coordination, were very obvious in 1989. While difficulties with these certainly remain, they seem to be of less importance to the case study authors. Other problems identified in 1989 are still present and the authors suggest a number of innovative solutions. These problems include: a shortage of funds; communication difficulties; a lack of institutional capacity to train personnel; poor collection, management, and dissemination of local information resources; and an absence of an enabling environment.

Shortage of Funds

Many countries in Africa are experiencing fiscal shortages and most of the case study authors write that their projects face a shortage of funds. Some of them resolved this problem by designing smaller, more manageable projects from the beginning. Look, for example, at the experiences described by Albina Kasango, Ermias Dagne, and James Muttunga. Others, such as Charles Musisi, Moussa Fall, and Paulos Nyirenda, have implemented cost-recovery systems that spread the costs of a service throughout the user community. Agnes Katama and Alex Tindimubona discuss their efforts to put their scientific presses on a sustainable footing by instituting sound business practices. Public/private partnerships are another solution for chronic funding problems and Neil Robinson discusses how ZAMNET was developed as a private company to provide Internet services.

Communication Difficulties

Communication difficulties, another problem identified in 1989, are still present in Africa. Maintenance of the telecommunication systems has suffered and, in many countries, it is often easier to telephone internationally than across the capital city, since the international service is usually the most profitable part of the service. The telecommunication monopolies in most countries still operate on the basis that they make their profits from international calls and from their services for a small number of large subscribers at relatively high cost, rather than from a large number of small local subscribers at low cost.

However, local networking initiatives are gaining ground in many African countries. Emerging as a logical path in the development of full Internet connectivity are a series of grassroots electronic networks that use robust and appropriate hardware and software tools. Fidonet systems that are able to use even poor dial-up telephone lines can provide electronic mail access to the Internet. Such systems are helping to build the local user base in many African countries and are proving to be highly effective feeder roads into the Internet. Because there have been few public subsidies for these grassroots developments, these networks have to be fully self-sustaining and capable of operating with only the simplest microcomputers, modems, and ordinary dial-up lines. Lishan Adam, Moussa Fall, Charles

Musisi, Paulos Nyirenda, and Neil Robinson each describe how they have achieved success in overcoming communication problems.

Shortage of Trained Personnel

Each case study author discusses the problems faced in training personnel. As the computer revolution creates a demand for computer-literate and specialized personnel, more and more people need to be trained. Training in the broadest sense, including computer literacy and consciousness-raising, is needed at all levels. Several authors remarked that the lack of training for senior level managers is limiting the adoption of newer technologies. The lack of training affects information systems in several ways: it limits the effectiveness with which new technologies are used and it causes users to lack confidence in their ability to master the technology. Training programs can help "demystify" information and communication technologies.

Most of the authors found that they had to provide their own training programs when they introduced a new information service or technology. John Newa and John Villars describe their consciousness-raising efforts with senior management. Helga Patrikios, James Muttunga, and Xavier Carelse describe the more in-depth and targeted programs they had to provide. Each of the networking authors faced an uphill battle to educate their users. Each found that the training burden would rest on their own shoulders since so few other options were available.

Poor Collection and Dissemination of Indigenous Information Resources

The intellectual output of many African countries is not being captured or deposited in a location where it can be maintained and made available to others. The research efforts of African scientists are not reported in the literature since the journals in which they publish are not indexed by the major bibliographic sources. The authors describe many solutions to these problems.

Stella Monageng maintains a program that systematically collects records for inclusion into a local database. Regina Shakakata and Helga Patrikios collect records from their own countries and contribute these to the *African Index Medicus.* They and James Muttunga also publish digests of relevant material that are disseminated to the research communities in their countries. Since African scientists face diminishing avenues of publication, Xavier Carelse, Alex Tindimubona, Albina Kasango, and Agnes Katama tackled this problem by improving the quality of local publishing houses through desktop publishing.

John Villars and Ermias Dagne take a slightly different approach in their case studies. The former discusses his efforts to launch a nationwide network for the dissemination of scientific information relevant to decision makers. The latter describes his discipline-oriented approach to uniting scientists interested in natural products.

Lack of an Enabling Environment

One of the most serious problems faced by the case study authors was the lack of an enabling environment within which they could begin to build an effective information service. Many felt they were working in isolation because the "computer culture" in their regions was so poorly developed. There was no support network—no back-up, no documentation, no service, nor any spare parts—and they often resorted to trial and error to get a project off the ground. While this experimentation eventually resulted in successful projects, it proved very frustrating along the way.

Several authors report that they had trouble dealing with vendors. Often they did not know exactly what to ask for—as a consequence they were given older, more complicated, or inappropriate technologies. Other times, they had difficulty communicating with vendors who did not respond to faxes or email, or who did not understand the situation in Africa. James Muttunga turned to mail order; Neil Robinson finally found a vendor who would deal with Zambia, and Helga Patrikios got the right combination of software and hardware only through perseverance. The ability to attend international trade shows and conferences improved the authors' understanding of the technology and allowed them to establish personal relationships with the vendors.

Another problem that was identified only by a few authors was the shortage of good, easy-to-use software in local languages. Lishan Adam reports that Ethiopia is one of the oldest countries using its own script. Generic native-language software interfaces that allow easier storage and retrieval of textual information in local languages and scripts are not well developed. Some new programs have features for processing data in all languages simultaneously but these are not readily available in Ethiopia.

Another manifestation of the poor information environment was the discovery that many researchers had little incentive to use information services. In some cases, they were unwilling or unable to pay for information even though they valued the information service. In other cases, they had little understanding of the value of electronic information resources as compared to more traditional information products. The deterioration of libraries due to poor storage conditions and lack of foreign currency to maintain journal subscriptions contributed to a serious underuse of information resources.

Such low expectations on the part of researchers had to be overcome by aggressive marketing techniques. Some of these are described by Regina Shakakata, John Newa, and James Muttunga. Helga Patrikios reports that the introduction of the CD-ROM improved the status of the library staff. By being in a position to provide better service, her staff was better able to interact with the requestor on a professional level. Using information technologies in an "everyday" setting demonstrates to the users that these technologies need not be feared, that instead they can be manipulated to give the user the information wanted.

Despite these adverse conditions, the case study authors found unique and innovative ways to create enabling environments within which their own projects could thrive. Many of the authors credit one or two individuals for helping and inspiring them. These experts served as support groups and as objective sources of advice—often filling in the gap caused by a shortage of journals, other literature, and conferences and exhibits. Other authors credit the donors, especially the Carnegie Corporation of New York, for having the vision to fund projects that involved new, untested technologies. Organizations such as the National Research Council and the American Association for the Advancement of Science also played enabling roles by helping with proposal writing, providing technical advice to the authors, and convening frequent meetings so project managers could learn new skills, share ideas, and foster collaboration.

LESSONS LEARNED

An examination of the case studies as a whole reveals several common conclusions that can be summarized quite briefly here.

- Pilot or demonstration projects play a critical role in the introduction of information and communication technologies. They allow for experimentation and demonstrate the use and costs of CD-ROM, desktop publishing, electronic mail and computer conferencing, and software development using personal computers and off-the-shelf database management software. They provide a low-risk, non-threatening environment in which users can try new services.
- Training programs—both for information providers and for organization directors and managers—are still badly needed throughout Africa. Training should include broad overviews of microcomputers and networking, as well as consciousness raising about the importance of information. It should include formal instruction through high-quality schools as well as shorter-term workshops, seminars, and computer-based instruction. Improved documentation and manuals will also help fill the training gap.
- The most sustainable projects are those that start small and follow a logical growth pattern. Local networks seem to be a prerequisite for the successful introduction of the Internet.
- The successful implementation of STI systems and services often relies upon a combination of technologies. Libraries need to offer both CD-ROM and network access. Publishers need desktop publishing and access to local information. No single technology will solve all the information needs of the research community and a suitable and coordinated mixture of technologies seems to help all parties.

- The informal networks, personal contacts, and user groups that have been formed in Africa have been very helpful in providing information about the costs and suitability of different technologies. Networks and professional associations are also good mechanisms for sharing information about innovative outreach and cost-recovery programs.
- The development of indigenous databases through the collection and publication of locally-produced material is extremely important. Local databases provide resources for solving local problems by assuring that the scientific research of a country is being captured and entered into a database to which others in the country have access. Once such databases exist, project managers must make major efforts to disseminate information about their availability to researchers in the country and region.

Many of the lessons learned by the case study authors should be self-evident but the fact that projects are still being designed, implemented, and managed without much thought to these lessons proves that more active dissemination activities are needed. *Bridge Builders* takes an important first step in outlining remaining problems and barriers to the introduction of information and communication technologies. It also demonstrates that innovative solutions to these problems are available.

Still needed are venues at which these lessons can be identified and discussed with others. Networks, professional associations, trade shows, and other events provide an appropriate meeting ground where project managers can discuss the choice of suitable technologies, get help in defining needs for information products and services, offer technical assistance to others, and share information about information services and technologies.

By reading these case studies, donors, government ministries, and project managers alike should be encouraged to see just how much can be accomplished with relatively small amounts of funding. Echoing the strongest recommendation from the 1989 Nairobi conference is this advice from the case study authors: small amounts of funds can be highly leveraged and can provide a low-risk environment that allows for experimentation and innovation.

The advisory committee sincerely hopes that *Bridge Builders* will help counterbalance the "afro-pessimism" that pervades the halls of policy- and decision-makers in both the United States and Africa. These people might choose to dwell on the institutional weaknesses, poor economic environment, inadequately trained manpower, cultural and attitudinal values, and generally low levels of technological awareness that work together to prevent the further development of effective STI systems and services in Africa.

Or they might look at the efforts of these few, representative individuals and be inspired by how their activities and efforts have helped to overcome these barriers. They too might find that the possibilities and the opportunities are limited mostly by their own imaginations; they too might be infected by the pioneering spirit demonstrated by these case study authors.

Then, perhaps, they will choose to help by working with these "bridge builders" and the many, many others whom they represent.

Appendix A
List of authors

Lishan Adam, UNECA - PADIS, P.O. Box 3001, Addis Ababa, Ethiopia
lishan@padis.gn.apc.org

Dr. Xavier Carelse, Department of Physics, Electronic Instrumentation and Design, University of Zimbabwe, P.O. Box MP 167, Harare, Zimbabwe
xcarelse@zimbix.uz.zw

Dr. Ermias Dagne, NAPRECA Ethiopia, Department of Chemistry, Addis Ababa University, P.O. Box 1176, Addis Ababa, Ethiopia
Chemistry_AAU@padis.gn.apc.org

Moussa Fall, Operatuer de Systeme, Enda-Tiers Monde, P.O. Box 3370, Dakar, Senegal
moussaf@endadak.gn.apc.org

Albina Kasango, Publications and Publicity Officer, Economic and Social Research Foundation, 51 Uporoto Street, Ursino Estate, P.O. Box 31226, Dar es Salaam, Tanzania
esrf@costech.gn.apc.org

Agnes Katama, Manager, ICIPE Science Press, P.O. Box 72913, Nairobi, Kenya
ICIPE@cgnet.com

Stella Monageng, Librarian, National Institute of Research, University of Botswana, Private Bag 0022, Gaborone, Botswana

Charles Musisi, Makerere University, P.O. Box 7062, Kampala, Uganda cmusisi@starcom.co.ug

James Muttunga, Senior Research Officer, Kenya Medical Research Institute, Mbagathi Road, P.O. Box 54840, Nairobi, Kenya jmuttunga@ken.healthnet.org

Dr. John Newa, Director, University Library Services, University of Dar es Salaam , P.O. Box 35092, Dar es Salaam, Tanzania lib@unidar.gn.apc.org

Dr. Paulos Nyirenda, Head, Department of Physics and Electronics, University of Malawi, Chancellor College, P.O. Box 280, Zomba, Malawi nyirenda@unima.wn.apc.org

Helga Patrikios, Medical Library, University of Zimbabwe, P.O.Box MP 45, Mount Pleasant, Harare, Zimbabwe patrikios@healthnet.zw

Neil Robinson, ZAMNET, University of Zambia, Box 32379, Lusaka, Zambia neil@zamnet.zm

Regina Shakakata, Medical Librarian, Medical Library, University of Zambia, Box 50110, Lusaka, Zambia rshakakata@unza.zm

Dr. Alex Tindimubona, Chairman, African Science and Technology Exchange (ASTEX), P.O. Box 10382, Kampala, Uganda ASTEX@mukla.gn.apc.org

Dr. John Villars, GHASTINET, Council for Scientific and Industrial Research, P.O. Box M32, Accra, Ghana jvillars@ghastinet.gn.apc.org

Appendix B
List of Acronyms and Abbreviations

AAS	African Academy of Sciences, Nairobi, Kenya
AAAS	American Association for the Advancement of Science, Washington, D.C.
AHILA	Association for Health Information and Libraries in Africa
AIM	African Index Medicus
APC	Association for Progressive Communications, United Kingdom
ARCT	African Regional Centre for Technology, Dakar, Senegal
BBS	Bulletin Board System
BITE	Bringing Internet To Ethiopia
BOSTID	Board on Science and Technology for International Development, National Research Council, Washington, D.C.
CABECA	Capacity Building for Electronic Communication in Africa
DTP	Desktop Publishing
EAIA	East Africa Internet Association
ELCI	Environmental Liaison Centre International, Nairobi, Kenya
ENDA	Environment and Development Action in the Third World
ESANET	Eastern and Southern Africa Networking Project
ESAP	Economic Structural Adjustment Program
FRD	Foundation for Research and Development, South Africa
FTP	File Transfer Protocol
GII	Global Information Infrastructure
GnFido	GreenNet/Fidonet hub
ICT	Information and Communication Technology
IDRC	International Development Research Centre, Ottawa, Canada

IFS	International Foundation for Science, Sweden
IGC	Institute for Global Communications, United States
IIP	Intergovernmental Informatics Programme (UNESCO)
ILL	Inter-library Loan
ISDN	Integrated Services Digital Network
LAN	Local Area Network
LEO	Low-earth Orbiting Satellite
MG	Megabyte
MHz	Megahertz
MIS	Management Information System
OCR	Optical Character Recognition
OIA	Office of International Affairs, National Research Council, Washington, D.C.
NGO	Non-Governmental Organization
NMR	Nuclear Magnetic Resonance
NRC	National Research Council, Washington, D.C.
PABX	Private Area Branch Exchange (switchboard)
PADIS	Pan African Development Information System, Addis Ababa, Ethiopia
PGI	General Information Programme (UNESCO)
PPP	Point-to-Point Protocol Connection
PVO	Private-Voluntary Organization
RAM	Random-access Memory
SANGONET	Southern Africa Non-Governmental Network
SAREC	Swedish Agency for Research Co-operation with Developing Countries
SDI	Selective Dissemination of Information
SLIP	Serial Line Internet Protocol
STI	Scientific and Technological Information
TCP/IP	Transmission Control Protocol/Internet Protocol
TDR	Tropical Disease Research
THF	The Health Foundation
TIFF	Tagged Image File Format; also .TIF
TWAS	Third World Academy of Science, Trieste, Italy
UNECA	United Nations Economic Commission for Africa
USIA	United States Information Agency
VSAT	Very Small Aperture Terminal
WAIS	Wide Area Information Server
WHO	World Health Organization, Geneva, Switzerland
WWW	Worldwide Web

Appendix C
Glossary

BAUD RATE
The transmission speed of an asynchronous communications channel. Technically, it refers to the maximum number of changes that can occur per second in the electrical state of a communications circuit. Often baud is used interchangeably with *bits per second.*

BIT/BYTE
All computer data is composed of tiny electrical pulses called **Bits** (short for binary digits). Each pulse represents a single digit of data. A group of eight bits is called a byte. Bytes are measured in units of a thousand, thus kilobyte.

BULLETIN BOARD
A system with a computer, modem, and phone line that acts as a central point for information exchange. It can be used for electronic mail and for storing files that can be downloaded.

CD-ROM
Stands for compact disc/read-only memory. A high density storage medium on which electronic data is etched and read by a laser beam.

COMPUTER CONFERENCE
A form of computer-based communications that emulates a face-to-face conference where people meet to discuss issues of common concern. Computer confer-

ences include a "messaging" module to simulate the private discussions that often take place at meetings but they also permit communication among multiple users and allow flexible treatment of conference comments.

DATABASE MANAGEMENT SYSTEMS (DBMS)
Databases are organized collections of information. They are used to file, search, and retrieve data.

DESKTOP PUBLISHING (DTP)
Publishing by means of a personal computer. DTP is the product of technological advances in personal computing, print graphics, and computer-generated typography. It synthesizes the capabilities of typesetting, graphic design, book production, and platemaking in one integrated, cost-effective hardware and software configuration.

ELECTRONIC MAIL
Computer-based messaging. The transmission of letters and messages from computer to computer over a network.

FIDONET
A robust network of individual computerized bulletin board services that uses regular dial-up phone lines and high-speed modems to move electronic messages.

FILE SERVER
A high-performance personal computer that serves all the users of a local area network. It provides access to files and software.

FLOPPY DISK
A magnetic storage medium. The floppy disk is compact, light, and portable. You can input or output data or software applications between a floppy disk and the computer.

FTP
File Transfer Protocol. Allows users to exchange files between their workstations and remote computers connected to the Internet. It is most useful for retrieving files from public archives that are scattered around the Internet.

GATEWAY
A device that connects two dissimilar LANs or that connects a LAN to a WAN, a server, or a mainframe. It reformats the data so that it is acceptable for the new network before passing it on.

HARD DISK

A hardware component used for storing software, applications, and data. It has a higher capacity and faster speed than a floppy. Hard disks are sealed units not usually meant to be removed from the computer.

HARDWARE

The central processing unit, monitor, keyboard, mouse, printer, and other equipment associated with a computer system.

INTERACTIVE

Used to refer to applications that engage the computer user by prompting for certain responses and then reacting to those responses in what seems like original ways.

INTERNET

A system of interconnected computer networks. Provides access to computers, electronic mail, bulletin boards, databases, and discussion groups, all using the TCP/IP protocol.

LEASED LINE

A dedicated private telephone line between two locations. Leased lines are often used to connect mid-sized local networks to an Internet service provider.

LOCAL-AREA NETWORK (LAN)

A method of connecting computers, peripherals, and communications equipment within a restricted locality, such as a building or campus.

MEGAHERTZ (MHz)

A unit of measurement, equal to one million electrical vibrations or cycles per second, commonly used to measure the clock speeds of computers.

MICROPROCESSOR

Hardware component responsible for the basic elements of computer processing: arithmetic, logic, and control. The microprocessor is an *integrated circuit chip*— a dense network of microscopic electrical pathways etched into highly refined sand, or silicon.

MODEM

A device that connects a computer to a telephone line and converts the digital data from the computer into analog (sound) frequencies. The modem sends the sounds through the phone line to a receiving computer's modem, which then turns the sounds back into a digital form that can be displayed on the receiving computer's screen. (MODEM is a contraction of *modulator/ demodulator.*)

MONITOR
The video display terminal (VDT); the part of the personal computer system that looks like a TV screen. It allows the user to see text and graphics as it is entered into the computer.

MS-DOS
An operating system for microcomputers. Short for *Microsoft disk operating system*, DOS has been perhaps the most common set of programs for controlling the microcomputer.

NETWORK
Individual computers linked in such a way that users can share software and hardware (for example, printers) and communicate with each other.

ONLINE
The "state" of being connected, either via a modem or a dedicated line, to a distant database or to another computer.

OPERATING SYSTEMS
The master program that controls the computer hardware and applications. Also called the system software.

PACKET
A "bundle" of data. In some types of electronic communications, data is broken into small chunks that traverse the networks independently.

PACKET-SWITCHING NETWORK
A wide-area network that achieves high data transmission speeds by dividing information into sections, called *packets*. The packets are then transmitted by the most efficient route and reassembled at their destination.

PERIPHERALS
Hardware components that are not essential to the basic operation of the computer but that may be necessary to perform certain applications. Peripheral hardware includes printers, scanners, and modems.

POINT
The lowest level of the Fidonet hierarchy. Points are connected to hubs and hubs to hosts in order to move mail through the system.

POLL
A method by which a central computer calls or "polls" another computer to see if that computer has electronic messages to transmit. Polls can be set up to automatically call another computer when the rates are lower or when traffic is minimal.

RANDOM ACCESS MEMORY (RAM)
The computer's short-term memory or the electronic "work space" in which software, programs, and data reside while they are active.

RESOLUTION
A measurement, usually expressed in linear dots per inch (dpi), of the sharpness of an image generated by an output device such as a printer or monitor.

ROUTER
A device that connects networks that use the same protocols together and passes information among them.

SCANNER
Hardware device that allows the transfer of photographs, graphic images, or text to the computer. Scanners convert the image to a form than can be manipulated and stored by the computer.

SOFTWARE
The applications, data, and operating systems associated with computer systems.

SPREADSHEETS
An electronic means of organizing, storing, and presenting numeric information in formats that allow for easy calculations. The most common means of handling numeric information.

TCP/IP
Transmission control protocol/Internet protocol. Connotes a full-time, interactive Internet connection.

TELNET
The Internet standard protocol for remote terminal connection service used for logging into and searching other computers connected to the Internet. It allows your computer to interact with a remote timesharing system at another site as if your terminal were connected directly to the remote computer.

UNINTERRUPTIBLE POWER SUPPLY (UPS)
Device that insures a steady and clean supply of electricity to the computer. A sudden loss of or change in power can destroy data and cause damage to a computer. UPSs give the user time to exit from all active applications and save all current data in the event of a power outage.

UNIX
An operating system for a wide variety of computers, from mainframes to personal computers. It supports multi-tasking and is suited to multi-user environments.

VIRUS
A program designed to enter a computer without the user's knowledge and perform tasks that can be destructive to the data and software stored in the computer.

WINDOW
A rectangular, on-screen frame through which you can view a document, worksheet, or other application.

WINDOWS
A windowing environment and application program interface for MS-DOS that brings to IBM compatible computers some of the graphical user interface features of the Macintosh computers.

WORD PROCESSOR
The single most universal application for personal computers. Word processing programs convert computers into writing and editing machines. Word processing easily allows revisions, formatting, and corrections.

WYSIWYG
Pronounced *wizzy-wig*, an acronym for What You See is What You Get. A term used in desktop publishing that means that what you see on the computer screen is exactly what you get on paper when you print.